The Poetics of Imitation in the Italian Theatre of the Renaissance

SALVATORE DI MARIA

The Poetics of Imitation in the Italian Theatre of the Renaissance

UNIVERSITY OF TORONTO PRESS
Toronto Buffalo London

Toronto Buffalo London
www.utppublishing.com

ISBN 978-1-4426-4405-2

Toronto Italian Studies

Library and Archives Canada Cataloguing in Publication

Di Maria, Salvatore, author
The poetics of imitation in the Italian theatre of the Renaissance / Salvatore Di Maria.

Includes bibliographical references and index.
ISBN 978-1-4426-4712-1 (bound)

1. Italian drama – To 1700 – History and criticism. 2. Imitation in literature. 3. Classical drama – Influence. I. Title.

PQ4139.D54 2013 852'.409 C2013-902844-7

This book has been published with the help of a generous grant from the University of Tennessee.

University of Toronto Press acknowledges the financial assistance to its publishing program of the Canada Council for the Arts and the Ontario Arts Council.

University of Toronto Press acknowledges the financial assistance to its publishing program of the Canada Book Fund.

Contents

Preface

This study is the outgrowth of my "From Prose to Stage: Machiavelli's *Mandragola*," *MLN* (2006), from which it takes both its critical approach and its thematic investigation. My principal argument is that the theatre of the Italian Renaissance, though inspired by the classical stage of Greece and Rome, grew into a theatre in its own right. Many *cinquecento* playwrights, though drawing mostly on old and recycled plot materials, were modern and original. They were original for the dramaturgical innovations they brought to the genre and modern in their representation of the living realities of their times. Writers strove to dramatize a fictional world in which the audience recognized significant aspects of their own society, including morals, aesthetic preferences, political issues, and sexual mores. My discussion proceeds from the humanists' debate on the poetics of imitation, because *cinquecento* theatre is largely based on the imitation of ancient drama, historical accounts, and fictional narratives. I dwell on the authors' treatment of the original sources, especially the variations and the novelties that distinguish their plays from the source. The differences between source and stage adaptation reinforce the argument that imitation *per se* does not imply lack of creativity, as has been suggested, for it often leads to the production of works that are original both in form and content.

I anchor my critical approach in the poetics of imitation and proceed to show how adapting old ideas to one's own times can often yield innovative works. Following the enthusiasm with which humanism revived and idealized classical antiquity, it was common for playwrights to rely on the *auctoritas* of the ancients because it lent legitimacy to their works and provided them with the opportunity to display their own creative genius. Dramatists achieved originality often by re-presenting old stories from a different point of view. A case in point is Machiavelli's *Clizia*. Though some critics labelled the comedy a "rewriting" or a "reduction" of Plautus's *Casina*, a close analysis shows that the plays are quite different. In the Florentine version, Nicomaco's amorous pursuit of his young ward does not arise from some perverted eroticism, as is the case with his Plautine ancestor, but from the delusory wish to fight off old age by a valiant display of virility. Thus, not by changing the original story but simply by altering the motives for the erotic pursuit, Machiavelli transforms the farcical representation of a foolish and lecherous *amator senex* into a quasi-tragic representation of an old man's desire to escape the ineluctable process of aging.

With regard to adaptations of prose narratives, the discussion centres on the implementation and thematic implications of the Aristotelian unities. In my discussion of Dolce's *Marianna*, a close adaptation of Josephus's account of the relationship between Herod and Mariamme (*History of the Jews*), I show that the play's originality lies mostly in the creative use of the unity of time. By concentrating in a single day several of the murders Herod committed throughout his reign, the dramatist turns Josephus's calculating king into a cruel and impetuous tyrant in the grip of blind jealousy. As for stage novelties, I call attention to the growing emphasis playwrights placed on the use of mechanical devices for the reproduction of visual or sound effects such as a flash of lightning, a clap of thunder, sounds of the hoofbeats of horses, and similar sensorial signs. When possible, the discussion includes the spectators' reception of the play and the extent to which it reflects the values and the aesthetic taste of the times. For instance, the audience's enthusiastic approval of the licentious world of Cecchi's *Assiuolo* may be seen as the spontaneous reaction of a permissive society that laughs at its own loose morals.

The book also challenges the traditional view that Italian dramatists were by and large slavish imitators of the classics. This notion, common among established literary critics, found its voice in America through Marvin Herrick (*Italian Tragedy in the Renaissance*, 1965) for whom Renaissance playwrights were largely "copyists" lacking creativity. This rather uncritical view has its roots in the heated arguments that fuelled the debate between moderns and ancients in sixteenth-century Italy. Now as then, however, there is a need to distinguish between slavish imitators and creative playwrights who produced true works of art. One of these authors is, of course, Niccolò Machiavelli. But he is not alone. Cecchi's *Assiuolo* is considered good enough to rival Machiavelli's *Mandragola*. For Ireneo Sanesi it is one of the best plays ("frutti") ever produced by the comic theatre of sixteenth-century Italy. Dolce's *Marianna* is undoubtedly one of the best Italian tragedies of the century. Some scholars, such as Luigi Tonelli, view Della Porta's *Gli duoi fratelli* as a play "worthy of standing next not only to the best Italian comedies, but also to the best of Calderon's and Lope De Vega's."

Admittedly, such a study might be successfully conducted on any of the numerous imitations of prose narratives or ancient plays that make up most of the comic and tragic theatre of the *cinquecento*. I limit it to well-known playwrights whose works have enjoyed considerable editorial attention and figure prominently in the histories and collections of the Renaissance theatre. Some of the plays, such as *Mandragola*, *Clizia*, *Assiuolo*, and *Gli duoi fratelli*, have been translated into English. Their popularity will undoubtedly win immediate recognition, making it easier for a broader readership to engage in the discussion. Lest the discussion become diffuse, I confine it to seven plays that illustrate, each in its own way, a particular aspect of the imitative process. *Mandragola*, for instance, borrows material from Boccaccio's stories and turns them into the most successful imitation of prose narratives. *Assiuolo* exemplifies creative imitation based on multiple sources, including Boccaccio's tales, Machiavelli's plays, and Plautus's comedies. *Marianna* showcases Dolce's imitative creativity in turning Josephus's historical account of Herod and Mariamme into a gripping stage representation. Groto's *Emilia* allows a critical insight into a unique form of imitation that arises from a plot based on the interlacing of contemporary war atrocities (the Turkish conquest of Cyprus) with a loose adaptation of an ancient comedy (Plautus's *Epidicus*).

The book joins and expands existing critical studies on the poetics of imitation as it relates to the theatre of the Renaissance. It adds new and concrete arguments to Carmelo Musumarra's general discussion of the poetics of theatre (*La poetica*, 1972), and Martin McLaughlin's philological study of the humanist theory and practice of imitation (*Literary Imitation in the Italian Renaissance*, 1995). It complements the recent and growing scholarship of well-known scholars, including Louise Clubb's seminal book on Della Porta (1965), Konrad Eisenbichler's work on Cecchi (1986), Michael Lettieri's critical edition of Aretino's *Orazia* (1991), Ronnie Terpening's monograph on Dolce (1997), and Mary Morrison's study of Giraldi's tragedies (1997). It also builds on and promotes the excellent translations of many comedies, including Clubb's *The Two Rival Brothers* (1980), Eisenbichler's *The Horned Owl* (1981), Sices' and Atkinson's *The Comedies of Machiavelli* (1985), Bruno Ferraro's

The Slave Girl (1996), Giannetti's and Ruggiero's *Five Comedies of the Italian Renaissance* (2003), and Donald Beecher's two-volume collection of eleven comedies, *Renaissance Comedy* (2008–9). As for the tragic stage, only a handful of tragedies have been rendered into English. Most recently, Trissino's *Sophonisba* has been translated by Gillian Sharman and Aretino's *Horatia* by Michael Ukas, both in *Two Italian Renaissance Tragedies*, edited by Michael Lettieri and Michael Ukas (1997). Finally, the present book builds on and complements my own scholarship on the Renaissance theatre, especially my *The Italian Tragedy* (2002).

I thank the following journals for their generous permission to use material from my previously published work: *MLN*, for "From Prose to Stage"; *Rivista di Studi Italiani*, for "Imitation and the Continuum of History"; and *Forum Italicum*, for "Cecchi's *Assiuolo*."

Unless otherwise indicated, all translations are my own. I usually cite in English. I quote in the original when, in my view, the text has particular linguistic nuances or implications.

I take this opportunity to thank all my family, friends, and colleagues (too many to name) who in one form or another encouraged and assisted me in this painstaking undertaking. The task would have been more difficult without their expert advice and endless patience. However, I would be greatly remiss if I failed to express my warmest appreciation for the generous and unconditional help I received from my dear friends and colleagues Salvatore Bancheri and Chris Craig. They read every single page of the entire manuscript and were never short of interesting comments and creative suggestions. Naturally, the blame is entirely my own for any flaws that may be found in the pages of this book.

The Poetics of Imitation in the Italian Theatre of the Renaissance

Chapter One

Imitation: The Link between Past and Present

"Books always speak of other books, and every story tells a story that has already been told."

Postscript to Umberto Eco's *The Name of the Rose*

This book builds on the premise that imitation is a means through which the present turns to the past for guidance and inspiration. As prevailing beliefs and value systems fail to provide adequate solutions to rising exigencies, society tends to look upon old models for lessons and suggestions on how to meet the new challenges. After all, as Machiavelli points out in his *Discourses*, men of wisdom remind us that all new things have their point of reference in the things of the ancient past.[1] This was the case in Renaissance Italy as it looked for a form of worldly entertainment more consistent with its secular preferences than the traditional *sacre rappresentazioni*. Italian writers proceeded to meet this emerging need by imitating the ancient theatre of Greece and Rome. The ensuing discussion focuses on the rise of the Renaissance theatre from a mere imitation of the classics to its modern form. Secular representations made their first appearance in academic settings, where university students performed Latin plays in front of their teachers and fellow students. But as interest in the genre spread beyond the walls of academia, scholars began to translate Latin plays into the *vulgare*, reaching an ever larger audience. Responding to the growing demand for stage performances, authors with a penchant for the stage took to writing their own plays, following the example of the ancients and borrowing from them. They imitated the comedies of Plautus and Terence and the tragedies of Aeschylus, Euripides, Sophocles, and Seneca. Mastery of the genre eventually led them to adopt plot material from historical accounts and fictional narratives that had never been staged before. Thus, building on the example of the past, they proceeded to establish a theatre of their own.

The process was lengthy and controversial, as not all playwrights agreed on the extent to which they might imitate old models. Some followed their sources so closely that they ultimately produced only *volgarizzamenti,* reworkings or rough translations of the original. Soon playwrights and stage theorists found themselves engaged in a debate on imitation centred mostly on the question of originality and on the issue of relevance to contemporary audiences. Some argued that it was permissible to adopt plot material from the ancients, since there was nothing that had not being said before ("nihil sub sole novum"). Even old material could be morphed into something new and relevant. After all, they insisted, the great Plautus and Terence did not hesitate to pilfer story lines from their Greek counterparts. Others countered that authors should base their works on recent events, that the stage should reflect living realities and not the ancient times of Athens and Rome. Though for them the issue of what might be imitated was as new as secular theatre itself, a general debate on the poetics of imitation had engaged scholars for several centuries. The following pages centre on the notion of imitation, the humanists' debate on literary imitation, and its effect on selected aspects of Renaissance culture. The discussion leads to a close analysis of the ways in which playwrights imitated ancient theatre and how they turned it into a modern venue of entertainment and social commentary.

Broadly speaking, the practice of imitation ranges from copying something to transforming it into something new. The first is the lowest and least desirable form of imitation because it tends to reproduce that which is or was. Quintilian, in his *Institutio oratoria* 10.2.7, calls this type of imitation dishonourable or "turpe." The latter is creative and, thus, instrumental to the re-evaluation and adaption of old models and ideas. Its most basic function is to link the present to the past by relying on the authority of proven examples in order to forge novel approaches to emerging needs. Machiavelli says it best when he notes that his precepts on princeship are mostly based on the highest examples of the past because humans almost always walk on trails blazed by others (*Prince* 6).[2] Of course, innovation is an essential aspect of the imitative process, for without it, Quintilian points out, nothing would have been invented ("nihil fuisset inventum"), nor would there be progress in the history of the world (10.2.4). The creative phase of imitation begins as imitators evaluate the past from a modern perspective and proceed to chart a course of action that, while informed by the past, is original and consistent with contemporary realities. This dialectical confrontation, which Thomas Greene considers typical of *heuristic* imitation (40), tends to power the flux of ideas and, inherently, the continuity of history.

The imitative process normally begins by identifying who and/or what is worthy of imitation. This is a most challenging first step, since there has never been a universally accepted definition of the concept. Following Plato's and Aristotle's contrasting and loosely defined ideas of imitation, successive generations dwelled on its meaning. Ultimately they favoured Aristotle's mimesis, the imitation of human actions as recorded by great authors. From classical Rome to the Renaissance, the concept went through various interpretations and modifications, without ever arriving at a precise definition.[3] Rhetoricians such as Cicero, Horace, Seneca, and Quintilian, saw *imitatio* as a mental process that morphs existing human achievements into new creations. For them, the realm of ideas is always in constant flux, partly because great minds reshape and adapt old models to new circumstances. In addition, they viewed ideas as a public domain. Thus they did not entertain the question of plagiarism, nor did they see any contradiction in the notion of imitation as an original activity. Virgil's *Aeneid,* for example, was for them a praiseworthy imitation of the Homeric poems and an original epic in its own right. Accepting the premise that successful imitation leads to innovative alternatives, they agreed on the three most important aspects of the process: what or who was worthy of imitation (*inventio*); the rearrangement or reshaping of source material (*dispositio*); and the creative ability to present it in its new form (*elocutio*). Seneca compared imitation to the work of a bee that gathers pollen from various flowers in order to produce honey, a product that resembles none of the collected ingredients.[4] Quintilian, exhorted writers to imitate the best authors and strive to produce something different and better. He believed that in the end they would be praised for surpassing those who preceded them and for teaching those who follow ("ut priores superasse, posteros docuisse dicantur," 10.2.28).

In the world of imitation, where originality rests largely on the dialectical confrontation between past and present, historical memory is fundamental in identifying and selecting the material to be imitated. The Roman rhetoricians' advice to draw from the best writers, though intended specifically for literary imitation, does not exclude the emulation of other human accomplishments, such as art forms, systems of education and government, and even aesthetic taste. They themselves, in fact, benefited immensely from their imitation of Greek civilization, which they saw as a source of intellectual wealth and social refinement.[5] Thirsting for social sophistication and intellectual stimulation, Rome sent its young to Greece in order to further their education or, as Horace puts it, to seek for truth among the groves of Academe ("inter silvas Academi quaerere verum," *Epist.* 2.2.46). The famed schools of Athens and Rhodes proved fertile ground for young Roman intellectuals, including Brutus, Caesar, Cicero, and Horace. Building on their assimilation and appreciation of Hellenic culture, they imitated and, in some instances, surpassed their ancient masters. Their works contributed to the rise of a civilization that went on to blaze its own path of lasting influence. It is a telling testament to Rome's enduring legacy that even after more than a millennium of neglect it would spur the "rebirth" of Western civilization. The *artes liberales* of antiquity not only "liberated" the humanists from the labyrinthine mentality of medieval scholasticism, they also encouraged a secular view of life as opposed to the world of the hereafter so vividly envisioned and exalted in Dante's *Comedia*.

The Humanists Turn to the Ancients

What aroused the humanists' interest in antiquity was, in part, the cultural vacuum that followed the waning of the Middle Ages. The crisis created the need for fresh values and ideals that would guide society through the realities of the rising new era. By the beginning of the fourteenth century, traditional beliefs and religious assumptions were proving ever more inconsistent with the commercial developments affecting people's way of life. The rising moneyed nobility, whom Dante disdained as the "gente nuova" with their "súbiti guadagni" (*Inf.* 16.73), redefined the social barriers that had stood for social harmony and class distinction. They also limited, and in some cases seized, the political power that in the past had been in the hands of the aristocracy. In 1293, Florence enacted a law mandating that only merchants and tradesmen could be elected to political office (Napier 348). In the schools, demand for the study of mathematics outpaced the traditional interest in philosophy, largely because of the growing need for trained agents in the evolving art of financial accounting.[6]

Clerks replaced clerics, profit-making upended the church's condemnation of avarice, and the detested usurers of old became the respectable bankers of the emerging new era. What was once considered sinful avarice had now become good business sense. New wealth inevitably led to an appreciation for material goods and became the perceived source of happiness. A popular refrain of the times proclaims that those who do not have riches cannot be happy: "Chi non ha oro o argento / non può aver nessun contento" (Macek 52). Affluence led to a new emphasis on refined fashion and personal appearance. Women, in particular, decked themselves in expensive clothes and jewellery and flaunted their looks, causing Dante to lash out against those who dressed in such a way as to reveal part of their breasts ("l'andar mostrando con le poppe il petto," *Purg*. 23.102).

As the heavily religious value system of the Middle Ages was becoming increasingly anachronistic for the cultural secularism and commercial dynamism driving fourteenth-century Italy, society and its intellectual leaders turned for guidance to the memorable example of antiquity. Their wish to learn from the ancients led to a widespread practice of imitation, perhaps one of the most significant forces behind the creative genius of Renaissance Italy. Artists and writers studied antiquity with the intent to learn from its celebrated culture and adapt it to their own circumstances. They engaged in intense debates on whether writers should imitate only famed authors, such as Cicero, or simply glean the best from various sources, as Seneca suggested in his apian metaphor. But before they could fully appreciate and imitate aspects of Graeco-Roman culture, they had to recover many of the ancient manuscripts that centuries of wars and neglect had nearly erased from historical memory. Not only did they need to find old manuscripts, they also had to restore them to their original integrity, as many texts had been altered and/or misinterpreted by overworked or unschooled copyists.[7] The task required both a fresh mental approach free of scholastic sophistry and a meticulous philological analysis based on the mastery of the classical languages. While wealthy patrons hired Greek natives to teach the language and translate major authors, several scholars went to Greece to search for new manuscripts and, as Eugenio Garin puts it, drink from the well of Hellenic wisdom ("abbeverarsi di sapienza," 32). As for the Latin writers, scholars turned to the works of acclaimed authors such as Cicero, Quintilian, and Virgil in order to refine their own linguistic skills and rediscover the true teachings of the great masters.

Unlike the Romans of antiquity, who could easily travel to Greece to behold its artistic splendour and learn directly from living scholars, most Italian *literati* had to rely on the testimony of written documents, many of which had yet to be discovered. They embarked on a frenzied and challenging search for original manuscripts lying under the rubble of the barbarian invasions that had followed the fall of the Roman Empire. Scouring libraries in remote and hard to reach abbeys and monasteries, they could hardly contain their excitement when they finally found an original text. Poggio Bracciolini (1380–1459), one of the most active book hunters of the time, gave testimony of such a pleasure in the many letters he wrote to his humanist friends about his findings. From Constance in 1416, he wrote to Guarino Veronese about his exciting discovery of several manuscripts, especially one by the "outstanding and extraordinary" Quintilian (Gordan 193).[8] Bartolomeo di Montepulciano, writing to Ambrogio Traversari about his exciting discovery of Flavius Vegetius Renatus's work on military strategy, noted the Roman writer's potential contribution to contemporary warfare: "he will do us good, if we ever use him sometimes in camp or more gloriously on a crusade" (Gordan 209). The search extended all the way to Greece, where scholars such as Guarino Veronese, Francesco Filelfo, and Giovanni Aurispa ventured in search of treasured manuscripts. Aurispa, the most successful of the three, in 1413 was on the island of Chios buying Sophoclean and Euripidean texts. He was so persistent in his hunt that in 1423 he returned from Constantinople with a collection of 238 works, many of which were unknown in the West.[9]

Patrons spent large sums of money for the pleasure and privilege of filling the shelves of their private studies with newly discovered books. In time, their collections served to build up public libraries in major cities such as Florence, Venice, the Vatican, and Urbino. Scholars, poring over the new discoveries, grew ever more appreciative of a sophisticated culture that had much to teach them about civic values and institutions, art and thought, literary taste and creativity. Their enthusiasm inspired them to imitate the works and the men that came alive from those yellowing and often mutilated pages. Petrarch emulated the classics to such an extent that Boccaccio and Salutati considered his style equal or superior to that of Cicero and Virgil.[10] He himself boasted that Cicero was not the only one to have devoted admirers; he too had his fans.[11] Men of letters such as Aeneas Sylvius and Giannozzo Manetti distinguished themselves as great public speakers by studying Quintilian's theoretical writings and by emulating Cicero's speeches. Jacob Burckhardt called Manetti an "orator the like of whom has not been often seen" (I.245).

Some writers Latinized their names and called themselves Franciscus, Marsilius, Albertus, and Machiavellus. They also developed school curricula based on the works of classical authors and taught young students to treasure the great masters and imitate them in both speech and writing style. Classical Latin became the standard diplomatic language for most European courts, where scholars were highly rewarded for their skills. Many actually lived off their rhetorical abilities, selling "their tongues and pens to the wealthiest and most prestigious powers that would have them" (Frazier 16). But Latin was not just a means for making a living or a common medium of communication for scholarly pursuit and diplomacy. It was also the language that gave status and credibility to the content it expressed. The prevailing assumption was that what was well written had to be true or, in the words of Cardinal Jacopo Ammannati, "Quod elegans legitur, hoc et factum creditur."[12]

In their endeavours to write elegantly, some imitated the classics so closely that their works often mimicked the original source, risking imitating like apes, parrots, and magpies. Petrarch considered it appropriate to imitate another's idea, but not his words, for the first creates poets, the latter makes monkeys ("illa poetas facit, hec simias"). Recalling Seneca's apian simile, he suggested that imitators gather ideas from various sources in order to produce something different and better ("aliud et melius," *Epyst. fam.* XXIII.19.13).[13] As the debate continued well into the next century and beyond, prominent humanists such as Poliziano, Barbaro, Cortesi, Pico, and Bembo focused on questions of originality, specifically which Latin authors were most worthy of imitation, and whether it was better to imitate one or more writers.[14] Whatever their arguments, there was general agreement that writers should aim to rival the source and produce something original. But many, lacking creativity, were satisfied to follow slavishly the source, reducing *studia humanitatis* to pedantry and lowering the conversation or dialectical confrontation with the ancients to a mere memorization exercise or, in the words of Garin, "un soffocante esercizio di memoria" (82). Society rejected their presumptuous erudition. Leonardo called them pompous windbags who recite and trumpet the works of others.[15] The comic theatre paraded them on stage and ridiculed them as fatuous and ostentatious pedants or "magisters." Michel de Montaigne made *péndatisme* the subject of his scathing criticism.

If, on the one hand, enthusiasm for the classics gave way to pedantry, on the other hand, it led to a meaningful appreciation of antiquity and, inevitably, to the realization that the ancients had already had their place and time in history. Any attempt to live by their values or speak their language was anachronistic. The awkwardness of expressing contemporary realities in an ancient tongue was all too obvious, especially when attempting to describe modern technological terms. Flavio Biondo (1392–1463) illustrated such clumsiness by using a thirty-eight-word Latin periphrasis to describe the verb to bomb ("bombardare"). Almost a century later, Bembo (1470–1547) expressed new concepts such as medieval jousts, cannon shots, and gunpowder by using long and obtrusive Latin circumlocutions. The word "gunpowder," for example, became "pulvere ad ignem celiter comprehendum idoneo" ("powder suited to catch fire quickly," McLaughlin 272). Most indicative of the growing preference for the vernacular over any ancient language was perhaps Martin Luther's claim: "thank God that I hear and find my God in the German tongue, whereas I, and they with me, previously did not find him in the Latin, the Greek or the Hebrew tongue" (31:75).

Though Latin began to give way to *vulgare*, its cultural models continued to be a source of inspiration well into the sixteenth century. In the field of historiography, for instance, humanists imitated the great historians of the past, especially Livy and Sallust. Felix Gilbert notes that in writing history, the humanists applied the principle of imitation "to all their literary efforts" (204). Moving away from the standard chronicles and commentaries, humanists framed their *historiae* in annalistic sequence, divided them into books, and indulged in set-piece speeches and battle narratives common in classical historiography (Ianziti 368). Following the example of Livy's *Ab urbe condita*, they wrote histories celebrating their own city-state: Florentine chancellors from Leonardo Bruni (1369–1444) to Machiavelli wrote histories of Florence; Flavio Biondo produced two histories of Rome; the Venetian senate was proud to learn that Sabellico's history of Venice (1486) elevated the city to a "new Rome" (Cochrane 84). Also, taking as models Caesar's *De bello gallico* and Sallust's *Bellum Catilinae*, they wrote histories limited to a single war. Giovanni Pontano (1426–1503) wrote on Ferdinand of Naples's war against the barons, Cicco Simonetta (1410–80) on Milan's war against Naples, and Bernardo Rucellai (1448–1514) on the 1494 French invasion of Italy. Of Rucellai's *De bello italico*, Erasmus wrote that "if you read it, you would say that it was written by another Sallust or at least in Sallustian times" (Gilbert 212).

Emulation of ancient historiography also led Florentine humanists, Bruni in particular, to dismiss the myth that Florence was founded by Caesar. They concluded with pride that the city was actually founded by Sulla's veterans during the republic. The implication was that the city descended not from imperial Rome but from the free men of the *respublica romana* and was, therefore, endowed with a birthright claim to freedom. Bruni amplified this claim by linking it to his criticism of Dante's condemnation of Caesar's assassins. He argued that Brutus and Cassius did not belong in the bottom of hell but on the altar of liberty. In his view, they killed in the name of the republican ideals that Caesar had crushed. He refuted the medieval celebration of the empire, agreeing with Tacitus that its dictatorial nature was inimical to freedom and to the flourishing of great minds.[16] Whether Bruni's historical perspective was merely literary or inspired by a cult of Ciceronian rhetoric, as some have argued, is not relevant here.[17] What is relevant is that it led to a heated debate on the merits of republicanism versus autocracy. The controversy first flared up between the Florentine chancellor Poggio Bracciolini and Guarino da Verona, a humanist at the court of Ferrara. The exchange and the invectives that continued to fuel the debate were not simply scholarly disagreements but the ideological confrontation between those (Florentines) who lived by the freedom of their republican principles and those, such as the Milanese humanists Decembrio and Loschi, who defended the advantages of monarchical rule. It was an example of literary humanism transitioning into civic activism.

While the debate was undoubtedly coloured by memories of Florence's valiant resistance against Milan's attempt to bring it under Visconti rule (1402), the controversy continued well into the sixteenth century. Donato Giannotti, for instance, based his brief *Dialogi* (1546) on conversations he supposedly had with Michelangelo about Dante's treatment of Brutus. The discussion between the two friends, culminating in Giannotti's denunciation of Dante's approval of Caesar, is not just an intellectual exercise. By and large, it proceeds from a strong belief in the civic ideals for which both he and Michelangelo fought in the struggle of the last Florentine republic and for which they were ultimately banished from Florence (1530).[18] Also, it should not go unnoticed that the dialogues, having taken place during Duke Cosimo's rule, imply the condemnation of Cosimo as a modern Caesar and usurper of republican institutions. Giannotti's denunciation of tyrants and the implied praise of their slayers went beyond a personal attack, for it actually reflected the established practice of elevating political assassinations to noble deeds. From the murders of Galeazzo Maria Sforza (1476), Giuliano de' Medici (1478), and Alessandro de' Medici (1537), tyrannicides evoked the ghosts of Brutus and Cassius. Lorenzaccio, the assassin of Alessandro, was one of the most celebrated tyrannicides of the times. His contemporaries honoured him with short Latin poems, and some went so far as to hail him as the new "Tuscan Brutus" (Varchi 1.15.23.420). Michelangelo, ever hopeful that freedom would return to Florence, sculpted a bust of Brutus to celebrate Lorenzaccio's deed.[19] It should not come as a surprise, then, that even Shakespeare's Antony lauds Brutus among Caesar's killers as "the noblest Roman of them all," and consigns him to literary memory with the epitaph, "This was a man!" (*Julius Caesar* 5.5).

Renaissance fascination with and imitation of the ancients extended to the visual arts, especially architecture. Unlike in literature and historiography, the imitation of classical architecture did not lead to debates but only to competition among the artists. Following the rediscovery of Vitruvius's *De architectura*,[20] Italian artists revived architectural planning and design in ways that met society's needs and even exceeded its expectations. Alberti, Serlio, and Palladio were among the most famous artists to emulate the Roman architect. Leon Battista Alberti (1404–72), who has been called the "new Vitruvius" (Lotz 146), wrote *Re edificatoria*, a critical reading of Vitruvius's work. He also helped to popularize the use of perspective both in painting and in architectural adornments. Sebastiano Serlio (1475–1554) established the standards for the construction of stage sets and the concept of theatrical space through the use of perspective. Andrea Palladio (1508–80), besides the construction of many churches and villas, is best remembered for his Teatro Olimpico in Vicenza, the first commercial theatre in Renaissance Italy. Bramante and Sansovino adapted many of Vitruvius's architectural notions to their works. The first worked in Sant'Ambrogio (Milan), the latter in Saint Mark's Library in Venice. But whether they built churches, palaces, stage sets, theatres, or mere façades, their works were more than just derivations from Vitruvius. They were the product of creative minds that imitated the example of the past in order to meet the needs and the aspirations of the present. In some instances, they even challenged the prevailing aesthetic preferences of the times. Speaking of Peruzzi's plans to remodel the dome of Siena's cathedral, Wolfgang Lotz notes that the architect's plans show that he had "broken away from the intellectual theories of Alberti and from the meticulous rules of Vitruvius' treatise" (49). Vasari, reflecting on the distance Renaissance architects had travelled from their Roman source, pointed out that the Sangallo brothers applied the Doric order in ways that surpassed the Vitruvian norm. They conceived and implemented it with more precise measurements and proportions than those prescribed by Vitruvius ("con miglior misure e proporzione, che alla Vitruviana opinione e regola," 4.290.91). Michelangelo's *David* might be regarded as a paradigm of Renaissance artistic originality. In Paul Strathern's estimation, the great statue reveals that the "Renaissance was now beginning to emerge in its full originality, surpassing and casting aside the classical exemplars that had initially so inspired its artists, poets, and thinkers" (311).

Unlike the imitation of ancient architecture, literary imitation was and continued to be a source of debate among scholars. But, when the controversy moved into the sixteenth century, it shifted focus, broadened the audience, and was no longer restricted to a handful of humanists. As Renaissance society grew ever more appreciative of classical theatre, the question of imitating ancient dramatists moved to the forefront of the dispute with renewed intensity and wider scope. Unlike other literary forms, such as oratory, poetry, and stylistics, on which the humanists had centred their arguments, secular theatre was new on the Italian cultural landscape. Only around the end of the fifteenth century did playwrights begin to experiment with the genre by performing Latin plays in university halls or in private residences. Having assimilated the basic elements of ancient stagecraft, authors from Ariosto to Bibbiena to Machiavelli began to write their own plays, borrowing freely from classical sources. Just as *cinquecento* Petrarchists looked upon Petrarch's poetry for inspiration, and generations of *novellieri* modelled their narratives after Boccaccio's *Decameron*, dramatists followed the example of Greek and Roman playwrights. They adopted basic structural elements, such as the prologue and the division into acts and scenes. But, with regard to imitation, though the *Poetics* of Aristotle and the *Ars poetica* of Horace provided valuable guidance, there was no consensus on how and what to imitate. The diverging views led to a debate that would characterize the Italian Renaissance theatre through most of the sixteenth century.

The debate was no longer limited to a few humanists, for the question of theatre imitation took place before large audiences, thus becoming a public and truly cultural issue. Playwrights usually discussed their notion of imitation in the prologue, where they argued for or against borrowing plot material from the ancients. It was common for them to claim that the material, though old, was relevant to the times. Most did not hesitate to mention their primary source(s), striving to benefit from its *auctoritas* and, at the same time, compete with it. Ariosto, for example, not only admits to borrowing the story for his *Suppositi* from Plautus and Terence, he also insists that such borrowing is not plagiarism. Through Prologue, he points out that both Roman playwrights – themselves imitators of Greek theatre – would call it poetic imitation rather than thievery. Castiglione, in his prologue to Bibbiena's *Calandria,* defends the playwright against charges of thievery, noting, tongue in cheek, that Plautus should not have left his property unguarded. In his own prologue, Bibbiena jokes that upon inspection there is nothing missing from Plautus's work. On the same humorous tone, Lorenzino de' Medici defends the old plot he used in his *Aridosia,* quipping that old plots are like old women, who, like old chickens, make good broth. On a more serious vein, Lodovico Dolce justifies his free adoption of old plot elements for his *Didone* by insisting that both Euripides and Sophocles took similar liberties.

These playwrights argued that it was impossible to find new things in a world that is always the same. The idea that there is nothing new under the sun was a common thread even among the Romans. Terence, for example, answered his detractors by pointing out that there was nothing that had not been said before ("nullumst iam dictum quod non dictum sit prius," *Eunuch,* prologue). The emperor and philosopher Marcus Aurelius expressed a similar view, noting that things have always been the same and will continue to be the same. In his view, one who has seen the present has seen all, "both everything which has taken place from all eternity and everything which will be for time without end; for all things are of one kin and of one form" (*Meditations* 6.37.77). Machiavelli returns to this theme in his prologue to *Clizia* as he states that human events and situations tend to reoccur over time, albeit to different people and in different settings.[21] Indeed, braggarts, misers, servants, tyrants, and old men in love have the same basic attributes in the Renaissance as they did in antiquity. As Machiavelli observes in his recommendation on how to deal with the rebels of Valdichiana, the world has always been inhabited by men who have always had the same passions ("le medesime passioni," *Opere* 802). Thus, the story of the despairing young lover who must compete with his old father for the same girl or the jealous husband who is ultimately cuckolded in spite of his precautions is the same in Machiavelli as it had been in Boccaccio, Plautus, and Aristophanes. But if individual types, passions, and situations remained the same, some argued, their meaning was different in that it was defined by the cultural context in which they reoccurred. In Annibal Caro's *Straccioni,* Prologue points out that the meaning of the source material has been altered because the times and costumes have changed ("sono alterati ancora i temi e i costumi").

Some authors, perhaps wishing to underscore their adaptation of old material to brand-new situations, claimed that their plays were actually new. Castiglione, for instance, calls Bibbiena's *Calandria* "commedia nuova," though the play is clearly an imitation of Plautus's *Menaechmi.* Ariosto insists that his *Suppositi* is "nuova" while admitting that he purloined a few elements from the Roman stage. Cecchi describes the story of his *Corredo* as a new event, though he concedes that it had happened in ancient Greece. Others, wanting to appear altogether original, presented their works as completely new. Dolce promotes his *Ragazzo* as a new comedy, not stolen from the ancients. Actually, the play owes much to Plautus's *Casina,* Machiavelli's *Clizia,* and Aretino's *Marescalco.* Prologue, in Francesco Belo's *Pedante* (c. 1536), calls the play "new" because, he explains to a presumably sceptical audience, people like novelties just as they abhor worn-out things, such as old women. Cecchi touts his *Pellegrine* as "nuova" because it had never been performed, though written years earlier. The adjective *nuova,* then, did not always mean original, since most plays featured borrowed elements, albeit altered and rearranged. The term clearly recalled the Terentian "novus," by which the Roman playwright meant the reworking of dramatic material he borrowed from various sources.

But reliance on the classics had its opponents, especially those who demanded that theatre be a *speculum vitae* or, in the words of Prologue in Grazzini's *Arzigogolo,* a reflection of truth, example of customs, and mirror of life ("immagine di verità, esempio di costumi, e specchio di vita"). Antonfrancesco Grazzini (1503–84) was a distinguished dramatist in his own right as well as one of the most outspoken critics of servile imitation. He did not hesitate to chastise fellow playwrights for the anachronism inherent in their adaptation of ancient material. In the prologue to his *Strega,* reiterating what he had already pointed out in his other plays, he insists that theatre should reflect the culture in which it is produced. Aristotle and Horace saw their times, he concedes, "but our times are different from theirs: we have other customs, another religion, and another way of life. [...] in Florence one does not live as one lived in Athens and in Rome." He also spoke against the ancient use of *ritrovamenti* or recognition scenes that reunited long-lost relatives separated by the vicissitudes of war, pirate incursions, or other such calamities. For him these scenes were anachronistic and silly, because the kidnappings and enslavements that in the past led to the dispersion of families were not happening anymore, at least not in Tuscany.[22] He also laments the rising importance accorded to intermezzi; though meant as a mere distraction between acts, they were becoming more spectacular than the play itself. He reserves his harshest criticism for those who mixed the old with the new and produced something that had neither head nor tail ("né capo né coda"). He advises these pedestrian writers to limit their literary activities to translating rather than mutilating their work and that of others ("non guastino l'altrui e il loro insieme," *Gelosia*, prologue).

Grazzini's call for total independence from the ancients resonated with fellow dramatists eager to appear modern and to meet the spectators' demands for fresh and entertaining material. Agostino Ricchi boasts that his *Tre tiranni* is a new comedy, "never seen before, never read or found in the ancients." Cecchi proudly calls his *Assiuolo* a new play taken neither from Terence or Plautus but from an event that had happened recently in Pisa. Giraldi Cinzio, claiming to depart from the norm in order to please the spectators, declares that his tragedy *Altile* dramatizes a story never told by ancient or modern poets. Francesco D'Ambra describes his *Bernardi* as a true product of the times, in that it features none of the long and tedious speeches found in Terence or other ancients. Grazzini shares this aversion to tiresome scenes, and has Prologue both in *Strega* and in *Spiritata* assure the spectators that they would not be burdened with lengthy and dull ("lunghi e fastidiosi") speeches. Reflecting his contemporaries' annoyance with wordy plays, the stage theorist and sometime director Angelo Ingegneri (1550?–1613) observes that spectators could actually fall asleep and wake up at the end of a long monologue without missing much of anything (284). The emphasis on holding the audience's interest was not purely rhetorical, for the public in general was growing tired of humdrum scenes and stale plots. Isabella D'Este, writing to her husband about two plays she had seen on the occasion of her brother Alfonso's wedding, complains that the first was long and boring ("longa e fastidiosa") and the other was wearisome, mostly because of its lengthy lines.[23]

The audience was an active participant in the debate on the poetics of theatre, and its expectations inevitably influenced the playwright's selection of plot material and its staging. After all, an author's reputation rested mostly on the audience's response, which alone determined the play's value as a form of entertainment and as a commentary on moral and social issues. In judging stage representations, the spectators could not help but compare the new theatre with that of the Greeks and the Romans, the only secular stage they had come to know and appreciate. Inherently, they expected an art form that, while emulating the ancients, offered a realistic representation of their own world. Eager to win the audience's approval, some playwrights called attention to their classical source and their implicit or explicit intent to compete with it. In his prologue to Bibbiena's *Calandria,* Castiglione reminds the audience that the author intended to vie (or "stare a paragone") with Plautus, the play's original source. Others emphasized the verisimilitude of the story by placing the action in contemporary and familiar settings. In Grazzini's *Frate,* for instance, Prologue informs the spectators that the story they are about to see happened in Florence during the 1539 siege of the city. Machiavelli underscores the actuality of his *Mandragola* by pointing out to the spectators that the action took place in their own city. But fearing a libel suit, he claims, he had to omit details that might reveal the identity of some citizens alluded to in the play.

From the Classical Stage to the Theatre of the Renaissance

Claims of originality such as these make it clear that many dramatists believed they had learned all they could learn from the classics and were now looking to create their own theatre. This was in no way a rejection of the great accomplishments of the past but an expression of the Renaissance belief in the potential of human ingenuity. Long before Ariosto argued that modern writers could be as good as their classical idols on the grounds that creativity is a God-given talent (*Cassaria,* Prologue), Petrarch had pointed out that it was foolish to trust only the ancients, for they were men, too. In his view, he writes to his friend Francesco Bruni, writers should strive to be original and not be influenced by that trite and vulgar saying that there is nothing new to be said.[24] Dolce reiterated this same belief in the prologue to his *Fabritia,* where two boys make a lengthy and detailed argument in favour of originality in imitation. After the first boy admits that there is nothing the ancients have not already said, the other young man points out that it is not at all paradoxical to imitate and surpass them at the same time. After all, the Romans excelled by imitating the Greeks, and the moderns have already surpassed the ancients in many things. It is not unreasonable, he continues, that today's authors surpass their classical models in the art of theatre ("che gli intelletti de' moderni non possano in questa parte avanzarli"). Of course, by imitation Dolce does not mean the reproduction of the old costumes, customs, and institutions but the adaptation of existing material or ideas to the living realities of his times.

What emerged from the ongoing debate was not a consensus or a manifesto on the poetics of theatre but a sense that imitation of the ancients was an acceptable way to vie with them. This did not preclude the production of original works that spoke directly to contemporary audiences about their world. Accordingly, playwrights set out to distinguish themselves by staging storylines at times taken from history or short story collections, at other times with characters and episodes from classical theatre. Often, they worked with plots and subplots gleaned from a variety of sources. To be sure, the presence of the ancients never fully vanished from the theatre of the Renaissance, as playwrights continued to adhere, albeit loosely, to the formal structure of classical drama and the teachings of Horace and Aristotle. A basic Horatian precept was the emphasis on the visual aspect of stage representation because, as Horace points out, spectators are impressed more by what they see than what they hear. However, he cautions that certain gruesome scenes should be kept off the stage (*Ars poetica* 179–88). Aristotle's *Poetics* helped to determine what topics were suitable for stage representation in both comedy and tragedy. Also, the Aristotelian unities allowed for a coherent representation and a degree of verisimilitude, both of which the spectators came to expect and appreciate.[25]

The extent to which the Renaissance theatre succeeded as a means of entertainment and as a forum for cultural debates hinged largely upon its appeal to the audience. The notion of verisimilitude, which proposed that theatrical representations bear a strong resemblance to actual reality, played an important role in suspending the audience's natural reluctance to be drawn into the fictional world of the stage. It was in this context that playwrights claimed that their works were a reflection of contemporary reality, took place in recognizable modern cities, and represented "true" stories. Dolce, for example, assures the audience that his *Ragazzo* is a real story ("ritratta dal vero"). Giraldi claims that the events in his *Antivalomeni* are cast in virtual reality ("con sembianza del ver"). Verisimilitude also extended to a realistic stage reproduction of natural phenomena, such as light and sounds. A luminous contraption representing the sun or the moon moving slowly across the fictional skies of the stage was often used to suggest the virtual time of the day and its passing.[26] The rolling of a large stone off stage produced the sound of thunder, while flashes of burning powder created the illusion of lightning. The effect of these technical innovations was both entertaining and engaging, as spectators, always eager for entertainment, undoubtedly marvelled at the ingenuity of the inventions. The architect Sebastiano Serlio, often hired to create stage sets, was a strong advocate of sensory devices because he believed that they delighted the spectators, excited their fancy, and predisposed them to accept more readily the illusion of theatre.[27]

But what really measured or challenged the playwright's poetic ability were his development of the plot and his treatment of the characters. What mattered was not so much the story as the disposition of the events and the novel way in which the characters experienced them. The tale in Machiavelli's *Clizia*, for instance, is roughly the same as that of its Plautine source, *Casina*, but the Italian characters experience it in a totally different way than their Roman counterparts. Admittedly, *Clizia*'s characters exhibit some of the traits displayed by their ancient models; however, the new values and ambitions informing their behaviour reflect the stage world in which they have come to live. In other words, they look, think, and act in ways that speak to the audience of their own culture. Like the characters in the story, the spectators, too, experience the stage events in the context of their times.[28] It is unlikely that they found humorous some of the situations that amused the Roman audiences. Nicomaco, *Clizia*'s *amator senex*, is hardly the ridiculous old man in love from the Latin source. If anything, he inspires compassion, whereas his Roman ancestor is a permanent source of laughter and ridicule.

This distinction warrants our paying particular attention to authors' treatment of the source, especially the alterations, the innovations, and the cultural context that ultimately define and distinguish a new play. The task is most challenging because the source is not always easily recognized. Though most playwrights revealed their theatrical source(s), albeit only in general terms and as a reminder that they were competing with the past, there are stage adaptations that feature characters, themes, and episodes borrowed from several sources. Some playwrights do not name a source at all. Agnolo Firenzuola, for example, does not identify the source of his *Lucidi*, although it is obviously a close imitation of Plautus's *Menaechmi*. Ariosto's *Cassaria* owes some of its themes to several Plautine and Terentian plays. Cecchi's *Assiuolo*, supposedly based on a recent event, is actually interwoven with material adopted from several Boccaccian tales. Also, the play's Ambrogio, an old lawyer given to sexual fantasies, brings to mind *Clizia*'s Nicomaco. As characters and situations tended to appear and reappear in various works, each with a particular emphasis or place in the story, it is important to identify and focus on the primary source(s). Only then can one determine what was imitated and whether or how it was modified.

It must be noted that in most cases playwrights adopted plot material either from existing plays or from prose narratives. In the first instance, they might choose to retain certain source elements, modify others, and/or add new ones. In the second case, the task was more engaging because they faced the additional challenge of transforming the medium of communication from storytelling to theatre. Unlike stage representations, prose narratives are not bound by realistic expectations. They may take place over an extended period of time and in various, distant places. Also, the world they depict rises from the suggestive power of the word that stirs the readers' emotions and incites their minds to wander beyond the confines of the written page. No such freedom is accorded to theatre audiences, whose perception of the fictional world is guided largely by the audible and visual signs of the stage. Here, the allusive nature of the word is somewhat restricted by the representation of a reasonably realistic world that defines and contextualizes it.[29] Renaissance audiences were usually shown a dramatic action that unfolded before their eyes and/or within earshot of the auditorium, leaving little to the imagination. The representation was expected to have the appearance of truth or verisimilitude, as Aristotle recommended. Accordingly, where the source story called for certain episodes to take place far away from the stage, such as in another city or country, the playwright changed the location to a place close enough for the characters to go to and/or return from during the performance. This concern for realistic representation also led dramatists to reduce to a single action source-stories consisting of several narrative strands.[30]

Though these formal requirements were meant to streamline the plot and, at the same time, give it a sense of realism, they often carried thematic implications of their own. In *Mandragola*, for instance, the change of location from the Boccaccian public baths to Nicia's own home is formally necessary because the baths are too far from the stage location. The spectators would find it unlikely that the lovers could travel to the baths, enjoy each other's company, and be back on stage (downtown) all within the action's time frame. But this change of location is not purely formal, for it also underscores the shift in the thematic emphasis Machiavelli places on the love affair. In the source (*Decameron* 3.6), the adulterous liaison between Ricciardo and Catella celebrates the power of love; in the play, the affair between Callimaco and Lucrezia makes a mockery of marriage, especially because it is perpetrated in the adulteress's own bedroom. With regard to the unity of time, the source dwells on Ricciardo's long and consuming wooing of young Catella, emphasizing the notion that love is all-powerful and that no human can resist its urge. The play compresses the lengthy courtship into a few days, causing young Callimaco to fall in love with Lucrezia even though he has never seen her (he had just heard of her great beauty). He conquers her within a short time after arriving in town. The sudden infatuation, narrated as *antefactum*, and the quick seduction tend to trivialize the importance Boccaccio placed on the labours of love, reducing the theme of love to a whimsical impulse and, therefore, to a theme of secondary importance in the world of the play.

All alterations tend to distinguish the adaptation from its original source, establish its own originality, and proclaim its relevance to the audience. These modifications are significant, for the way in which they transform the source into a new product leads to a deeper understanding of the Renaissance notion of imitation. It also allows for a higher appreciation of the cultural dynamics that characterize the world of the author and his audience. But the variety and the specific functions of the innovations are such that an attempt to compile a list of conceivable changes would be impractical, if not futile. Better results are obtained by concentrating on the basic elements of theatre, especially the characters, the distribution of the dramatic sequences, and the spatial/temporal settings in which the action unfolds. Emphasis must also be placed on the linguistic peculiarities of the new text. Particular attention must be paid to staging features, such as physical appearance, movements, noises, and all other audio-visual effects that tend to place the old in a modern context. When available, the spectators' reception must be taken into account, for their approval or disapproval tells us of their values, aesthetic preferences, and social concerns.

The Poetics of the New Theatre

The ensuing chapters focus on these aspects of theatre, with particular emphasis on the ways individual authors treated the source and on their effort to engage the audience. The playwright's innovations not only afford us a comprehensive appreciation of the poetics informing his choices but also help to evaluate his creative ability to morph the original into something new. Naturally, the most immediate assessment comes from the spectators. Likely familiar with the source(s), they were in a position to compare the adaptation with the original, note the novelties, and assess its relevance to their world. As the success of a representation rested almost entirely on the spectators' favourable reception, playwrights were most anxious to please them with their stagecraft and literary skills. Unfortunately, there is very little documented testimony regarding the audience's reception of any given performance. The void leaves today's readers to look for any textual or extra-textual evidence that might help determine how a play was received and which aspects, if any, the spectators found of particular interest. In most instances, Prologues provide bits of information that may lead to plausible assumptions regarding the audience's reception of a particular play. It was usually in the prologue that playwrights, before proceeding with the actual representation, introduced themselves and reminded the audience of their previous stage successes.

All dramatists accepted the premise that the main function of theatre was to teach and delight ("giovare e dilettare"). This they usually promised through Prologue, who welcomed the viewing public and asked for its undivided attention. Like their Latin models, they spoke directly to the spectators, mostly with the intent to predispose them favourably towards the representation. For the benefit of the audience, they provided a brief summary of the plot, identified the source(s), and, when appropriate, defended or explained their poetics. Always through Prologue, they also took the opportunity to advertise their own plays, much as some of today's book covers provide a list of the author's previous works. Cecchi, for instance, in his *Sciamiti*, tells the spectators that he is the author of *Servigiale*, *Medico*, and many other comedies. In his *Maschere*, he reminds a Florentine audience that he has written eighteen plays, fourteen of which take place in "your city." Lelio Gavardo Asolano, in dedicating the 1590 performance of Sforza Oddi's *Prigione d'amore* to Galeazzo Paleotto, writes that the play was so popular that many people from various regions were asking for a copy. The only way to satisfy such a great demand, he continues, is to have the text mass-produced ("col la stampa").[31] In the case of comedy in particular, some playwrights called attention to their new comic style. In the prologue to his *Cortegiana*, Aretino boasts of a comic style different from that of the ancients. Though he does not dwell on the nature of this new "stil comico," it definitely includes witticisms ("giochi") with which, according to Prologue in Ariosto's *Cassaria*, one can make a story less dreary ("men trista").

It was quite common for authors of comedies to warm up their audiences with witty remarks, puns, or plays on words often charged with lewd allusions. In addressing the women in the audience, playwrights, always through Prologue, would thank them for the festive mood their beauty and elegance brought to the auditorium and for luring male spectators to the theatre. Drawing on the feminine gender of the word "comedy," at times referred to as lady comedy ("madonna commedia"), authors did not hesitate to push the analogy woman/comedy to the obscene. In Ariosto's *Lena*, Prologue plays on the double meaning of the word "tail" ("coda") as he refers to the female character Lena and the *comedia* of the same name. Noting that the play's new version features two additional scenes attached at the end (the tail), he points out that Lena (the play/the character) is proud of the tail tacked on her back. She is like "all the other women who want to feel a tail behind them, but despise those who don't want one, or those who cannot have one. No woman, [...] who can put one on," Prologue concludes mischievously, "refuses to do so." Other Prologues were even more obscene, especially when playing on the double meaning of the word "Argomento" as either plot summary or male organ. In Firenzuola's *Trinuzia*, Prologue advises the ladies to induce their lovers to fantasize during the day about things they could do with them at night. If you want baby goats, he tells them, you must mount the goats good and early. He also reminds them that he is too tired to do the *Argumento* (give a plot summary), which stretches the eardrum or the "hole" ("buco") of the mind and "penetrates or slides in more easily."[32]

One must assume that the audience approved of these salacious witticisms, for playwrights had to be careful not to offend the prevailing sense of decorum, lest they jeopardize their good reputation. The audience's acceptance of Prologue's libertine allusions as legitimate forms of amusement reveals a society with rather tolerant moral standards. This is especially true when one considers that some of these plays were written by members of the clergy (Cardinal Bibbiena's *Calandria*) and were often performed in convents and even before the Roman Curia. Of course, if the spectators found the Prologue's coarseness amusing, certainly they would not object to what they were about to hear and see on stage. On this premise, a jovial Prologue invited them to watch and enjoy the performance.

Not so jovial, of course, was the Prologue of tragedies. His role was in many ways similar to that of his comic counterpart, including addressing the audience, discussing the author's poetics, and fending off potential detractors. However, his primary goal was to prepare the spectators for the human suffering and the violent death(s) they were about to witness on stage. He spoke to them of innocent victims and bloodthirsty tyrants, of gruesome deeds and savage revenge that, though inhabiting the fictional world of the stage, could potentially befall real people just like them. He then invited an apprehensive audience to behold the play's performance, promising them a cathartic experience. Before exiting the stage, he usually turned to the ladies in the audience and asked them not to hold back their tears, a true sign of their approval.

In all stage dramatizations, when the curtains came up (as was the custom then), the spectators beheld a fictional world that proposed to move them to tears or laughter, depending on the comic or tragic nature of the representation. Whatever their emotional experience, they were treated to a stage spectacle and a literary exhibition that inevitably prompted them to assess the playwright's creative ability. We may never be able to fully determine the extent to which Renaissance audiences appreciated the novelties of a given play. We can only attempt to identify some of them and discuss their cultural and dramaturgical implications. In this sense, we must, like virtual spectators, note the differences between the adaptation and its source, observe the ways in which the old inspired the new, and determine to what extent the imitation is an original work. This will help us to gain a better understanding of what contemporary audiences were likely to find amusing and engaging, and what issues and values defined the ethos of Renaissance society. Established scholars of the Italian Renaissance theatre such as D'Ancona, Apollonio, Sanesi, Neri, Borsellino, Herrick, and Radcliff-Umstead provide insightful comments on major differences between adaptations and sources. However, their observations tend to be too sweeping for a comprehensive appreciation of the complexities of stage adaptation. They also tend to limit their analyses to the literary text, glossing over the stagecraft that normally informs the genre. They seldom focus on the thematic implications of stage sounds or visual props; nor do they dwell on the impact that such sensorial percepts might have on the audience's emotional and intellectual response.

The present book centres on the confrontation between imitations and their original sources, highlighting the themes and the stagecraft that distinguish the "new" plays as original works in their own right. It attempts not a chronological or systematic evolution of the genre but a fresh perspective on how Renaissance playwrights moved forward by looking back. Its purpose is to show creative imitation at work by focusing on source elements that playwrights chose to adopt, omit, or modify. Each chapter deals with particular aspects of the imitative process that make the work original and relevant to contemporary audiences. *Mandragola,* for instance, shows how Machiavelli borrows material from Boccaccio's stories and turns them into a play that speaks to Florentine audiences about their city and social mores. *Clizia,* though a close imitation of Plautus's *Casina*, stages a fictional world that gives pause to those who expected a farcical *pièce* along the lines of its Roman source. *Assiuolo* exemplifies literary *contaminatio* in that its author borrows plot elements from several prose and stage sources and moulds them into one of the best comedies of sixteenth-century Italy. Groto's *Emilia* is a unique imitation with a plot drawn from a mixture of ancient stage and current history. Mixing comic forms from Plautus's *Epidicus* with unhappy memories of the bloody fall of Cyprus, the author forces his Venetian audiences to reflect on the humiliation Venice suffered following its surrender of the island (1571). Della Porta's *Gli duoi fratelli rivali,* though reminiscent of some of Plautus's plays, is a close imitation of one of Bandello's *novelle* set in 1283 in Sicily. The playwright skilfully moves the action to early sixteenth-century Salerno, highlighting the city's Spanish rule and its realities. Interestingly, as in Groto's case, here too the comic element does not seem to blend with the sombre mood of the situation. Thus the comic seems to exist for its own sake rather than as an integral part of the play.

The tragedies that follow, Giraldi's *Orbecche* and Dolce's *Marianna,* are two unique examples of imitation in that they both draw their material exclusively from prose narrative sources: the first from fiction, the second from history. Here, the emphasis is on the playwrights' stagecraft, especially on how they interweave events that happened at various times and in several locations and reduce them into a single action that takes place in one day and in one location. The authors' choices to modify and rearrange source materials allow for the dramatization of cultural issues of particular concern to their audiences. *Orbecche* dramatizes the ongoing debates on the Renaissance notion of princeship and on the status of women; *Marianna* stages the tragic consequences of the destructive forces of a tyrant's political insecurity and jealous love. A short conclusion points to the future of tragedy on the Italian stage, noting that, while it never rivalled the best of Shakespeare or Racine, it produced excellent works. Among the most memorable dramas, it suffices to mention Giovambattista Andreini's *Adamo* (1613), Carlo De' Dottori's *Aristodemo* (1670), and Scipione Maffei's *Merope* (1713). It will find its greatest champion in Vittorio Alfieri (1749–1803), the best and most prolific tragedian in the history of Italian drama. Tragedy also became a major source of inspiration for seventeenth-century melodrama, a genre that eventually evolved into opera as we know it today. The conclusion also reflects on the absorption of neoclassical comedy by the increasingly popular commedia dell'arte, an art form that dominated the theatres of Europe until Carlo Goldoni (1707–93) brought it back to its literary tradition.

Chapter Two

Machiavelli's *Mandragola*

Machiavelli's *Mandragola* is considered one of the best comedies of the Italian Renaissance and, arguably, the most successful imitation of prose narrative. We do not know exactly when it was written, but most scholars agree that it was composed either in 1518, on the occasion of Lorenzo de' Medici's wedding with Madeleine de la Tour, or the following year.[1] We know from contemporary sources that it was received enthusiastically in several Italian cities. Giovio reported that the 1520 performance in Rome provoked great laughter even among the most sober of spectators ("vel in tristibus risum excitavis"). Marin Sanudo recorded in his *Diaries* that in the 1522 performance in Venice the audience was so large that it poured onto the stage, preventing the actors from finishing the last act. The comedy was performed again, without interruption, three days later.[2] Through the centuries, the play's critical fortunes continued to grow, winning the endorsement of scholars who praised its artistic and ideological qualities as well as its originality.[3] To be sure, the work is not altogether original; it owes much of its storyline to Boccaccio's *Decameron*. However, adapting or imitating known sources is not necessarily evidence of lack of creativity, as is often alleged, but a viable approach to producing new works of art. In the following pages, the discussion centres on how Machiavelli adapted Boccaccio's story to the stage, and how the world it reflects is original and relevant to contemporary audiences.

The play is a free adaptation of Boccaccio's story of Catella and Ricciardo (*Dec.* 3.6), although aspects of some of its themes and characters may be traced to other sources – namely, Boccaccio's Calandrino stories and Bibbiena's *Calandria*.[4] The Boccaccian tale takes place in fourteenth-century Naples, where the nobleman Ricciardo Mutolo is hopelessly in love with Catella, the beautiful and jealous wife of Filippello. Unable to win Catella's affection after a long and frustrating courtship, Ricciardo devises a plan that brings about the immediate satisfaction of his desires. Taking advantage of the woman's excessive jealousy, he dupes her into believing that her husband is cheating on her. She readily accepts his story that her husband is courting his (Ricciardo's) wife and that lately, through the services of an old woman they have arranged to meet in a room at the local baths. The susceptible Catella quickly resolves to go to the baths and take the place of Ricciardo's wife so that she may surprise her own husband in the act. When she realizes that the man making love to her in that dark room at the baths is not her husband but Ricciardo, she is furious and threatens to tell her husband. But Ricciardo dissuades her, warning of the grave consequences that would befall them both should the incident become public. Her reputation would be ruined, and her husband would kill or be killed in his attempt to avenge his honour. The impetuous young woman, still savouring the passionate experience with Ricciardo, agrees to keep quiet and to continue the love affair for as long as they take pleasure from one another. The story concludes with the female narrator's envious wish that God should grant her and her audience such pleasures ("Iddio faccia noi goder del nostro," *Dec.* 236).[5]

In adapting the story, Machiavelli proceeded to make the necessary alterations to transform it into a dramatic representation. The task was not an easy one, for, apart from Ariosto's plays, there was hardly any established theatrical tradition on which to build. According to Richard Andrews, "pioneers such as Ariosto and Machiavelli were inventing a new mode of theater from scratch" (205). Formal guidance came mostly from the example of what was known of ancient theatre, from the *Poetics* of Aristotle, and from Horace's *Ars poetica*. However, criteria for retaining elements from the source or adding new ones rested largely on the playwright's stagecraft and on the view of the world he wished to represent. For such a world to be accessible and meaningful to the intended audience, the representation had to feature thematic and formal novelties that were both engaging and entertaining. This involved selective, but significant, modifications that affected both the plot and the characters. Elements commonly requiring changes included the place and times in which the action took place. Formal innovations such as these followed by and large the poetics of verisimilitude inspired by the Aristotelian concept of mimesis or the imitation of truth. In the first half of the *cinquecento*, long before a full-blown debate erupted over the appropriateness of verisimilitude in theatre,[6] it was a common expectation for stage action to develop according to some realistic premises.

Whether a play was based on an old story or on a recent event, authors tended to situate the action in familiar places and times in order to make stage representations somewhat believable. To this end, they normally located the action on a major street or central *piazza* of a modern city. Machiavelli's *Mandragola* takes place in Florence, though Prologue tells the audience that the story is so universal that it could easily be imagined as taking place in cities such as Pisa or Rome.[7] In describing the stage, Prologue alludes to a central square or intersection featuring a doctor's house on the right, another house occupied by a young lover on the left, the street of Love on the corner, and a church across from it. The need to provide a Florentine audience with spatial markers of a street or square in their own city implies that the scene is not clearly depicted and thus not easily recognizable. Some see this form of unrefined sketching as an early or precocious example of the use of perspective in theatrical representation.[8] But the vagueness may actually be intentional in order to avoid easily identifiable locations that could compromise the line between fiction and reality. Conceivably, Machiavelli could have risked a libel suit if the audience had recognized the house belonging to the aging cuckold Messer Nicia and identified him with its actual owner. This fear is openly expressed in *Clizia,* where Prologue warns the audience not to expect to recognize the scenic setting or the characters because the author has changed names and places in order to avoid a libel suit ("per fuggire carico"). Be that as it may, there is plenty of textual evidence to establish with certainty that the action takes place in Florence. It suffices to recall that Ligurio looks for Callimaco "in Piazza, in Mercato, al Pancone delli Spini, alla Loggia de' Tornaquinci," all landmarks that a Florentine audience would easily recognize (4.2).[9] As for the historical context, Machiavelli sets the play's events between Charles VIII's invasion of Italy (1494) and the menace of the Turkish incursions on the Italian coasts during the first quarter of the sixteenth century. These familiar spatial and temporal settings not only conveyed a strong sense of realism to the fictional representation, they also helped to lull the spectators into a sense of proximity with the world of the stage.

The poetics of verisimilitude went hand in hand with the observance of the unities of action, time, and place that characterized ancient theatre and later became known as the Aristotelian unities. With regard to the unity of action, though an increasing number of playwrights favoured story lines interwoven with a variety of intrigues and subplots, Machiavelli chooses to develop the action in the same linear fashion as the original tale. Simply told, the play follows the Boccaccian source to the extent that it too proceeds from a young man's determination to win the affection of a beautiful young woman. Callimaco, Ricciardo's counterpart, is passionately enamoured of the virtuous Lucrezia, the wife of Messer Nicia, a Florentine lawyer. The young man overcomes all obstacles and, like Ricciardo, achieves his goal through deception. He spends the night in bed with Lucrezia under the pretence that he is an innocent victim of Nicia's scheme to get her pregnant. While in bed, he tells her of his undying love and of Nicia's help in bringing about the amorous encounter. Lucrezia, deeply hurt by her husband's loathsome complicity in the whole affair and greatly satisfied by the sexual experience with young Callimaco, readily agrees to continue the relationship. The play ends as Nicia, the young lovers, and several other characters go to Sunday Mass. This conclusion, suggesting the church's sanction of the adulterous union,[10] recalls the sacrilegious tone of the original story, which ends with the plea that God grant the narrator and her audience the same pleasures accorded to Catella and Ricciardo.

The transition from the narrative to the stage does not present great obstacles with regard to the unity of time largely because the play focuses solely on Callimaco's seduction scheme. In the prose source, the narrator, after providing the basic elements of the story's background, recounts Ricciardo's persistent and vain efforts to seduce Catella and concludes with the final and successful attempt. Machiavelli skilfully compresses the events leading to the play's action and turns quickly to the development of the plot. The play's action begins immediately after a short verbal exposition of the historical circumstances that caused the Florentine Callimaco to move to Paris. While living in Paris, he happens to hear of the legendary beauty of the Florentine Madonna Lucrezia and, smitten by the description of her looks, decides to go see for himself. Having thus established Callimaco's instant passion as the force behind the story, Machiavelli proceeds to build the plot by announcing that Callimaco has just arrived in Florence and has hired the middleman Ligurio to help him conquer the irresistible Lucrezia. The play ends the following morning as Callimaco and Lucrezia, having spent the night in each other's arms, go to church accompanied by those who helped to bring about their happy, albeit adulterous, encounter.

Though time compression is primarily a formal expedient for limiting the stage action to a twenty-four-hour period, it usually affects the content of the story. In Boccaccio, the female narrator announces that the tale is about Ricciardo and Catella, two young Neapolitans happily married to their respective spouses. She then proceeds to describe Ricciardo's obsession with Catella and the various ways in which he tried to seduce her. The long and detailed account of Ricciardo's unrelenting courtship underscores the consuming power of love and the irrepressible urge to satisfy one's natural passions. By contrast, Callimaco falls in love with Lucrezia immediately upon hearing about her beauty and manages to bed her within a short time after arriving in town. This expeditious treatment of the theme of love tends to diminish the importance the Boccaccian source places on the power of love. Indeed, Callimaco's impetuous passion for a woman he has never met before reduces love to a whimsical impulse and, therefore, to secondary importance in the world of the play. To be sure, love is the ostensible force behind the scheme to secure Callimaco's success. However, the actual focus is not so much on love as on the personal motives that cause each character to take part in the scheme. And it is from the dramatization of these motives that there emerges the view of the world the author intends to represent on stage.

The change in thematic emphasis is also apparent in the action's location. The scenic space consists of the usual *piazza* with streets leading to and away from it. To achieve this unity of place, the playwright found it necessary to modify the Boccaccian story, which unfolds in various areas of Naples, including the local baths. *Mandragola*'s characters live or work in buildings situated on the streets and / or on the square featured on stage, so that the action can unfold mostly in one area. Even the lovers' trysting place, which in the source is located in a distant bathhouse, is moved to Nicia's residence on one of the streets converging on the piazza. Ligurio calls attention to this change of place as he advises Nicia to take Lucrezia to the local baths, thus recalling for the audience the Boccaccian location. But Nicia, claiming that the baths are too far away and alleging logistical difficulties, discards the idea (1.2). Instead, he agrees to help arrange in his own house an encounter between his wife and the first "young rascal" found wandering around the neighbourhood that evening (2.6).

From a dramaturgical point of view, it may be argued that the location of the trysting place is not important. After all, the spectators do not witness the amorous encounter, and therefore it does not matter where it takes place. But it does matter, because spatial proximity goes to the heart of theatrical representation. Dramatic space, whether on stage or near it, reduces the need to narrate what happens offstage. An event that requires narration, John Storey points out, tends to rob "the stage of its most important function, that of representing and referring."[11] Also, spatial proximity reinforces the notion of verisimilitude, which helps to foster the theatrical illusion of reality. As Renaissance commentators on Aristotle's *Poetics* argued, an event that by its nature takes a long time to develop should not be represented in a short period. A messenger sent from Rome to Egypt who returns to Rome within hours tends to undermine credibility. Callimaco would do just that if he, having travelled to the baths and spent time in bed with Lucrezia, were to return to the *piazza* (on stage) within the hour. In addition, the dramatic space would be so far removed from the stage that the episode would have a limited dramaturgical effect on the audience. Instead, with the action unfolding within the scenic space, the spectators can actually see the abducting party (Ligurio, Siro, Fra' Timoteo, and Nicia) seize Callimaco and force him into the house where he is to lie with Lucrezia. The house stands in front of them as the symbol of a moral fortress (the virtuous Lucrezia) whose defences have finally succumbed to the corrupting ways of its assailants. Though the bedroom is not visibly accessible, the proximity of the house excites the spectators' imagination and allows them to witness through their mind's eye the terms of the surrender being negotiated within its walls. They are undoubtedly all ears when Callimaco finally comes out of the house and, presumably still dishevelled, gives an excited description of the pleasures he and Lucrezia took with each other.

The new trysting place has also a thematic significance in that it is not a mere public place, like the baths in the source, but the very home of the man being cuckolded. Adultery, in addition to being a serious breach of the wedding vows taken before God and the community, makes a mockery of marriage when it is perpetrated in one's own home, the very temple of holy matrimony. Nicia's consent to induce his wife to commit adultery in their home and their own bed defines him as a shallow individual incapable of appreciating the serious implications of his actions. His willingness to be cuckolded undermines the integrity of the family he is trying to raise. It also implies the renunciation of his role as a true *paterfamilias* and, at the same time, the reduction of his standing in the community. His wife scoffs at his stupidity, while others ridicule him. Thus, a seemingly simple change of location emerges as a symbol of a social institution under assault and underscores the moral indifference of its chief custodian. Pointedly, it calls attention to the change of focus from the Boccaccian emphasis on the power of love to the concern for a society undermined by the corruption of its members.

The Characters: Source versus Imitation

This thematic novelty becomes more apparent when one considers the extent to which Machiavelli changed or modified the roles of the original Boccaccian characters. Though the characters in *Mandragola* differ in various ways from their counterparts in the source, the similarities with their prototypes allow for a close look at the story's evolution from its prose source to the stage adaptation. Lucrezia is a beautiful woman and a faithful wife, just like Catella. She, too, is induced to have an extramarital affair and, like Boccaccio's heroine, decides to continue the intrigue. Callimaco is a young nobleman driven by the same natural passions that drive his counterpart Ricciardo, and, like Ricciardo, resorts to artful means in order to achieve his goal. The cunning Ligurio brings to mind the old woman, the supposed messenger in the alleged affair between Filippello and Ricciardo's wife. Nicia is reminiscent of Filippello to the extent that both are cuckolds or *cornuti*. Though distant, these similarities help to confirm Boccaccio's story as the primary source of Machiavelli's play. The connection not only confers the authority of literary tradition on the new text but also establishes the cultural environment from which the world of the play evolves. Ultimately, the similarities tend to highlight the alterations that lend originality to the imitation.

The likeness between Catella and Lucrezia inevitably calls attention to their differences, especially the flaws and the virtues that mark their behaviour. Catella's swift decision to go to the rendezvous at the baths reveals her blinding jealousy and at the same time underscores the impulsive nature of her personality. Also, her hasty consent to continue the secret amour with Ricciardo calls into question her passionate declarations of conjugal fidelity, as it emphasizes the power of human passions to override one's commitment to social conventions and institutions. Such behaviour contrasts sharply with the prudence and rectitude of her stage counterpart. Lucrezia finds abhorrent the suggestion that in order to get pregnant she must sleep with a man other than her own husband. Only after persistent threats from her husband, nagging pressure from her mother, and absolving assurances from her confessor does she agree to commit adultery. Her resistance not only underscores the depth of her moral convictions but also allows the playwright to highlight the hypocritical roles that church and family play in undermining the very same values upon which they stand. Quite clearly, their involvement sanctions Lucrezia's grudging decision to continue the adulterous relationship, which she carries out openly and without regard for decorum.

This behaviour sets her apart from her predecessor in several ways. First, unlike Catella, who decides hastily and on her own initiative, Lucrezia follows the counsel of her confessor and her family, emphasizing the public domain of the affair. Second, she resolves to continue her liaison with Callimaco not out of mere sexual gratification or fear of social repercussions, as does her Boccaccian counterpart, but mostly out of contempt for her husband, who pressured her into the illicit affair in the first place. Third, unlike Catella, who keeps her intrigue secret, Lucrezia parades hers in public. Catella's secrecy highlights her awareness of the unlawful and sinful nature of her deed. Lucrezia's openness, in contrast, shows her intent to flaunt the approval of society and the blessing of the church. She insists that Callimaco befriend Nicia, that he go to church with her family the morning after and, afterwards, to the house for dinner (5.4). And, having proposed to Callimaco that they be together as often as they wish, she tells Nicia to give the young lover the key to the house so that he may come and go as he pleases (5.6).

The comparison distinguishes Lucrezia as a woman of high integrity who succumbs reluctantly to the corrupting pressure of family and friends. Some scholars suggest that she is a victim of rape. Others, focusing on her decision to continue the love affair, liken her to a Machiavellian hero or "savio," who recognizes and seizes the opportunity to act.[12] Though these suggestions are not without merit, they offer a limited view of Lucrezia's character because they do not take into full account the factors that contribute to her decisions. In 5.1, Callimaco reveals that Lucrezia decided to continue the relationship or, if one wishes to use a Machiavellian phrase, "seize the opportunity" because of Callimaco's shrewdness, her husband's foolishness, her mother's simplicity, and the friar's wickedness. This is hardly the resolve of the typical Machiavellian hero or *virtuoso* who seizes the moment with speed and determination. Nor is it the reaction of a sacrificial lamb, as Roberto Alonge suggests. Alonge goes so far as to liken Lucrezia's anguish to Christ's agony, elevating her night with Callimaco to a "Gethsemanic night."[13] More likely, it is the response of a woman who feels betrayed by the very defenders of her integrity. At best, she is a moral casualty reminiscent of the city of Florence, which, according to the political allegory originally suggested by Samburg and later developed by Parronchi, was allowed to come under the control of the francophile Lorenzo de' Medici (Callimaco), while the Florentine Gonfalonier Soderini (Nicia) remained the nominal head of state.[14] Be that as it may, the relevance of these critical views to the present discussion is that they call attention to the ideological relevance of Lucrezia's role and, inherently, the extent to which the play evolved from its narrative source.

Another equally important distinction is the way in which Machiavelli modified the character of the middleman. Though the parasite Ligurio retains certain distant traits of the Boccaccian old woman, his role is infinitely more essential to the development and the representation of the story. The similarity between the two characters begins and ends with their roles as intermediaries in the amorous encounters between the lovers in the respective versions of the story. In the original, the old woman exists not as a real character but only as a verbal construct of Ricciardo's invention. She is the go-between "femina" that Ricciardo mentions in his tale of the fictitious love affair between his own wife and Catella's husband, Filippello. Even in this fabricated existence, the old woman is but a narrative expedient that allows Ricciardo to dupe Catella. In *Mandragola*, the intermediary is an actual character who is central to the plot and instrumental in our appreciation of other characters.

Ligurio is a crafty parasite with an uncanny discernment of the motives and ambitions that drive others to action. His keen assessment of Nicia's wish to beget an heir allows him to deceive the old *messere* and cause Lucrezia to accept Callimaco as her lover. In his view, Nicia is so engrossed in his desire to have a son that he will not hesitate to accept as real the tale of the mandrake potion and its miraculous powers to impregnate infertile women. He knows how to convince the cowardly old lawyer that for the plan to be safe and successful another man must lie with Lucrezia. First, he scares him into believing that because of the potion's fatal side effects the first man to sleep with Lucrezia may die soon afterwards. Considering the risk, it is only wise that a man other than Nicia be the first to lie with Lucrezia. Then, he proceeds to overcome the old fool's hesitation by appealing to his vanity. He pretends to be highly disappointed that a man of letters and prestige, such as Nicia, would be so provincial as to hesitate to do what the French aristocracy has been doing for years. Ligurio is equally insightful in assuming that the lure of money will spur the grasping Friar Timoteo to advise the pious Lucrezia that it is not sinful to commit adultery when the intent is to have a child. With regard to Sostrata, Lucrezia's mother, he rightly assumes that she is worldly enough to go along with the scheme and help overcome her daughter's moral reservations (2.6).

Ligurio's character, though a radical modification of the Boccaccian old woman, recalls obliquely that of Ricciardo himself, especially his scheming ability. Also, to the extent that he is Callimaco's *alter ego*, he shares with Ricciardo the same goal: the fulfilment of his amorous desires. Nonetheless, there is a significant difference in the motives that determine their individual actions. Ricciardo schemes in order to obtain what long months of courtship have failed to produce: Catella's love. Ligurio's motive is not love but a smouldering resentment of Nicia's undeserved social standing. He is hired to help Callimaco conquer Lucrezia with the understanding that if he succeeds he will receive a good sum of money, a meagre supper if he fails (1.1). But, as the play develops, it becomes clear that what drives him is not so much the promise of material gain or, as some critics believe, a natural predisposition to trickery[15] but a deep-seated animosity towards the undeserving Nicia. At the end of the first act, he actually assures Callimaco that he is so eager to see him conquer Lucrezia that he would help him even without remuneration. He sees Nicia as a simpleton, undeserving of his privileged social status and unworthy of the young and beautiful Lucrezia. He suspects, among other things, that the old *messere* is not only too old to have children but possibly sterile and conceivably a homosexual. Alonge believes that Nicia's obvious pleasure in describing how he saw and touched the "young rascal's" male organs (5.2) suggests that he indeed harbours latent homosexual tendencies (249). Ligurio is convinced that the rich lawyer owes his wealth and his enviable marriage not to his own merits but to the whims of fortune (1.3). This resentment raises him above the status of a mere parasite in search of a good meal and reveals his intent to expose the undeserving Nicia to public ridicule. Unlike Ricciardo, who uses his intelligence to satisfy his sexual desires, Ligurio is willing to forgo his own gain in order to denounce those who do not deserve the social honours and privileges they enjoy (1.3). The distinction not only points to the evolution of the story from the private affair of two individuals (Ricciardo-Catella) to a situation involving various members of the community but also elevates the tale to a public censure against pretentious and unworthy individuals.

Ligurio's ridicule of Nicia, then, may be seen as a statement against the cultural bestowing of privileges according to one's birth. Scholars have compared Ligurio's resentment to Machiavelli's own frustration at being restricted to the role of secretary of the Second Chancellery largely because of his humble origins. He was never considered for the First Chancellery, assigned to his boss, Marcello Virgilio Adriani, a man better suited to the study of literature than the scheming world of politics. One can easily imagine Machiavelli's humiliation when a "wellborn" emissary, his friend Francesco Vettori, was chosen over him to lead the Florentine diplomatic mission to Emperor Maximilian in the summer of 1507.[16] "Machiavelli took it hard," writes Maurizio Viroli; "all his work and sacrifice, the splendid reports that had astounded everyone: everything subordinated to considerations of family and birth."[17] We cannot say with certainty whether and to what extent Machiavelli's own experience informs Ligurio's resentment. But it is not unreasonable to assume that the parallel reinforces the argument that the parasite's exposure of Nicia to public ridicule tends to highlight the need to place more emphasis on a system of merit and less on family names and connections.

Nicia's character and shortcomings distinguish him considerably from his Boccaccian analogue, Filippello. Although both characters are cuckolds, wealthy, and married to beautiful women, they could not be more different both formally and thematically. Unlike Nicia, who consents and contributes to his own victimization, Filippello is the unwitting victim of his wife's excessive jealousy. Formally, his role is peripheral to the plot and, much like the old woman in the story, he is virtually absent from the narrative. The reader learns of his existence through comments made about him. The narrator refers to him as a young nobleman, Ricciardo fashions him as an adulterer, and Catella complains about his recent lack of attention towards her. The purpose of these testimonials to Filippello's existence is not to establish his relevance in the story but to bring out Catella's character and explain her actions. His nominal role is in marked contrast with that of the ubiquitous Nicia, who is actively engaged in the development of the plot and in the celebration of his own wife's adultery.

The Critics

There is general agreement among established literary critics that Nicia's fatuous behaviour defines him as a pompous old fool wallowing in shallow values. Lately, however, some scholars have taken the unconventional view that the old *dottore* may not be the simpleton he appears to be. Harvey Mansfield, exhorting readers "not to be prisoners of convention," thinks that it is not wise to consider Nicia "stupid because he is a cuckold." If adultery brands a man as a cuckold, he argues, it does not necessarily make him "stupid." In his opinion, the aging *messere* is a shrewd individual who uses others to achieve his goal, namely, to have an heir (27–8). While it is true that Nicia should not be considered stupid because of his cuckoldry, he is hardly the "shrewd" schemer who uses others for his purpose. Besides Machiavelli's expressed view that Nicia is a simpleton,[18] textual evidence shows overwhelmingly that he is a pretentious fool guided by superficial values and thus easily duped. It suffices to recall the soliloquy in the third act in which he declares himself totally confused as to what is happening all around him. Following the meeting with Ligurio and Fra' Timoteo, he wonders rather pathetically,

> Is it night or day? Am I awake or dreaming? I haven't had a drop today, and yet I must be drunk, to go along with all this horseshit! We stop to talk about one thing with the friar, and he [Ligurio] says something completely different. Then he wants me to play deaf [...], God knows for what purpose! Here I am, out twenty-five ducats already, and nobody has talked about my real business yet. Now they have left me hanging around here like a doughnut on a stick. (3.7)

Clearly these are not the inner thoughts of a shrewd schemer but those of a confused simpleton who fails to grasp both Ligurio's crafty approach to lure Timoteo into the scheme and the latter's keen ability to see through it. At best, he is what Borsellino calls a dim-witted *dottore* with very few scruples ("corto d'ingegno e pochi scrupoli," *Commedie* xxvi). It should be reiterated that Nicia is laughable not because of his cuckoldry but for his pretensions and trivial values. For example, he takes pride in his knowledge of Latin, yet he fails to notice the nonsense of Callimaco's Latin commentary on the properties of women's urine (2.6). He recalls how hard he had to study jurisprudence just to learn a modicum of law (2.3), unaware that he is calling attention to his intellectual mediocrity. Reacting to Ligurio's baiting insinuation that his refusal to take Lucrezia to the baths is due to his lack of travelling experience, he brags about his trips to faraway places such as Livorno, Pisa, and Prato (all within a few miles of Florence). In Livorno he saw the sea, which, he marvels, is at least seven times wider than the Arno river and one sees nothing but "acqua, acqua, acqua" (1.2). Finally, a doctor of law who claims erudition and social status in most coarse language,[19] who considers himself a seasoned traveller for having been just a few miles away from home, who believes in miraculous plants, and who allows his wife to commit adultery upon being told that it is a common practice among French nobility is not a "shrewd schemer" but an inviting target for ridicule. Commenting on Nicia's pedantry, Sices and Atkinson point out that the old lawyer "represents a threat to society because he has misconstrued the proper use of education" (20).

This characterization of Nicia as an object of laughter points to a significant departure from his prototype and, inherently, from the scope of the source. In Boccaccio, Filippello's actual absence from the plot allows the narrative to move beyond the shopworn attacks on husbands and their inadequate manhood and to centre on the natural urge to satisfy one's passions. The story is a reflection of a world that celebrates intelligence (Ricciardo's trickery) as the driving force behind the accomplishment of one's goals, including the enjoyment of worldly pleasures, especially the pleasures of the flesh. Though *Mandragola* builds on values similar to those of the *Decameron,* its focus is on society's need to deal with the threat that its unprincipled and undeserving members pose to its integrity. Machiavelli's intent to draw attention to the widespread corruption undermining some of society's basic institutions may also be seen in the greater number of characters populating the world of the play.

New Characters

In addition to the four characters retained from the original story, Machiavelli introduced four new characters: a servant (to Callimaco), a friar, Lucrezia's mother, and a pious woman on her routine visit to a local church. Some of them appear on stage only briefly, but their number and respective roles are significant both formally and thematically. Dramaturgically, a large cast fulfils the theatrical necessity to dramatize in physical terms characters and situations that can only be imagined when reading a story. In prose fiction, characters exist only as verbal constructs and act out their parts in the reader's mind. In theatre, by contrast, they rise to their full essence through their physical presence and deportment. They appear not as the reader may imagine them but as the playwright wishes the audience to see them. Also, the stage would seem empty and practically devoid of action if only two or three characters were to dramatize the story. On the contrary, the bustling about of many people, the frequent comings and goings, the various sounds of rushing footsteps and excited voices, the rapid succession of scenes, and similar stage trappings tend to enliven the action and capture the attention of the viewing audience. One only needs to consider the theatrical effect of the riotous scene in which the masked, abducting party jumps the disguised Callimaco, blindfolds him, gags him, and drags him into Nicia's house for the encounter with Lucrezia (4.9).

From a thematic point of view, the large number of characters belonging to different levels of society, from servants to masters to clergymen, tends to reinforce the idea that the story involves a whole community. It clearly accentuates the departure from the private amour of the Boccaccian lovers to a love affair that is arranged with the help of various people, and thus with public knowledge and approval. In the *Decameron*, the story is confined to two individuals who give full expression to their natural desires. Their sworn secrecy guarantees the privacy of their actions and, as Ricciardo points out, protects Catella's reputation. It also prevents the involvement of other individuals, such as her husband, who would undoubtedly try to avenge the slight to his honour. Inevitably, the altercation would provoke the intervention of the authorities, causing the affair to become public knowledge and thus ruining everyone's reputation. In the adaptation, there is no secrecy, as Callimaco does not hesitate to make public his determination to conquer the beautiful Lucrezia. At the beginning of the play, he informs his servant Siro that, having considered the difficulties in seducing such a virtuous woman, he has secured the services of the shrewd middleman Ligurio. As the plot develops, Ligurio engages the help of Lucrezia's husband, her confessor, Friar Timoteo, and her worldly mother, Sostrata.

The introduction of additional characters, besides filling the stage and making it livelier, helps to place the action in a larger social setting. The servant and the pious woman have limited but important functions. The first serves to emphasize the social status of his master, Callimaco. He adds a sense of realism to the ruse, for it would be difficult to have Callimaco pass for a renowned doctor from Paris if he were not attended by the customary servants. As for the church-going woman, though she appears only once, she reinforces the historical context of the action by referring to the Turkish coastal incursions during the first quarter of the sixteenth century. Her fear of being impaled ("ho una gran paura di quello impalare," 3.3) certainly resonated with contemporary audiences, who were fully aware of and highly apprehensive about this most barbaric form of execution. Roger Crowley, speaking of the Europeans' fear of impalement, writes that the Ottomans used it as shock tactic, "especially as a means of demoralizing besieged cities" (154). As impalement consisted of hammering a long pole up the victim's rectum,[20] scholars have used the woman's reference to it to support their view that her speech is coloured with sexual allusions. Roberto

Alonge, for one, believes that she represents a society whose desires rotate around money, pleasure, and sex.[21]

But more to the point, she helps to expose Timoteo's grasping nature and willingness to sell his services. The unscrupulous friar, though a perennial literary commonplace, is yet another reminder of the corruption embedded in society and, more precisely, in the church. He follows in the long tradition of depraved clergymen populating the world of the *Decameron*, always ready to bend or compromise religious beliefs for private gain.[22] Within the context of *Mandragola*, however, the friar may also be seen as an instrument of society because in encouraging Lucrezia to procreate he helps to promote society's survival and continuity. From this perspective, the friar's role reflects Machiavelli's view of religion as an *instrumentum regni*, that is, as an institution that may be used for social and / or political needs.[23] It must be noted that such a practice makes use of any available resources, including the most abject means and / or ignoble individuals. To be sure, the "service" to society does not erase or mitigate the baseness of the means or individuals employed. In the case of the corrupt friar, his usefulness to society does not excuse his defilement of his religious commitment. Machiavelli may be irreligious, or a "writer of rabid anti-Christian sentiment," as some critics insist,[24] but he does not condone ungodly behaviour for its own sake. He simply believes that the state / society may resort to whatever means are at its disposal, good or bad, in order to preserve or advance its cause. Such a belief is rooted not in religion but in a socio-political morality based largely on secular values.

The other additional character, Sostrata, though not driven by the desire for material gain, exercises a seemingly corrupting influence on Lucrezia and, implicitly, on the integrity of the family. She does not hesitate to disregard all moral reservations and joins forces with those pressuring her daughter to submit to the potion experiment. Her behaviour confirms Callimaco's characterization of her as a fun-loving woman or "buona compagna" (1.1). It also bears out Ligurio's belief that she will be happy to assist with the scheme. He should know, for she is an old acquaintance of his ("é mia nota," 2.6). Even Friar Timoteo relies on her corrupting assistance, drawing on his view of her as a real fool or "una bestia," and thus easily manipulated (3.9). In fact, she is so uncritical of the friar's argument that the adulterous encounter is not a sinful act that she has no qualms about advising her daughter to go through with the mandrake trial (3.10). It was perhaps this flexible sense of morality, together with that of the other characters, that led

Eugenio Camerini to label the play immoral beyond words ("immorale oltre ogni dire," 22).

Machiavellian Morality

There is no question that the community represented on the stage regards Sostrata as a woman of not-so-high moral standards. Building on this negative image, scholars such as Alonge have labelled her a dissolute woman, fascinated by erotically perverse situations (246). However, a closer look at her role reveals that what defines her character in the play is not moral indifference but an overriding concern for her daughter's well-being. For her, for a woman to have a child is a question not of morality but of prudence. A wise person, she argues in a typically Machiavellian fashion, must always choose the lesser of two evils (3.1). She is aware that adultery is sinful, but she is equally aware that without children her daughter would have no respectable place in society. This is a society that by and large measures a woman's worth in terms of her childbearing function. "Can't you see," she pleads with her daughter, "that a woman without children has no home?" And, worse, should a childless woman become a widow, she would be left alone "like an animal, abandoned by everyone" (3.11).

This is not the hyperbolic apprehension of an overanxious mother but the stage reflection of a harsh reality of the times. That Lucrezia could become a widow at such a young age is by no means farfetched. In the Renaissance, women were often much younger than their husbands, and usually outlived them. It was common for young women to marry older men, in some instances men who were more than a quarter of a century their elders. Poggio Bracciolini, for instance, was fifty-five when in 1435 he married the eighteen-year-old Selvaggia Buondelmonti. Cosimo I de' Medici's mistress, Eleonora degli Albizzi, was twenty-four years younger than he. His other known mistress, Camilla Martelli, was twenty-six years his junior. He eventually married her, but upon his death, the young widow was confined to a convent for the rest of her life.[25] Speaking of the destitute conditions of some widows in Renaissance Florence, Margaret King notes that "half of the women who sought assistance from the Ospedale dei Mendicanti were widows" (61). The spectre of this harsh reality, which gives Sostrata reason to worry about her daughter's future, was likely to resonate with contemporary audiences, especially the women. Widows of the comic stage of the Renaissance often served as a reminder of this ugly aspect of their culture. In Grazzini's *Pinzochera*, Antonia, the hapless widow-turned-prostitute, speaks poignantly for most of them as she laments her own wretched condition. In a cheerless soliloquy, she explains that, when she had lost all means of livelihood following her husband's death, poverty forced her into the shameful profession. Now, a *pinzochera* or bawd by necessity, she finds herself "alone and abandoned by all." She has fallen so low that she wishes she had not been born (3.1).

From this perspective, Sostrata is hardly a woman of questionable morals, as other characters depict her, or a woman of lewd tendencies, as some readers suggest. She is a caring mother whose role in the play should be defined not by her colourful past but by her deep concern for her daughter's future. Indeed, it is not Sostrata's morality or lack thereof that is relevant to the outcome of the play but her pragmatism in seeking to insure her daughter's well-being. As such, her character is more significant than her limited stage appearance would suggest. Although she appears in only five of the play's thirty-seven scenes and has very short lines,[26] she calls attention to the unfortunate status of women in *cinquecento* patriarchal society. Her concern for her daughter reflects that of many Renaissance mothers who feared that their daughters would become social outcasts and never have a family if they did not fit or grow into the traditional role of women. Understandably, it was a mother's duty to see that her daughters were raised to be suitable for marriage and, it was hoped, motherhood. In some instances, women discouraged their own daughters from pursuing an education for fear that their intellectual maturity would intimidate and scare away prospective husbands. Christine de Pisan, for instance, was educated with the approval of her father and against her mother's wishes. The mother, herself raised according to the "usual feminine ideas," wanted her daughter to spend her time "spinning, like other women."[27] It is out of this realistic, motherly concern that Sostrata advises her Lucrezia to put aside all moral reservations.

Sostrata's subordination of morality to "actual" reality defines her as a truly practical character in pursuit of an immediate and tangible good, or *utile*. Her behaviour, detached from rigid moral standards, is informed by the Machiavellian "necessità" of the moment, in this case a woman's need to procreate. Such a need was especially significant at a time when, as Daniela Frigo points out, the decreasing fertility of the upper classes represented a menace to the survival of the family (82). To be sure, the existence of the family was also threatened by wars and by natural disasters such as famines and plagues, which, as Herlihy and

Klapisch-Zuber point out, could induce "temporary sterility" (81–3). In a world where a healthy and prolific family was fundamental to the very survival of society, Sostrata's pragmatism may be seen as the key to the whole play. Accordingly, given Nicia's sterility, Lucrezia's adultery is a necessary transgression because it provides for the procreation of children and the establishment of the family. Inherently, it assures the regeneration and preservation of society.[28] The threat that moral corruption poses to social and religious institutions is definitely a lesser evil than the risk of extinction. Friar Timoteo uses this same argument to convince Lucrezia that the act of adultery he is advising her to commit is not a sin but a service to humanity. He illustrates his point by recalling the biblical episode in which Lot copulated with his own daughters (Genesis 19). The two sisters were fully justified in sleeping with their father, the friar reminds Lucrezia, because they believed that the survival of the human race rested solely on their duty and ability to give birth (3.11).

In Machiavellian terms, the friar's argument, though inspired by monetary motives, exemplifies the notion that an institution, be it religious or secular, does not hesitate to adjust its values for the sake of its survival. Accordingly, the play's community avails itself of any means at its disposal, including the foolish *messere,* the ignoble friar, and the "unethical" mother. But the effective use of these contemptible individuals in no way excuses their baseness. Indeed, though valuable instruments of a social cause, they continue to be symbols of the corrupting forces that undermine the integrity of social and religious institutions. The paradox inherent in the utilization of evil means for a good cause should not offend our sense of ethics or logic, for it has always been a common practice among societies to do whatever is necessary for their preservation. In theory, the play's use of depraved characters for a common good is similar in many ways to the employment of destructive and / or unethical means for the defence of a nation, or to law enforcement's reliance on lowlife snitches in its war against crime. The nobility of these ends does not redeem the wickedness of the means, which remain "destructive" and "lowlife," just as the play's characters remain the object of scorn and / or ridicule.

As we have seen, *Mandragola* stages a world hardly reminiscent of the Boccaccian tale that inspired it. Machiavelli took a medieval tale of love and natural passions and turned it into a dramatized view of society's need to expose those who corrupt and debase its institutions. The play also dramatizes the notion that in order to ensure its own survival, society must be ready to use all available means, however undesirable. Love is no longer the story's main theme but the pretext for directing attention to the motives behind the actions of its characters. Their individual interests come together to inform a social context that ultimately shapes the view the playwright intended to dramatize. Of course, Machiavelli could have expressed the same view through a poem, a treatise, or even a prose narrative without having to borrow from Boccaccio or any other author. But only through the dialectical confrontation between source and imitation could the spectators appreciate the formal and thematic changes that inform the stage representation. The inevitable juxtaposition of the genres offers them a critical and entertaining perspective upon their own world. It is only through the stage and his stagecraft that Machiavelli could dramatize his view in all its dynamism and provoke a lively and immediate dialogue with his audience.

Finally, Machiavelli's skilful transformation of the source not only attests to his creative ability and keen sense of theatre but also vindicates his choice to dramatize an old story in order to represent a fresh point of view. The adaptation of Boccaccio's tale serves to confer upon the play the legitimacy of tradition and, more importantly, to provide a point of departure for measuring the extent to which the playwright has modified the source. And it is out of this contrast that there emerges distinctly the play's relevance. Machiavelli accomplished the transformation of the original prose fiction into a theatrical text primarily through formal changes, such as time compression and space selection. Additional changes may be observed in the adherence to the poetics of verisimilitude that characterized the Italian Renaissance stage. Of the original story only a few, barely recognizable elements remain. Places and times are changed, and characters are modified in such a way as to recall only faintly their original roles. One might say that he took an old portrait, refurbished its frame, and put a new picture in it. In this sense, *Mandragola* is an imitation in the classical sense of the word: it does not reproduce the original but morphs it into something altogether different, just as the Senecan bees turn pollen into honey. Ultimately, what Machiavelli took from Boccaccio was not a view of the world but the inspiration to represent his own.

Chapter Three

Clizia: From Stage to Stage

Machiavelli wrote *Clizia* in a hurry (early January 1525) and perhaps on request to celebrate the return of his friend Jacopo di Filippo Falconetti from exile. It was first performed at Falconetti's house on the thirteenth of the same month with music by Philippe Verdelot and scenes by Sebastiano Sangallo, the same Sangallo who had designed the scenery for *Mandragola*. The representation earned the play immediate and widespread success, as attested to in a letter Filippo Neri wrote to his friend Machiavelli a month later. Neri emphasized that he had heard of the great performance not through letters from enthusiastic friends but from unbiased travellers who had nothing but high praise for the play's splendid scenery and comic situations ("gloriose pompe e fieri ludi").[1] This success notwithstanding, *Clizia* was never as popular a comedy as *Mandragola,* mostly because it does not rise to the same artistic level as the earlier play. Scholars consider it too slavish an imitation of Plautus's *Casina* (185 BCE), one of the most imitated comedies in the Italian Renaissance.[2] In the early acts in particular, Machiavelli follows the Latin source so closely that some critics have spoken dismissively of translation and reworking rather than adaptation.[3] Even in the Renaissance, close imitations were spurned for their alleged lack of originality and anachronistic subservience to the ancients. But *Clizia,* though indeed a close version of the Roman play, is actually a good example of how imitation can yield original works. The ensuing discussion attempts to show how Machiavelli's sense of theatre turned the Latin source into an authentic stage representation of his own world.

Though literary imitation was common among Renaissance playwrights, many thought of it as an intellectual activity lacking originality. Grazzini, for instance, in the first prologue to his *La gelosia,* chastises fellow dramatists for mixing the old with the new and producing works of doubtful value. He reserved most of his criticism for those who use new cities and modern times but introduce old costumes with the excuse that they are following the example of Plautus and Terence. These remarks, though directed against a general trend in mid-*cinquecento* Italy, may conceivably extend to Machiavelli and his *Clizia*. The play, like many other comedies of the time, blends the old with the new to represent a story that, according to Prologue, took place in ancient Athens, happened again in classical Rome, and recently re-occurred in Florence. But to lump *Clizia* with the legions of mediocre imitations that drew Grazzini's scorn would be shortsighted. In fact, the play presents a world that, though seen through the ancient tale, is Florentine through and through. Machiavelli makes it a point to tell his audience that although the story has remained the same, those experiencing it have changed. And it could not be otherwise, for, as Prologue argues, if humans reappeared in the world "in the same way as do events, not a hundred years would go by before we would find ourselves together once again, doing the same things as now."[4] The novelty, then, is not in the story, but in the characters who live it and, inherently, in the spectators who view it through their cultural values and aesthetic expectations. As John Storey points out, "different people have different interpretative resources, just as they have different needs" (60).

Briefly, *Clizia*'s plot follows Plautus's dramatization of Lysidamus's vain attempt to bed his young ward, Casina. Unfortunately for him, his son Euthynicus is also in love with the girl and wishes to marry her. Lysidamus removes this minor obstacle by sending the young man off to their country home with instructions to stay there until further notice. Though the tale proceeds from this father-son amorous rivalry, the plot centres on the clash between old Lysidamus and his wife, Cleostrata, who has vowed to foil his plans. The old man schemes to marry the girl off to his slave Olympio so that he may then enjoy her for himself. Cleostrata, aware of her husband's sham, counters with her own ruse. She proposes to marry the girl to the slave Chalinus, who, unbeknown to her, is actually a stand-in for Euthynicus. They finally agree to settle the dispute by drawing lots, hence the title of the original Greek play *The Lot-Drawers*.[5] The drawing favours Lysidamus, but Cleostrata, refusing to accept defeat, arranges for Chalinus to disguise himself as Casina and pose as the "bride." The trap is set for old Lysidamus to enter the bedroom and face the humiliating virility of the young male slave. However, he does not suffer the full impact of the painful experience, as Olympio, eager to be first with his "bride," ignores the arrangement he had made with his old master and decides to go in first. His impatience earns him a sound beating, originally intended for Lysidamus. When the old man arrives to take his pleasure with the young "bride," he is chased by the male slave. He manages to escape unharmed but leaves behind his cloak and staff. On the street and all roughed up, he is scolded by his wife, ridiculed by his servants, and humiliated before the entire community. The play ends with Lysidamus's promise to behave and with Epilogue informing the audience that Casina is actually a free-born Athenian and that she will soon marry Euthynicus.

Except for minor variations, Machiavelli re-enacts the same series of events, retains most of the original characters, and adds few details that reflect the modern "re-occurrence" of the old story.[6] Considering *Clizia*'s close imitation of the Roman play, one should not expect significant formal changes, especially with regard to the Aristotelian unities. Basic alterations underpinning the poetic claim of novelty may be observed in the new location, in the historical context of the action, and in the various references to contemporary events and localities. There is sufficient textual evidence, including allusions to the city's prisons ("Stinche") to establish with certainty that the action takes place in Florence. However, the scenic space itself is not easily recognizable, for, as Prologue explains, the neighbourhood ("casato") as well as the names of the personages are fictitious lest the author be cited for libel.[7] We also know that the events occurred in 1506 or, as young Cleandro recalls, twelve years after the 1494 French invasion of Italy (1.1). More precisely, it is in the early winter of 1506, as one can deduce from Nicomaco's sarcastic comment about Sofronia's religious habits. Meeting her on her way to church, he observes derisively, "And yet it is only Carnival; imagine what you will do during Lent" (2.3). In keeping with the new cultural backdrop, the slaves from the source are now servants and farmhands: Pirro, in the role of the Roman slave Olympio, is a servant; Eustachio, in the role of Chalinus, is a farmhand; the foundling Clizia, just like the slave Casina, is actually the daughter of a rich gentleman. Both plays end as the girls' respective fathers claim the young ward as their long-lost child.

The most obvious textual indication that the play evolves in a Florentine environment is of course the language, especially the use of local proverbs and colloquialisms. Allusions to popular ceremonies and activities, such as Nicomaco's references to San Biagio's day (2.3) and to the game of soccer (3.1), help to locate the story's events in contemporary Florence. Another reminder that the tale is set in the contemporary city is Nicomaco's allusion to *Mandragola,* especially his cunning reference to Friar Timoteo's "ludicrous" miracle. Taking up Sofronia's suggestion to let a religious man settle their disagreement over Clizia's marriage, Nicomaco proposes to consult Friar Timoteo. After all, he quips sarcastically, the friar is their confessor and, above all, a little saint "that has already worked a few miracles" (2.3). Clearly, such a modern setting for an admittedly old story does not reduce *Clizia* to the category of the anachronistic imitations that drew Grazzini's censure. The basic function of the new setting is to serve not as backdrop to "old costumes" but as a bridge between theatrical fiction and living reality. There is no question that the spectators are more easily drawn into the fictitious world of the stage when it resembles their own. Undoubtedly, a strong sense of affinity draws them close to characters who speak their language, live in the same city, and share the same values. As the line between fiction and reality gradually fades, the spectators begin to soften their natural hesitation to enter the world of make-believe. They become more predisposed to appreciate the teachings and the entertainment normally expected of good theatre.

It is in this new cultural setting that history repeats itself, as events that occurred in antiquity now befall a Florentine family. Though the roles of the Florentine characters follow closely those of their Roman prototypes, the times have changed and so have the values that inform their behaviour. What sets them apart from their source models are the reasons behind their actions and the way they act and interact with each other. Nicomaco's plot to bed Clizia is similar in many ways to Lysidamus's plan to sleep with Casina, just as Sofronia's resolve to thwart Nicomaco's scheme parallels Cleostrata's determination to foil Lysidamus's game plan. But what stirs Nicomaco's passion for the girl does not arise from the same need as that of his predecessor, just as the reasons for Sofronia's resolve are different from those that motivate Cleostrata's trickery. Also, Cleandro's wish to marry the young ward recalls Euthynicus's intent to marry Casina, but the nature of their love is quite different. Thus, while the similarities confirm that the play is a re-presentation of an old story, the differences tend to distinguish the modern from the ancient. At the same time, they articulate the dynamics that inform the new dramatic conflict. More specifically, they call attention to the values that define the world of the new characters, making the old story relevant to contemporary audiences.

The Sons: Euthynicus versus Cleandro

Cleandro's role is analogous to that of Euthynicus to the extent that they are both in love with the foundlings in the custody of their respective parents. They are also in competition with their own fathers, who are determined to have their own young wards for themselves. While these similarities confirm Machiavelli's retention of the original character, significant modifications distinguish Cleandro from his prototype. The most obvious difference is that Euthynicus is never seen on stage, whereas Cleandro appears frequently and has numerous speeches, including several soliloquies.[8] The distinction is critical, both formally and thematically. Formally, it denotes that Cleandro, unlike his Roman counterpart, is within the spectators' sensorial perception: they can see and hear his physical and verbal expressions as he externalizes his sentiments. Such proximity causes the spectators to appreciate better his dilemma and grow more sympathetic to his cause. As both young men are driven by their passion for a girl, their words and deeds tend to qualify the depth, or lack thereof, of their personal feelings. They also help to establish to what degree and in what way the theme of love is relevant in each version of the story.

In the Roman account, the spectators never see Euthynicus nor do they hear him talk about his love for Casina or the obstacles he faces in his amorous endeavours. They learn about him from Prologue, who states that Lysidamus sent him away in order to get rid of the competition. Before leaving, the young man arranged for Chalinus to stand in for him at the wedding. As a reward, Prologue continues, he promised the young slave that he would share the girl with him, once she became his wife. Thus, even before the play proper begins, the spectators are told that this young lover is essentially a libertine. Also, his departure from the city without attempting to challenge his father's intent is tantamount to a cowardly surrender of his amorous ambitions. It causes the audience to question the seriousness of his feelings for the girl. Significantly, his depraved willingness to share his "wife" with another man not only emphasizes the casualness of his love but also reflects the author's intent to treat love as a licentious, erotic passion.

In the Florentine imitation, the theme of love is equally central, albeit in a much different way. Cleandro's role is to rival his father and do all he can to disrupt his scheme. He complains repeatedly about the old man's ignoble wishes and never tires of reminding the audience of his own undying love for Clizia. From the beginning of the play, he declares that his affection for the foundling has steadily grown ever since he was ten years old. Now, he is prepared to take her as a wife, a mistress, or in any way he can (1.1). He also laments the misery of those lovers who, like him, waste away in constant torment (3.2). At times, he inveighs against Fortuna for favouring the old instead of the young (4.1).

Just before learning that he can marry Clizia, he lapses into a maudlin soliloquy against Fortuna and bad luck ("mala sorte," 5.5). This insistence on love and all its misery not only confirms the centrality of the theme of love, it also reminds the spectators that in *Clizia* love is a noble sentiment and not a mere sexual whim as in the source.

The Fathers: Lysidamus versus Nicomaco

The contrast between the two young men and the different types of love that inform their roles set the stage, as it were, for a comparison between their respective fathers. In the case of Lysidamus, love is purely carnal and instinctual. His pursuit of Casina arises mainly from a whim or an implied desire to exercise some sort of *ius primae noctis*. The spectators often hear him talk about his plans to bed Casina but seldom about his feelings for her. In the few instances where he expresses his views on love, he tends to debase it through a series of banal similes and metaphors. When he first appears on stage, for instance, he sings that love is a very sweet spice and that all cooks should use it in their recipes, for no dish, he intones jokingly, "can taste sweet or sour if love's not there" (2.3). A little later, having placed all his hopes for his lewd scheme on the chancy lot-drawing, he resolves that if he loses the contest "my sword shall be made my bed and upon it shall I die" (2.4). In translating this line, James Tatum emphasizes that the old man delivers it "in tragic style, à la Ajax" (104). But the line appears equivocal, for it may be taken as an obscene allusion equating sword to a male organ, and thus foreshadowing the unhappy encounter with the supposedly new "bride." It can also be construed as a mockingly chivalrous deed. In either case, it tends to reduce the dignity of love to a crude, sexual image.

Through most of the play, Lysidamus's speech is peppered with analogies trivializing the nobility of love. When he can no longer contain his anxiety to be with the girl, he asks in a highly rhetorical and, presumably, despairing tone, "What brought this love to my heart? Was it a Roman omen? What was it I did to offend Venus? Why does she make so many delays for me and my love?" (3.4). The clash between the high, quasi-epic tone of the language and the vulgarity of the love it evokes tends to betray the lewdness of the speaker's intent. In another instance, lapsing into a melodramatic tone of self-pity, he declares to the audience, "There is not now, nor has there ever been, an old man in love more wretched than me" (3.5). Here, the aberration in the implied incongruence between "old man" and "in love" calls attention to the ridicule normally associated with the topos of the *amator senex*. These and similar comparisons not only belittle the notion of love, they also cast Lysidamus as a droll character. Marvin Herrick, in his discussion of the Renaissance notion of the risible, writes that Donatus, commenting on examples of laughter in Terence's comedies, recognized the incongruous contrast between the serious and the trivial as "one of the main sources of the risible" (*Comic Theory* 39).

To be sure, Lysidamus is the object of ridicule not so much for being in love but for his vulgarity and his pursuit of base love. As other characters point to his depraved habits and preferences, the spectators begin to see him as a lecherous old man lacking in pride and dignity. His wife, upon smelling the perfume he is wearing, asks, "what brothel have you been lying in now? [...] what whorehouse were you visiting?" She rounds off her tongue-lashing by swearing that no old man is more ignoble than he ("neminem esse ignaviorem," 2.3).[9] This reproach tends to depict Lysidamus not as a man who has recently lost his way but rather as one who has always led a wicked life, constantly seeking the company of young men and women of pleasure. But he is not just a frequenter of whorehouses; he is also a sexual pervert. The spectators see him kissing Olympio and hear him whisper, "touching you is as sweet as honey on my tongue." Not satisfied with the kiss, he clasps the slave from behind and begins to bump and grind until the young man complains "not on my back, lover boy" (2.8). The scene prompts the eavesdropping Chalinus to observe, "Lysidamus seems to prefer grown-up boys" (3.4).[10] The remark is clearly a sarcastic allusion to the "amorous" encounter between the old man and the young male slave Chalinus, the "bride" who will take Casina's place in the nuptial bed. Of Lysidamus's depravity, Timothy Moore writes that Plautus "makes him even more ridiculous and lecherous than other *senes amatores*" (166). George Duckworth calls him the "most lecherous old rascal in Roman comedy" (165).

There is no question that some of Lysidamus's character traits and behaviour resurface in Machiavelli's Nicomaco. Like Lysidamus, Nicomaco behaves in ways unbecoming to a respectable old man: he wishes to bed a young girl, drinks and eats aphrodisiac foods, wears perfumes, seeks the company of young people, frequents houses of ill repute, and is ultimately ridiculed. But there are significant differences between the two men. Unlike his Roman prototype, Nicomaco is not a habitual frequenter of whorehouses; nor is he a depraved "lover of boys." He is undergoing a serious personal crisis. As recently as the previous year, his wife tells the audience, he had been a prudent and respected old merchant, whose life was a model of social and moral propriety. But since he began to fancy young Clizia, Sofronia continues, he has become a totally different man: always shouting, mindless of his affairs, and wandering aimlessly in and out of the house (2.4). Sofronia appeals to his former sense of dignity as she chastises him for his unseemly new ways. She reproaches him for hanging around young men, spending time at the tavern, and frequenting bawdy houses and gambling dens (3.4). The cause for such a change is not clear to Nicomaco himself, who, when first coming on stage, asks in bewilderment, "What the devil is wrong with my eyes this morning? I seem to have flashes that don't let me see the light, and yet last night I could see well enough to split hairs. Could I have had too much to drink?" Though confused, he knows that his loss of inner peace has to do with his desire for young Clizia. He refuses to accept the limitations of old age, insisting that he is not too old yet "to break a lance" with the girl (2.1).

One must regard with caution the suggestion that Nicomaco is an old man who still feels the urges of the senses (Russo, *Commedie* 160). Such a view would reduce him to a commonplace *amator senex* and trivialize the seriousness of his bewilderment. Nor is there any textual evidence to support the suggestion that his desire to sleep with Clizia represents a wish to subvert social norms and/or the domestic rules that govern family life (Pesca 64). Prior to his crisis, Nicomaco is said to have been a respected member of society and, implicitly, a champion of its respectable values. No one in the play's community, including Nicomaco himself, knows why he has lost his way. Sofronia speaks for everyone when she wonders what could have caused her model husband to turn into an erratic and shameless juvenile. Some critics suggest that he is looking for a miracle that, like the mandrake potion, would give him back his youth and "fertilità" (Pesca 64). But such a suggestion founders on the simple question: why would he want to regain his fertility? Nowhere in the text is there any indication that the old man wishes to start a new family. It is more plausible to agree with Giulio Ferroni that Nicomaco's bizarre actions are fuelled by a deep desire for youth ("brama della giovinezza," *Mutazione* 113).

Indeed, Nicomaco's pursuit of the girl arises not from perversion, as in the case of his Plautine model, but from the delusory wish to fight off old age by a valiant display of virility. Aware of the challenges inherent in such a battle, he adopts a diet of spicy foods to build his strength and begins to wear strong perfumes to project his youth. Unlike Lysidamus, who buys perfumes to "please" Casina (Prologue), Nicomaco wears them to appear young or, as Sofronia puts it, "gagliardo" (4.4). Pirro facetiously warns him to conceal his old age by "arming" himself in such a way as to *appear* young. His strategy for the fateful night is to wear perfumes strong enough to "wake up a regiment" (4.5). The desire to be young is also apparent in the youthful company he keeps and in the carefree lifestyle he adopts – mimicking youth from a wish to deny the reality of old age. For him, Clizia is not a mere sex object but the symbol of the youth he intends to recapture through a brave show of his virile "dagger." As expected, in the bedroom encounter with "Clizia" (in reality the male servant Siro disguised as Clizia) he is mercilessly defeated. By his own account, not only was he bruised by the servant's kicks and punches, he also felt the young man's attempt to penetrate him: "I felt myself being jabbed in the rump, and I got five or six of the damnedest pokes right under the tailbone!" (5.2). Ironically, he is defeated by the same means with which he intended to win his "battle" and by the same youth he fancied to conquer.

Though Machiavelli takes the episode straight from Plautus, he alters its meaning significantly by shifting the role of the victim to the main character. In the Plautine version, the unfortunate recipient of the scene's obscene and violent skirmish is the slave Olympio, one of the play's marginal figures. He is the victim of his own impatience, as he decides to be the first with his "wife," ignoring his promise to let Lysidamus go first. By the time the old master arrives to take his pleasure with the "bride," the episode is practically over. Thus, as the neighbour Myrrhina points out, the joke is on Olympio.[11] With the young slave bearing most of the brunt, the old man is spared the humiliation and the beating meted out to his Florentine counterpart. The episode affects him only to the extent that he fails in his attempt to have sex with Casina. He is also forced to beg for his wife's forgiveness before a laughing crowd of neighbours and servants. But his public *mea culpas* are hardly sincere, judging by his clownish denial of his lascivious scheme. While Cleostrata is still fuming over his shenanigans, he asks childishly "did I do that? […] Did I do all those things you say?" He also winks at the audience as he prides himself on having the best wife in the world (5.4). In the end, there is no doubt that his plan to bed Casina was but a game for him, and that, given his lecherous nature, he will play it again with some other woman at some other time. Thus, a story that in its Roman occurrence serves to frustrate an old man's attempt to satisfy his erotic fantasies, in its Florentine re-occurrence turns into a clash between young and old, whereby the old is beaten back and brought face to face with his diminished virility.

Nicomaco's hankering after youth points to the very essence of his drama, that is, the tragic desire to escape the fated misery of old age. The nobility of this very human urge marks a profound difference between him and his lewd and buffoonish source model. The distinction is fundamental to the play's entire structure in that it tends to define the rapport that the two men have with other characters, especially with their respective sons and wives. In *Casina*, the relationship between Lysidamus and Euthynicus, though cast in rivalry, follows the traditional lines of parental authority and filial obedience. The young man submits to his father's wishes and, albeit reluctantly, goes off to the country house. As his absence makes it practically impossible for him to vie for the girl, it is his mother, Cleostrata, who takes his place in the competition. With the household largely under her control, she is in a formidable position to oppose her husband's scandalous scheme. She seizes with confidence the opportunity to measure up against the old man and foil his plan. In the end, not only does she beat him into submission, but she also affirms her complete independence from his patriarchal authority. With the actual contest taking place between husband and wife, the son's role is but a word construct, a rhetorical reference necessary to frame the story in the traditional father-son rivalry.

In the Machiavellian version, by contrast, the father-son competition is maintained throughout the play, underscoring the thematic relevance of the opposition between youth and old age. Admittedly, the contest is not on a level playing field, since young Cleandro cannot compete with the power of the purse that Nicomaco wields as head of the household. Largely because of this disparity, the contention never rises to the level of direct, open confrontation. However, young Cleandro, though helpless and dispirited, remains a serious contender, doing what he can to disrupt his father's plans. In 4.2, after eavesdropping on Nicomaco's and Pirro's conversation about their plot, he rushes to apprise his mother of what he has heard, trusting that she will thwart their scheme. His constant sighs and imprecations against Fortuna and his frequent appearances on stage not only emphasize his adversarial relationship with Nicomaco, they also remind the audience that the contest is very much alive and that he is in it come what may. The sustained rivalry anticipates and reinforces the play's central theme, whereby youth fights off an old man's deluded attempt to conquer it.

The Wives: Cleostrata versus Sofronia

The conflict defining the father-son relationship is but a prelude to the outright antagonism that characterizes the relationship of husband and wife in both plays. Cleostrata and Sofronia are actively engaged in preventing their own husbands from having sex with their respective wards. But the reasons behind their determination are profoundly different, and the difference informs their personalities, marital relationships, and the cultural values authorizing their behaviour. Cleostrata's motives arise largely from a personal disdain towards the cultural expectation that a wife should submit to the husband's overbearing rule and recognize him as the absolute master of the household. She complains to her friend Myrrhina that she is mistreated in her own home and that she has lost the freedom to exercise "my rights" ("ius meum," 2.2). Her repeated reference to her lost "ius" not only distinguishes her from a typical, obedient wife like Myrrhina but also defines her as a troublesome shrew who, as Timothy Moore points out, "seeks to invert the proper power structure of her marriage" (170). Her resentment against patriarchal imperatives and her intent to subvert them may be seen in her low opinion of her husband. In her view, he is a cesspool of iniquity, an oversexed antiquity, and a living disgrace who would defy everyone just to satisfy his lust. But she "will make him pay" and promises to serve him

No food or drink.
Just fag and nag;
I'll dish it out
Till I see him gag. (Act I, Casson trans.)

Her unbending resolve to make him pay unmasks her festering desire to bring her "master" to his knees and wield power over him. A clear expression of such power lies in her ability to defend her property, the ward Casina. Her motives for frustrating Lysidamus's lascivious attempt on the girl's chastity do not arise from moral indignation or from the wounded ego of a jealous wife but from the will to protect what belongs to her. She makes no secret that the young "slave" is hers and that she brought her up at her own expense ("mea est, quae meo educta sumptu siet," 2.2). To defend the girl, then, is to vindicate her own "ius" to personal ownership, thus affirming her marital independence. She is clearly challenging established traditions whereby, according to Myrrhina, everything in the household belongs to the husband. Daring to own things behind the husband's back is risky because, as Myrrhina cautions, it may prompt the husband to sue for divorce or simply repudiate the wife: "I foras, mulier" (2.2). Heedless of her friend's warning, Cleostrata continues to wage her power struggle and ultimately succeeds in reducing the old man to an inferior role in the family hierarchy.[12] The image of Lysidamus on his knees begging for forgiveness is perhaps the most telling testament of her success. Her victory is also expressed eloquently by her servant Pardalisca, who encourages the "bride" Chalinus

> To stand over your husband,
> To be stronger and never give in,
> To defeat him and so
> Be his conquering heroine!
> Let your voice, your authority rule everywhere
> Let him load you with clothes, while you strip him bare.
>
> (Act 4, Casson trans.)

Cleostrata's triumph is so complete, her position so secure, that she can safely forgive her husband. Consistent with her forgiveness, she gives him back the mantle and the staff he left behind when fleeing the bedroom where the "bride" Olympio threatened to thrash him (5.4). But this conciliatory gesture does not imply her intent to go back to the *status quo ante*, for the household hierarchy has been subverted forever, and real power now lies with her. The return of the mantle and staff, the respective symbols of authority and manhood, signals Cleostrata's self-assurance in her new role. It would be naive indeed to view her magnanimity as an indication that she is fully satisfied with her triumph. By her own admission, she forgives Lysidamus not out of compassion or belief in his contrition but out of consideration for the spectators who have endured a long play that need not be any longer ("longiorem ne faciamus fabulam," 5.5).[13]

This purely formal reason for letting go of her animosity towards her husband leaves the distinct impression that she will continue to "fag and nag" him until he "gags," long after the play is over. Such an insatiable vindictiveness robs her of the opportunity to be a noble *vincitrix* and relegates her, instead, to the world of typical Plautine shrews. From this perspective, it is difficult to accept the view that the play, unlike

Machiavelli's *Clizia*, is anchored to a "predominantly moral resolution" (Faulkner 40). There is hardly any moral value in Cleostrata's vengeful resolve or Lysidamus's histrionic repentance. What could have been a moral victory or, arguably, a feminist struggle *ante litteram* remains a farcical squabble between a nagging wife and a ridiculous old man. At best, the play might be seen as the celebration of a wife's successful attempt to take control of the household by subduing a husband who was a "shameful sower of scandal and a cesspool of iniquity" (2.1).

Much different and more complex is her Florentine counterpart, Sofronia. Though in the same role as that of Cleostrata, Sofronia inherited only the determination with which the Roman matron opposes her husband. Unlike her Latin model, Sofronia is not a vindictive wife; nor is she driven by a need to subvert the family power structure. She is determined to preserve such a structure by inducing Nicomaco to resume his place of authority within the family hierarchy. She reproaches him for his unbecoming behaviour and foils his unseemly scheme, but she does not wish to reduce him to his knees. Her only interest is that he return "al segno," that is, to the respect he commanded both within the family and the community prior to his infatuation with Clizia. It is conceivable that her opposition to her husband's erotic fancy might be partly provoked by jealousy, as her son Cleandro speculates (1.1). However, one must be careful not to limit the play's dramatic conflict to a simple family quarrel reminiscent of the Latin source. Sofronia's fight is much nobler than Cleostrata's squabble. She is guided not by ambition and vindictiveness but by a genuine concern for the girl's well-being and the family's integrity.

For Sofronia, Clizia is not an issue of personal property, as Casina was for Cleostrata, but a cause for humane regard and moral scruples. She reminds Nicomaco that the girl is so virtuous and beautiful that it would be a shame to "throw her away," that is, marry her to Pirro, the good-for-nothing servant. She raised her with too much love and care to stand by idly as unscrupulous men scheme to use and defile her. She threatens to turn the house and the city upside down to prevent that from happening (2.3). Towards the end of the play, she chastises her husband for having attempted to bed a girl they raised as their own daughter with such "decency as proper girls are brought up" (5.3). Caring and righteous expressions such as these call into question the view that she treats the girl "as a potential asset." It is difficult to see how a decent and loving surrogate mother like Sofronia could consider the girl's physical and moral virtues "as qualities useful for the market, that is, as adding value to a commodity, which they [Sofronia and Nicomaco] should make the most out of" (Faulkner 44).

Such a characterization of Sofronia as a business-minded woman is not convincing for two basic reasons. First, it assumes that she is trying to protect Clizia not out of genuine affection and decency but mostly for material gain. This is mere speculation, for there is nothing in the text that could lead one to question, even remotely, the sincerity of her repeated claims of motherly solicitude. Second, the suggestion that the young lady is but a marketable asset implies erroneously that there is a profitable market for foundlings. One wonders what a bourgeois family like that of Nicomaco and Sofronia could possibly gain from the modest marriage of a young ward. For Clizia, a woman of uncertain origins and without a dowry, the best that could be hoped for was to marry her off to a poor man. In Nicomaco's words, one cannot do better than marry her off to Pirro, for there are not many choices. A match like this, he argues, does not grow on trees ("[non] se ne truovi ad ogni uscio," 2.3). Also, one must not forget that the play's drawing of the lots purportedly was meant to determine whether to give her in marriage to a beggarly servant (Pirro) or to a rustic farmhand (Eustachio). In either case, there would be no significant material gain for the family. Admittedly, Sofronia suspends all marriage talk after she foils Nicomaco's plot, and tells the young pretenders not to get their hopes up. In the end, she warns, none of them might have her. However, this should not be viewed as an indication that she is looking for a more profitable marriage arrangement but only as her intent to proceed with prudence, now that Nicomaco has come to his senses and the family predicament is resolved. Her wish to go inside and straighten up the house ("rassettare la casa," 5.4) stresses her need to reassess the girl's marriage options and determine which of the applicants is the most suitable candidate.

Sofronia's strong sense of family also informs her resolve to prevent a public scandal. Fearing that without God's help the house is going to go to rack and ruin, she decides to sabotage her husband's plans and goes to church to commend herself to God (2.4). Unlike the Plautine matron who finds gratification in humiliating her husband, Sofronia has no choice but to expose Nicomaco to public ridicule. "I never wanted to make a fool of you," she reminds him. "You were the one who tried to do it to everyone of us, and you ended up doing it to yourself" (5.3). This righteousness has earned her the approval of some critics, who characterize her as a paragon of religiosity and incorruptible morality.[14] Religion, moral scruples, humane concerns, and social good standing are the principal values that strengthen her resolve to oppose her husband and, at the same time, define her character. Her integrity not only distinguishes her from her vengeful Roman counterpart but also elevates the play's dramatic conflict to a clash between a wife's rectitude and a husband's aberration, between right and wrong. Her final triumph, then, is a vindication of the prevailing social values, as it leads to the re-establishment of the old order, with Nicomaco as a good family man and a respected merchant. She hopes that her husband will want to go back to being the model citizen he once was, for if he does, they will all be happy to resume their place in the family hierarchy. "If you want to make a clean start, and go back to being the Nicomaco you once were a year ago," she tells him, "we shall all go back, too, and nobody will know a thing" (5.3).

Some scholars view with suspicion this return to the old order, insisting that the play's conclusion points to a new family structure with Sofronia in charge.[15] They base their argument on Nicomaco's virtual abdication of his authority and Sofronia's newly found power. Following his emasculating defeat, the old man retreats to his bedroom for a much-needed rest, telling his wife to do what she pleases with Clizia. He does not wish to see the girl's suitors (Cleandro, Eustachio, Pirro) much less discuss the marriage business with them. Having given carte blanche ("foglio bianco") to Sofronia, he simply wants to lie down because he is so tired that he can barely stand up straight ("non mi reggo ritto," 5.3). This apparent devolution of power and the admission that he is too weak to stand up straight may indeed be taken as an allusion to his loss of standing within the family. Feeding this perception is also the fact that Sofronia seems to enjoy her newly acquired authority now that she is free to manage the household as she pleases. Not only does she decide to place Clizia in the protection of a local convent; she also admonishes the young men to forget about the girl. Her sense of power is best illustrated in her claim that she alone will decide whether and when the girl comes home from the convent. Answering the young suitors' inquiry about Clizia's return home, she tells them that maybe she will come home, and maybe she won't, "as I see fit" ("come mi parrà," 5.4).

This lordly tone and the humiliation she brought on her husband have led some critics to call her a disdainful and unbearable winner, a "*woman in career,* sprezzante e quasi insopportabile" (Malara 237). Others, seeing her as a Machiavellian virtuoso who rises to the "unequivocal if indirect control of the house," have concluded that the play subverts the traditional family structure (Faulkner 48). Interesting and provoking as these rather novel approaches to *Clizia* may be, they fail to negotiate important textual evidence. The suggestion that Sofronia is an "unbearable" winner, much like her Roman counterpart, cannot be accepted because it treats her moral integrity as mere personal ambition. It also dismisses without argument her deep sense of family and social decorum. The view that the play subverts the family hierarchy and that it represents a Machiavellian lesson in "liberating and reforming the little republic of the household" (Faulkner 53) is also untenable because it ignores Sofronia's wish that everyone return "al segno." In the absence of acceptable textual evidence confirming Sofronia as an ambitious wife intent upon subverting the traditional family structure, one must accept at face value the sincerity of her wish to return to the old order. From this perspective, her taking control of the household is not a threat to the family hierarchy but a necessary step to preserve it. She will continue to fill the power vacuum only until her husband recovers. There is no doubt that, following his humiliating experience, Nicomaco will be better prepared to resume his patriarchal duties, returning Sofronia to her proper place in the household.[16]

In this sense, the play's resolution follows the typical comedy format whereby the represented world, having been thrown into turmoil, returns to a state of normalcy. The old order is fully restored, and the community is assured of its continuity as the union between Clizia and Cleandro promises a stable and productive family in the bourgeois tradition of their parents. On the formal level, this conclusion follows closely that of its Roman source: both plays resolve the conflict between husband and wife and conclude with the wedding of the young lovers. On the thematic level, however, the conclusions could not be more different. In *Casina*, the old order is subverted, and the return to normalcy rests on a new family structure headed by the wife. Also, the union between Casina and Euthynicus, unlike that of their Florentine counterparts, builds on a corrupt view of marriage. One must not forget Euthynicus's willingness to share his future wife with the slave Chalinus as a reward for the latter's help in securing her hand. These subverting and libertine elements are no longer present in the imitation. Machiavelli turns the old story into an example of social stability and traditional values. In the words of Giulio Ferroni, *Clizia* may be seen as an affirmation of family and bourgeois morality ("morale familiare e borghese," *Mutazione* 135).[17]

A Machiavellian Perspective

But there is more. Nicomaco's wayward behaviour and his return to his initial place of respectability underscores the moral of the story alluded to in the *Canzona* at the end of the play. The song reminds spectators that the play has just shown them what to eschew and what to pursue in order to go to heaven ("per salir dritti al cielo"). There is nothing unusual about this reminder, for, as Prologue points out, the avowed purpose of comedy is to amuse and to teach. What is remarkable is that immediately after stating the play's moral purpose, *Canzona* alerts the audience that there are other lessons hidden under a "thin veil." Admittedly, the view of the play as a vindication of bourgeois values cannot be seen as its most comprehensive message because it does not take into full account the quasi-tragic nature of Nicomaco's erotic vagary. Very unlike his buffoonish and depraved Roman model, he is a grave and respected old man experiencing an existential crisis typical of those who suddenly realize that old age has crept up on them. In a dramatic monologue more suited to tragedy than comedy, he reflects with anguish on the aging effect that time has had on him: "Oh God, old age is creeping up on me with all its misery" (2.1). These are not the words of a ridiculous old man but the voice of human angst in the face of the merciless passage of time and the fleetingness of life. His is but a temporary delusion bound to clash with naked reality. On the stage, the clash is played out in the bedroom, where a toothless old man ("non molti denti," 4.2) is crudely beaten by a palpably virile young man.

In Machiavellian terms, Nicomaco's crisis may be expressed as a human struggle against the ineluctable forces of nature, that is, the "factual reality of things" often associated with Fortuna. Speaking of the old man's passion for Clizia, Ferroni points out that it is aroused by an attempt to establish an active rapport with Fortuna or with exterior reality (*Mutazione* 112). The stage character most closely associated with adverse reality is Sofronia, the architect of Nicomaco's defeat. The *Canzona* at the end of act 3, points to this aspect of Sofronia's role as it alludes to her in ways that bring to mind Fortuna herself:

> He who offends a *lady* at any time
> Whether right or wrong, is crazy if he believes
> He will find mercy in them by prayers or tears.
> *As she descends into this mortal life*

Together with her soul she brings
Pride, cunning, and unforgiveness,
Deceit and cruelty are her escorts,
And all these evils help her
To gain her desire in every enterprise;
And if anger or jealousy moves her,
She looks for and employs harshness and wickedness
And her strength exceeds the strength of mortals. (Trans. Pansini; italics mine)

In the context of the play, the "offended lady" is Sofronia, of course; but her *descent* among mortals and her *superhuman* strength are attributes peculiar to heavenly creatures, such as Fortuna. Cleandro calls attention to this association in 4.1, as he remarks that Fortuna is a "woman" just like his own mother. He mentions the two "women" in the same context, and refers to them as the two forces that can deny or fulfil his wishes. He laments that they both hindered him in the pursuit of his love: his mother by leaving Clizia's marriage up to chance (lot-drawing), Fortuna by favouring the old man instead of being a friend to the young. Towards the end of the play, he complains again about having to fight Fortuna's forces and his mother's ambition at the same time (5.5). Incidentally, Damone's advice that Nicomaco place himself in the hands of "Sofronia tua," alludes to Fortuna by way of the anagram soFRONia TUA (5.2).

The association of Sofronia with Fortuna allows us to lift the "thin veil" draped over the other possible meanings mentioned in the last *Canzona*, and to view the husband-wife conflict as man's vain attempt to fight off the inexorable aging process. From this perspective, *Clizia* emerges not as a mere vindication of bourgeois values of *cinquecento* Florence but also as the dramatization of the existential crisis that afflicts humans as they come face to face with old age. Such a reading reinforces the view that the play alludes to autobiographical anxieties.[18] Some scholars have suggested a parallel between Machiavelli and Nicomaco, noting the similarity in their names: *Nico* = Niccolò + *maco* = Machiavelli).[19] Though the analogy is based on extra-textual evidence, it is not inconceivable that at age fifty-six, Machiavelli, too, was experiencing the limitations of age. His friends often teased him about his love interests, especially his involvement with the actress Barbara (or Barbera) Raffacani Salutati. Filippo Strozzi, in his letter of 31 March 1526, after informing Machiavelli that Barbera had arrived in Rome and that he would do his best to make her stay pleasant, goes on to joke that he would not dare kiss her because he knows of his [Machiavelli's] jealousy or "sottile avaritia."[20] Others tend to see Nicomaco's defeat as a metaphor for Machiavelli's own vain attempt to re-establish a role in active political life.[21]

Be that as it may, it is clear that the fictional world of *Clizia* is hardly a "reduction" or a "translation" of the Plautine source, as most literary criticism has characterized it.[22] It is a creative example of true imitation, an exemplary instance of moving forward by turning back. Machiavelli took Plautus's stage and filled it with fictitious Florentine characters and their living realities. Contemporary audiences were not treated to the farcical squabble that entertained their Roman counterparts but to a human drama veiled in comedy. The playwright simply rearranged some of the source's incidents and altered the ambitions of the characters experiencing them. The story's new version underscores Machiavelli's contention that the importance of an event is not in itself but in the way it affects people of different worlds in different times. By imitating the past, Machiavelli offered his spectators the opportunity to reflect on the dialectical contrast between the new and the old. Undoubtedly, they appreciated the innovations that spoke to them about their values and met or surpassed their aesthetic preferences. No wonder they received the play's first performance with enthusiasm and praised its great staging and hilarious entertainment ("gloriose pompe and fieri ludi").

Chapter Four

Cecchi's *Assiuolo*: An Apian Imitation

Giovan Maria Cecchi (1518–87) is perhaps the most prolific playwright of the Italian Renaissance. He wrote dozens of comedies and religious plays, all in a language punctuated with colourful sayings of his native Tuscany.[1] Fellow playwright Grazzini grumbled sardonically that for the Florentines, especially the women, Cecchi had eclipsed most of his fellow dramatists, including Grazzini himself.[2] Though popular with the theatre audiences of his time, Cecchi's work did not exhibit exceptional theatrical qualities that might have won him lasting approval among literary critics. Most of his plays, as he readily admits in some of his prologues, are largely based on the Roman comedy of Plautus and Terence. They usually feature the typical dispersions of family members that predictably lead to reunions and happy weddings. Of his vast theatrical production, *Assiuolo* (1550) is perhaps the best example of his stagecraft, particularly his knack for lively action, social satire, and entertaining scenes. Ireneo Sanesi, a most influential scholar of the Italian Renaissance theatre, called it one of the best piéces ("frutti") ever produced by the comic theatre of sixteenth-century Italy.[3] Unlike his other plays, often mired in multiple plots and sub-plots, *Assiuolo* features a two-pronged plot that develops in a linear, uncomplicated fashion and without any last-minute surprises. *Cinquecento* audiences received it with great enthusiasm, and some considered it good enough to rival Machiavelli's *Mandragola*, the best comedy to come out of Renaissance Italy. Unfortunately, Cecchi's work lost its appeal as time went by, and only in the nineteenth century did it begin to see a revival of its editorial fortunes (Rizzi 22). Since then, *Assiuolo* in particular has enjoyed considerable success among critics and editors, as attested to by its inclusion in most anthologies of Italian Renaissance comedies and by Eisenbichler's excellent English translation.[4]

Cecchi took pride in his play, proclaiming it new and original and claiming that it was written specifically for his Florentine audience ("fatta a posta [...] per voi").[5] He calls it a new story based not on the classics but on events that had happened recently in Pisa. He adds that it is free from the usual situations that wind up in marriages, as many comedies are wont to do (Prologue). To be sure, the plot borrows from several of Boccaccio's tales, Machiavelli's plays, and, to a limited extent, from Plautus's comedies. But such a *contaminatio* or pilfering from different sources does not diminish Cecchi's originality, which lies in his ability to modify borrowed elements and invest them with new narrative functions and fresh meanings. The wife who in the original source commits adultery, for example, in the adaptation also commits adultery but for different reasons and under circumstances that tend to redefine her character. The *amator senex*, a staple of the comic stage, fancies erotic encounters for different reasons from those of his source models. The ambitions and the reasons that determine the behaviour of these adapted characters tend to reflect the realities of the social milieu in which they have now come to live. Contemporary spectators saw on the stage before them a mirror or *speculum* of their own world and approved with enthusiasm its realistic representation. The extent to which *Assiuolo* spoke to the audience of their world and won their approval underscores Cecchi's originality in weaving a new fabric out of various strands of used "old cloth," to borrow a phrase from Lodovico Dolce's *Medea*.

The Plot: A *Contaminatio* of Sources

The play's tale takes place in Pisa and consists of three love situations involving two students, their respective ladies of interest, and a decrepit old man. The plot develops from young Rinuccio's physical attraction towards Oretta, the young wife of the old lawyer Ambrogio. Giulio, a Florentine student living in Rinuccio's house, also nourishes carnal desires for Oretta, but, fearing that he might jeopardize his friendship with Rinuccio, who is both his classmate and his landlord, suffers his love pangs in secret. The jealous Ambrogio is in love with the lovely widow Anfrosina, Rinuccio's mother. The action begins when Rinuccio, determined to be with Oretta, lures Ambrogio away from his home by sending him an invitation, purportedly from Anfrosina, to come to her house that evening. In the meantime, Giulio's servant, unbeknownst to his master, sends a letter to Oretta, also in Anfrosina's name, telling her that Ambrogio will be in Anfrosina's house that night and that she should come and surprise him in the act. When the disguised old

Romeo arrives at Anfrosina's house, Giulio, also in disguise, locks him out in the courtyard where he is left to cool off his "burning desires."

The action intensifies as Oretta arrives, also incognito, and is shown into Giulio's bedroom, where she expects to find her old Ambrogio waiting for "his" Anfrosina. Astounded to learn that the man in bed with her is not her husband but young Giulio, she eventually agrees to become his lover. While this is taking place at Anfrosina's house, Rinuccio steals into Ambrogio's residence and into Oretta's bed. He is hardly disappointed to find himself in bed not with "his" Oretta, but with her beautiful sister, Violante, who is covering for her older sister. Matters get more complicated when Ambrogio, reeling from the chilling experience in Anfrosina's courtyard, arrives home and, hearing a man's voice (Rinuccio's) coming out of his bedroom, immediately summons Oretta's brother so that he may witness for himself the dishonour Oretta has brought upon the family. But, as Rinuccio has managed to escape, Violante, disguised in men's clothes, comes downstairs and explains that the voice Ambrogio heard was hers. She insists that the old man, not Oretta, should explain where and how he spent the night. In the end, Ambrogio is forced to make amends, promising never again to look at another woman and to curb his unbearable jealousy of his young wife. The play concludes with the understanding that Oretta will continue her affair with the two young students.

Assiuolo's main situations are clearly derived from Boccaccio's *Decameron*: Oretta's attempt to catch her husband *in flagrante adulterio* recalls the story of Catella and Ricciardo (*Dec.* 3.6); the summoning of Oretta's brother brings to mind the tale of Monna Sismonda (*Dec.* 7.8); and Ambrogio's nocturnal vigil in Anfrosina's courtyard is reminiscent of the frigid night the amorous Rinieri spent in Isabella's courtyard (*Dec.* 8.7). There are also specific references to some characters of the *Decameron* and to Boccaccio himself. For instance, Rinuccio, when told of Ambrogio's cold night out in the open, is greatly amused and is reminded of the proverbial experience of "messer Rinieri del Boccaccio" (5.2). Also, the servant Giorgetto, mocking Ambrogio's sexual prowess, compares him to the elderly judge Ricciardo da Chinzica. The judge is a Boccaccian character who kept a calendar by his bed and every night invoked the chastity of the saint honoured that day as an excuse to abstain from having sex with his young wife (*Dec.* 2.10). In other cases, some characters behave in ways that bring to mind Machiavelli's stage characters. For example, Ambrogio, anticipating an intense sexual experience in the arms of Anfrosina, stops by the pharmacy to buy a potion or "lattovaro" that will enhance his sexual performance (3.4). This is the same aphrodisiac that Machiavelli's Nicomaco purchased (at the same Florentine pharmacy?) as he readied himself for the amorous encounter with young Clizia (*Clizia* 4.2). Also, Oretta's rationale for agreeing to become Giulio's paramour brings to mind Lucrezia's own arguments for accepting Callimaco as her lover. Like Lucrezia, she decides to continue her adulterous affair primarily because of her husband's stupidity and her lover's guile ("la pazzia sua [...] e l'astuzia vostra," 5.1).

These similarities establish beyond doubt Cecchi's sources and, at the same time, cause one to wonder why the dramatist, who claims to be original, made them so easily recognizable. Certainly he was aware that most contemporary theatre audiences were familiar with the proverbial names "Rinieri del Boccaccio" and "Ricciardo da Chinzica." It is likely, indeed, that even the least literate among them had read or heard of Giovanni Boccaccio or, as one of the narrators in Grazzini's *Le cene* calls him, "Saint John Golden tongue."[6] He also expected the spectators to see the connection between Oretta's and Lucrezia's individual decisions to pursue their respective illicit affairs. Surely they recognized Ambrogio's and Nicomaco's reliance on the same aphrodisiac, the miraculous *lattovaro*. This obvious pilfering of old sources is clearly at odds with Prologue's claim that the comedy is *nuova*, unless one considers the meaning of this adjective as the author's intent to show how he turned tried and proven models into something new. The sources, then, stand as terms of comparison that allow the audience to behold the novel ways in which the old elements were altered and how they ultimately came to signify something altogether different from their original meaning.

The first challenge facing Cecchi was to weave the material from various novelistic and theatrical sources into a cohesive dramatic text with characters and a story suitable for stage representation. With regard to the story, he modified borrowed scenes and situations, making sure they were closely related to one another. Also, he set them in a logical narrative sequence, creating a plot that, though consisting of interrelated subplots, is essentially linear. The three love situations are arranged in such a way that one leads to or justifies another: Ambrogio's pursuit of his erotic fancy causes Oretta's attempt to catch him in the act, which, in turn, leads to her love affair with young Giulio. With Ambrogio and Oretta out for the evening, Rinuccio can finally get into their house and, instead of spending the night with Oretta, as he expected, finds himself in the loving arms of the surprised but willing Violante. This last episode is perfectly placed in the development of the plot in that it allows Oretta, back from her amorous encounter, to refute Ambrogio's charges of adultery and turn the tables on him. Cecchi knew that he had successfully woven several narrative strands into a cohesive plot when he proudly announced to his audience that the story consisted of a single event or "caso" that lasted about ten hours.

In plotting a unified action, the playwright also casts events from various sources and distant periods into a twenty-four-hour time frame. The courtyard sequence, for instance, which in Boccaccio lasts the whole night, in the play is reduced to a few hours. Also, the encounter between Oretta and Giulio, reminiscent of the Catella-Ricciardo episode, is limited to a short scene. And the scene of the adultery charges and counter charges between Ambrogio and Oretta is relatively short compared to Sismonda's rather lengthy episode. The time compression, while helping to bring the action into formal compliance with the Aristotelian unities, allows for the audience's entertainment and points to a shift in thematic emphasis. The concentration of the courtyard scene, for example, limits the long exposure to the cold that nearly killed Boccaccio's Rinieri and focuses, instead, on Ambrogio's comic effort to get out. Undoubtedly, the spectators appreciated the humorous irony issuing from the contrast between Ambrogio's discomfort and Oretta's pleasure: while the first cools his hot flashes out in the courtyard, the latter is enjoying a passionate encounter inside the house. This simultaneous occurrence enhances the comic effect of Ambrogio's cry "Chiù, chiù," the password to summon his servant, Gianella.[7] In the silly cry, the spectators surely recognized the hooting of the horned howl (thus the play's title) and did not fail to appreciate the metaphor transferring the bird's horns to Ambrogio's head as symbol of his cuckoldry. The audience must have found it rather amusing to see and hear Ambrogio unwittingly proclaiming himself a cuckold while his wife was in fact making him one, and doing so just a few feet away.

The dramatic space in which the story's events take place consists of Ambrogio's and Anfrosina's respective houses, most likely located across the street from one another. Though this unity of place is a formal arrangement, its dramaturgical effect is significant. It is not hard to imagine the spectators' amusement as they become aware that old Ambrogio, in his vain pursuit of his amorous fancy, has come to the same place where his wife is actually having sex with a vigorous young man. The spatial proximity makes him a witness, as it were, to his own cuckoldry and, at the same time, ridicules his fanciful sexual prowess. Undoubtedly, the audience appreciated the irony inherent in Rinuccio's encounter with Violante in that it takes place in the very bed where Ambrogio should or could have sex. The mocking commentary on the socially accepted practice of old men marrying young women now reaches its height as the young couple make effective use of the very bed old Ambrogio neglected or was too feeble to enjoy. Admittedly, because of the genre's decorum, these events do not unfold in plain view for everyone to see. But the fact that they take place within earshot of the hall must have stirred the interest of an audience ever so curious to learn what was really happening inside the two houses.

The other challenge facing the playwright was the creation of characters who, while exhibiting behavioural patterns gleaned from several source models, were actually authentic. The spectators might recognize, for example, that certain traits of Ambrogio's character are reminiscent of this or that character from the stage and/or the *novellistica*. However, as has been noted, none of his predecessors exhibits all the unpleasant qualities that define his multifaceted personality (Radcliff-Umstead, *Carnival Comedy* 88). Ambrogio is unique in that, unlike any of his source counterparts, he is a doddering old man driven by sexual fancies and at once credulous, a cuckold, jealous, miserly, and pedantic. Renaissance spectators surely had no difficulty in recognizing that Ambrogio's experience is similar to that of Boccaccio's Rinieri: both are blinded by their passions, easily lured into a courtyard, and forced to spend the frigid night in the open rather than in bed with the women they fancy. But their similarity begins and ends here. The first is old, foolish, and presumptuous; the latter is young, daring, and intelligent. Rinieri is a learned young scholar passionately in love with a beautiful and flirtatious widow. The woman, Isabella, is so vain that, though already engaged in an amorous relationship, she encourages the young man to persist in his courtship. Eventually, she invites him to her house only to lock him in the courtyard throughout the snowy night, while she and her paramour laugh at his misery. Such cruel treatment did not go unpunished, for, the narrator notes approvingly, the young man soon took his just revenge upon the "silly" woman. In a world that celebrates youth, vigour, and intelligence, both the narrator and the audience praise Rinieri's vindication of his reputation and call him a hero.[8]

Ambrogio: An Original *Amator senex*

One can hardly characterize Ambrogio as a hero. If Cecchi modelled the old barrister after Rinieri, he certainly omitted the very qualities that distinguish the young student. The only experience they share is the dreadful night they spent out in the cold. But the reasons and the events that bring them to these humiliating and painful moments are totally different. Unlike young Rinieri, whose amorous ambitions are within the social norm, Ambrogio is an old *amoroso*, reminiscent of the indecorous and ridiculous *amator senex* of ancient comedy. Also, in the Boccaccian source, the flirtatious Isabella stokes Rinieri's amorous desires; in the adaptation, the chaste Anfrosina is not even aware of Ambrogio's craving for her. In fact, she is never seen or heard on stage, and her absence emphasizes the notion that Ambrogio's love is a chimera, a mere figment of his imagination. Thus, unlike Rinieri, who has every reason to accept as real the invitation to go to the rendezvous, Ambrogio has no reason whatsoever to assume that the invitation is genuine. Another detail that underscores their differences is the fact that Rinieri is unmarried and understandably in need of an object for his passions. In the case of Ambrogio, not only is he married, but he is married to a woman who grumbles about his lack of virility. "Because of his jealousy," she complains, "I'm deprived of pleasure outside the house and, because of his age, of pleasure inside the house" (4.3).[9]

More than a faithful adaptation, then, Ambrogio is a distortion of his Boccaccian counterpart; he is almost the opposite of Rinieri in every aspect of his personality. Unlike his prototype, who is noble, learned, and highly respected in the community, Ambrogio personifies socially repulsive practices and values. To be sure, like his predecessor, he is an educated man. But whereas the young Florentine is praised for his nobility and his learning ("onorato molto sì per la sua nobiltà e sì per la sua scienza," *Dec.* 8.7.571),[10] Ambrogio is derided as the most foolish and miserly man in all of Pisa. It takes almost an entire scene for the procuress Verdiana to get him to pay for her services with something more substantial than his precious old sleepers. Only after mocking his offers of used clothing (sleepers, socks, etc.), does Verdiana manage to get a few ducats from him (2.2). And when he parades his erudition by using Latin phrases that testify to his legal background, she mocks his pretentious rhetoric. She scoffs at his promise of free legal advice by turning his "gratis et amore" into "gratis e di amori" (2.2). He flaunts his rather mediocre Latin with the hardly literate Giannella, as he reminds the simple servant that all rewards presuppose work ("omnis proemium praesupponit laborem"). The poor fellow asks him to speak in plain language and not in Greek or Hebrew (3.5).

He also tries his erudition on Rinuccio, who hired him as his legal counsel in a civil suit before the local court. He greets the young student with "O bene veniatis domine," tells him that he expects the court to rule generously in his favour or "cum quibus," and assures him that the court will soon adjourn for the holidays, in "civilibus" (2.7). Rinuccio is hardly impressed with this pedantry. His reason for approaching the old lawyer is not to hear him speak Latin or to inquire about his legal suit but to make him believe that he and his friend Giulio will be going away to Florence that evening. With the students out of town, Ambrogio begins to imagine a passionate night in the arms of his "beloved" Anfrosina, just as the two young men expected (2.7). Lost in his reverie, he falls victim to the students' scheme and becomes a source of laughter for the spectators, who enjoy the ironic contrast between Rinuccio's devious plan and Ambrogio's infantile credulity. It never occurs to Ambrogio to question why Rinuccio needs to tell him about the trip to Florence. Had he been less concerned with flaunting his erudition and more suspicious of Rinuccio's true motives, he might have been circumspect enough not to take the bait so readily.

If some of Ambrogio's experiences reminded the spectators of Boccaccio's Rinieri, it was largely because of their differences. The latter personifies and champions important social values, such as intelligence and youthful love; the former is the negation of them. Rinieri is socially acclaimed for his virtues; Ambrogio is ridiculed for his shortcomings. The young man manages to retain his dignity; the old lawyer loses his. In allowing the young scholar to avenge the insult to his honour by means of an ingenious *controbeffa*, the Boccaccian narrator underscores the high value society placed on the resourcefulness of human intelligence. In the punishment of Ambrogio, one sees the reaction of a world that laughs at the aberration of a rich old fool taken by jealousy and lost in fantasies of youth. His ordeal in the courtyard highlights society's rejection of his miserliness, pretentious erudition, and unbecoming sexual pretensions. The rejection is so pronounced that he is victimized a second time when he is forced to relax his watchfulness over his wife, leaving her free to continue her amorous liaisons with both Giulio and Rinuccio. Surely the spectators did not fail to appreciate the irony that a creaky old man, given to extramarital fancy, winds up with a set of horns on his head. In Boccaccio, the story goes on to focus on Rinieri's revenge, leading the narrator and the audience to approve of his actions. Far from eliciting approval for Ambrogio, however, *Assiuolo*'s plot contrives an additional humiliation for him, as if to stress society's scorn for the old lawyer's hideous flaws.

The circumstances surrounding Ambrogio's additional punishment are similar to those in *Decameron*, 7.8, where the rich merchant Arriguccio accuses his noble but impoverished wife of adultery. In the end, it is Arriguccio who is scorned and humiliated by his adulterous and quick-witted wife. She convinces her brothers that the merchant's accusations against her are the result of his excessive drinking and womanizing. If the situations in the source and its imitation are similar, the characters and their experiences are not. Arriguccio had solid proof of his wife's cheating: not only did he discover the string that went from her foot out the window and down the street to alert her paramour, he also gave chase to the young lover in the middle of the night. Ambrogio has hardly any reason to be suspicious of his wife's behaviour; he simply hears a male voice coming out of his house and, conditioned by his excessive jealousy, immediately concludes that his wife is entertaining an inamorato. Unlike Arriguccio, who is an innocent victim of his wife's wit and sexual appetites, Ambrogio is a victim of his own adulterous fantasy and extreme jealousy. The coarse merchant is punished primarily for his "foolish" wish to become a nobleman by marriage ("ingentilire per moglie," *Dec.* 7.8.511); the old barrister is chastised for his loathsome ways. The Boccaccian denunciation of marriage based on monetary interests (sought by Sismonda's brothers) and on social climbing (Arriguccio's ambitions), in Cecchi's adaptation becomes a rejection of unnatural marriages between young women and rich old men.

But Ambrogio is not just superannuated, he is also a fanciful lover, somewhat reminiscent of the farcical Lysidamus, the *amator senex* in Plautus's *Casina*. There is no doubt that Cecchi knew the Roman play and that he was influenced, as in most of his other plays, by ancient comedy.[11] However, it is immediately clear that Ambrogio hardly resembles Plautus's buffoonish and depraved prototype, whose perverted sexual fantasies lead him to pursue young men as well as young women. Cecchi's direct source is definitely Machiavelli's *Clizia* (a close imitation of *Casina*), as attested by character similarities and specific textual allusions. Both plays open the second act with their respective *vecchi amorosi* reflecting on the intense passion that is affecting their individual daily lives. Nicomaco awakens with dismay to the realization that he is helplessly in love; Ambrogio laments his loss of peace of mind as he finds himself thinking day and night of his Anfrosina. Both men invest in perfumes, buy aphrodisiacs, and feast on strengthening foods in preparation for their individual, amorous jousts. Nicomaco eats a fat pigeon ("pippione grosso," 4.2) and takes his "lattovaro" potion in order to be vigorous or "gagliardo" (*Clizia* 4.4); Ambrogio takes the same aphrodisiac and eats the same food ("pippion grossi") in order to invigorate his manhood or, as he puts it, "ingagliardirmi" (3.4).[12]

Though these linguistic similarities establish *Clizia* as one of Cecchi's most immediate sources and make Ambrogio a mirror image of Nicomaco, the affinity between these two characters is only formal. The erotic desire underlining their resemblance arises from different needs that in the end distort their likeness and distinguish their individual characters. Nicomaco's plan to sleep with his young ward issues from his wish to prove to himself that, though old in years, he has plenty of vigour left in him. But this whimsical attempt to conquer the process of aging is but a tragic delusion that ultimately brings him face to face with the harsh reality of life. To be sure, Ambrogio, too, fails in his erotic pursuit, but his failure hardly resembles Nicomaco's defeat.

Nor does it stem from the same reasons. Unlike his Machiavellian model, Ambrogio does not seek a sexual contest in order to reassure himself that he is not a feeble old man. He can always prove his manhood with his young and beautiful wife, should he ever wish to do so. His servant Giannella wonders why he wants to be with another woman when he has a very beautiful one at home ("una sì bella in casa," 4.9). In the old man's erotic fantasy, Anfrosina is a symbol not of youth (with a son in his twenties, she is hardly a young maiden) but merely of an opportunity to expand his male prerogatives and feed his male ego. For him, to bed her would be another feather in his manly cap, another notch on his belt. His is but a whim that distinguishes him as a laughable old fool who pretends to do with other women what he cannot do with his own wife. His pursuit of another woman perturbs his wife, who complains repeatedly about his physical weakness and lack of sexual desire. It also draws Rinuccio's ridicule when he quips that the cowardly page (Giannella), as good at arms as his master (Ambrogio), is a worthy lover in bed ("valente cavalier nel letto," 4.5). In the end, unlike his Machiavellian counterpart, Ambrogio is not beaten but merely ridiculed and cuckolded. His failure implies not the rejection of his manhood, as it does for Nicomaco, but the censure and the mockery of his conceited view of himself as a desirable sex partner. This is the very presumption that causes him to accept as real the false invitation to Anfrosina's house.

Throughout the text there are plenty of obscenely charged references to Ambrogio's questionable manhood. A reference prevalent throughout the text is the salacious play on nouns such as "stocco" (a short dagger, and by extension one's manhood) and "uscio" (entrance door, and by context a woman's genitalia). For instance, he tells the panderer Verdiana that he must lock the *uscio* to his house for fear of what might wind up on his head ("quello che mi potrebbe tornare in capo," 2.2). The allusion, here, is that someone might enter the house and have sex with his wife, thus placing a set of horns on his head. Also, Giannella, as he prepares to accompany Ambrogio to the alleged assignation with Anfrosina, points out the paradox inherent in his master's intent to bang on the *uscio* of others while expecting that his own be left untouched (4.4). When the old man returns home from his failed adventure, he is furious to find the *uscio* open. There is no question in his mind that someone used a key ("chiave," hence the verb *chiavare* or to have sex) to unlock it. Immediately, he suspects his wife of adultery and sends for her brother. One can only imagine the spectators' laughter as they transfer the meaning of the sexually charged metaphor *uscio/chiave* to Oretta's encounter with young Giulio and Violante's night in bed with Rinuccio. Also, Ambrogio, before leaving for the supposed rendezvous at Anfrosina's house, tells Giannella that they need to take along their daggers for the "job." When the servant asks, with obscene intent, if he, too, might do the job, the old Casanova retorts with annoyance that he alone will enter Anfrosina's house (3.5). As it turns out, neither of the two gets to do the job: the servant loses his *stocco* when he fearfully runs away from imagined assailants; the old man breaks his while trying to force open the *uscio* of the courtyard. Here, too, the spectators undoubtedly appreciated the double meaning of the failed use of *stocco* as they recalled Ambrogio's suspicion that Giannella might be homosexual (2.2) and Oretta's complaints of her husband's lack of virility. They must have found amusing Violante's view that superannuated husbands are like a gardener's dogs in that they do not eat the cabbage they guard yet allow no one else to touch it (5.6).

Though Ambrogio's virility is the source of laughter throughout the play, it is important to keep in mind that, unlike his Machiavellian precursor, his failure does not imply the dismissal of his manhood but the collapse of his inflated notion of it. In *Clizia*, Nicomaco, alarmed by the creeping effects of age, rejects the possibility that he might be too old (2.1). In *Assiuolo*, the idea never occurs to the aging barrister, although it is obvious to everyone that he is a crotchety, senile, doting old fool. Violante alludes to him as a feeble old man on his last legs (3.4); Rinuccio refers to him as a dope or *rimbambito* with one foot in the grave (4.1). It must have been easy for the audience to share such a view, especially when they heard Violante's remark about how slowly he walks down the street (3.4). They also heard Ambrogio complain that his eyesight is failing so fast that he has difficulty recognizing people he knows (2.2). Thus, unlike Nicomaco who tries to defy the natural course of aging because he wishes to cling to the vitality of youth, Ambrogio, foolishly unconcerned with his age limitations, chases a whim. He pursues Anfrosina because, in his view, when one is burning inside, one must let out the smoke ("chi ha 'l fuoco dentro, bisogna che ne mandi fuori il fumo," 2.1). Thus, the nobility of Nicomaco's stand against the ineluctable becomes Ambrogio's farcical attempt to let off some erotic steam. In the end, the Machiavellian prototype is forced to accept the inevitability of aging and returns to his place of authority and respect within his family and the community. Ambrogio, on the other hand, becomes the laughing stock of Pisa and an enduring example of what to eschew.

It is not difficult to envision how ridiculous Ambrogio must appear as he, in his silly disguise, stirs a great hullabaloo in front of his house and in the presence of his brother-in-law. One can readily imagine the stage commotion with all the play's characters milling about while the neighbours, awakened by the fracas, look from their windows, laughing and commenting on the spectacle. Surely the spectators found the scene most amusing as they beheld the supposedly venerable old man disguised as a young page in a ragged outfit, holding his broken *stocco*, and frantically accusing his wife of adultery. For the spectators, who know where he spent the evening, the ironic tension arising from his hypocrisy earns him additional scorn. Also, the spectators' awareness that he is unwittingly accusing Violante, instead of Oretta, tends to amplify his foolishness and make him a sure target for ridicule. Both the contemptuous laughter he draws on himself and the miserable experience in the courtyard are indeed appropriate forms of punishment. The cold of the night cools his amorous flame, or, in his words, "il fuoco di dentro" (2.1); the laughter trivializes his presumptuousness in seeking to do with other women what he could not do with his own wife.

But perhaps the worse part of his punishment is the loss of his wife's chastity, as she is ultimately free to enjoy the pleasures he is too old to give and too jealous to let others provide. Like the freezing cold in the courtyard and the public ridicule, this aspect of the punishment is quite fitting because it is in direct response to his oppressive jealousy. By his own admission, he never allowed his wife out of his sight, always fearing the threatening presence of other men. He is especially suspicious of those Pisan students (how ironic!) with a lot of time on their hands and always looking to woo young women, in particular a beautiful one like his Oretta (2.1). He recalls that whenever she went to the monastery to see a religious play or do charity work, he escorted her and waited outside for hours patiently, like a "doctor's mule" (1.2). He seldom left the house, and when he had to go out, he ordered Giannella to lock the door and let no one in or out. But all these precautions could not prevent the cuckoldry he ultimately brings on himself. It is because of his whimsical desire to bed Anfrosina that Oretta, wanting to catch him in the act, winds up in the arms of young Giulio. And from then on, just like Machiavelli's Nicia, he will wear on his head the disgraceful horns of the cuckold, the very thing he has always feared the most. And so, as the servant Giorgetto predicted, Ambrogio, though keeping the devil's ring on his finger to assure himself of his wife's chastity, grew a set of horns bigger than those of Acteon when Diana turned him into a stag.[13]

Undoubtedly, Ambrogio should be added to the long list of credulous, cuckolded, and jealous husbands who crowd the world of the comic stage and the *novellistica*. However, his character exhibits a unique male ego caught between a naturally diminished sexual drive and an enduring pride in his manhood. The first leads to his insecurity and jealousy; the latter feeds his preposterous idea of himself as a sexual prize in demand. Thus, though showing inherited characteristics from his prose and stage ancestors (Plautus's Lysidamus and Demipho, Machiavelli's Nicia and Nicomaco, and Boccaccio's Chinzica), Ambrogio is different from them all in that he is unusually jealous of his wife and deeply concerned with his honourable standing in the community. In his view, a question of honour can be a matter of life and death ("dove ne va l'onore ne può ir la vita," 4.9). Honour is the driving force of his excessive jealousy, which arises from the fear of being cuckolded. He lives in the constant and prophetic apprehension that some young man – and there are many of them in Pisa – might seduce his wife and stain his reputation (2.1). Characteristically, his first concern, upon suspecting that someone has entered the house while he was out for the evening, is the loss of his honour ("oimè! l'onor mio," 4.10). It is out of this anxiety that he calls on Oretta's brother to come and take responsibility for his sister's adulterous behaviour. But in so doing, he brings shame on himself, for Oretta, with the brazen defiance reminiscent of Boccaccio's Monna Sismonda, accuses him of being the one who is in fact chasing other women. It is heavily ironic that a man so deeply concerned with his "honour" should bring about his own dishonour before the entire community.

To be forgiven, Ambrogio agrees to renounce his excessive jealousy and implicitly gives his wife freedom to do what she wants and with whomever she wants. The resulting cuckoldry is the most severe blow to his honour and male ego, as Oretta engages in a lasting love affair not just with one man but with two. In time, the play's community might forget the humiliating episode in the courtyard and the degrading scene in the street in front of his brother-in-law and the entire neighbourhood. But the neighbours will be constantly reminded of his dishonour and living shame as they see the two young men coming and going from his house. Adding insult to injury, the students will become "rascal godparents" ("compari [...] alla romanesca") to the child expected to be born in nine months (5.8). This ending is somewhat similar to the conclusion in Machiavelli's *Mandragola* in that both husbands are cuckolded by their own doing, become fathers to another man's child, and go on living with the dreaded shame of a set of horns on their heads. Also, it may be argued that the plays convey the message that in a society seriously preoccupied with its survival, not only because of rampant homosexuality (Machiavelli's Nicia and Cecchi's Giannella are both believed to be latent homosexuals)[14] but also because of a widespread practice of infertile old men marrying young women, the union of young and productive couples is a welcome assurance of its continued existence.[15] Indeed, both plays conclude with the understanding that the two childless households will soon be enlivened with the cries, the joys, and the noise of young children.

This conclusion, while underscoring the plays' similarities and, indirectly, Cecchi's debt to Machiavelli, points to important differences between the individual characters and their behaviour. Nicia and Ambrogio are two pedantic old fools who bring on themselves their own cuckoldry, but the way and the reason they come to their social shame set them apart. Unlike Nicia, who goes out of his way to have an heir and is happy to be a "father" (of another man's child), Ambrogio never thought of having children, nor is he aware that he will soon be a "father." In all likelihood, he will see the newborn as a living stain on his lost honour. In the source, Lucrezia's pregnancy is the outcome of intricate planning and efforts involving the entire stage community, including the friar, the husband, and Lucrezia's own mother. In Cecchi's imitation, the pregnancy is an inconvenient consequence of the trick that brought Oretta into the arms of young Giulio. In *Mandragola*, the wish to have a child is a prevailing theme that helps to determine the course of the play's action; in *Assiuolo*, there is no mention of such a wish. The noble desire to have a family mitigates somewhat the disgrace of Nicia's cuckoldry, just as the young couple's intent to be married some day (when old Nicia passes away) extenuates the immorality of the ongoing adultery. By contrast, the incident that brought about Oretta's love affair (neither she nor Giulio was aware of the ruse that brought them together), its brash and lascivious continuation, and the unexpected pregnancy, conspire to make Ambrogio the laughing stock of the community.

Oretta's wanton amour not only contributes to Ambrogio's public shame but also sets her apart from literary source models such as Catella, Mona Sismonda, and Lucrezia. Like Catella, Oretta, in her attempt to catch her husband in the act, finds herself in the arms of a young man and decides to continue the affair indefinitely. Also, like Catella, who reminds Ricciardo, mistaking him for her "unfaithful" husband, that she has had him watched ("io t'ho avuti miglior bracchi alla coda che tu non credevi," *Dec.*, 3.6.235), Oretta tells Giulio, believing him to be Ambrogio, "io t'ho avuti miglior bracchi alla coda che tu non credesti" (5.2). But the similarity is purely formal, for Oretta retains none of Catella's traits. Catella is madly in love with her husband; Oretta detests hers. In a monologue typical of the "malmaritata," Oretta complains about being married to a man old enough to be her grandfather and about her life of deprivation and restrictions. She considers herself the miserable wife of a crude and inhuman old man ("rozzo e inumano," 4.3). Unlike the jealous Catella, who believes the tale of her husband's adultery and goes to the rendezvous solely to catch him *in flagrante*, Oretta's primary intent is to avoid a major scandal and bring her delusional Ambrogio home ("riguidarlo a casa").[16] Catella agrees to continue the amorous relationship under duress ("piangeva forte") and only after being made aware that its disclosure would be ruinous to all the parties involved. By contrast, Oretta decides to continue the affair mainly because of her husband's foolishness, her wounded pride, and her lover's astuteness ("la pazzia sua, la gelosia mia, e l'astuzia vostra," 5.1).

These reasons bring to mind Machiavelli's Lucrezia, who, like Oretta, agrees to an adulterous relationship in part because of her lover's wit and her husband's stupidity (*Mandragola* 5.4). Also, just as Lucrezia is most virtuous and altogether averse to affairs of the heart (1.1), Oretta is said to be as far removed from the affairs of love as "roses are from January" (2.5). The plays end with both women engaged in adulterous relationships that promise to go on for a long time. Blessedly unaware of the women's adulterous affairs, the husbands unwittingly allow their respective wives to continue to see their lovers. Renaissance audiences found these similarities so striking that one evening both plays were performed in the same hall on two facing stages, alternating the acts of one play with those of the other. In Doni's *Marmi* (1552), a series of dialogues said to take place among young Florentines during the hot days of summer on the cool marble steps in front of the Duomo, one of the speakers recalls that the audience received the performance with great enthusiasm. He calls the two comedies "delightful and original" ("piacevolissime e di nuova inventione"), and praises both dramatists for their skilful use of material they borrowed from Boccaccio.[17]

Oretta's Immorality as a Reflection of the Times

Formal and thematic similarities between source and imitation notwithstanding, the morals and ambitions of the adapted characters distinguish them from their predecessors and ultimately point to their originality. Unquestionably, both Machiavelli and Cecchi modelled their female protagonists after Boccaccio's Catella, but the two stage characters are as different from each other as they are from their narrative source. Oretta complains about her husband's jealousy, old age, lack of virility, and the resulting deprivations. His controlling jealousy prevents her from attracting the attention of young men in town, and his old age, she adds, excuses him from giving her adequate marital attention. Though one may speculate that, given the opportunity, she would not hesitate to engage in a love affair with a virile young man, she goes to the rendezvous for the sole purpose of bringing the old man home and avoiding a scandal. Lucrezia, instead, never once complains about deprivations or her husband's lack of desire. She is so committed to her morals and religious convictions that only after unrelenting pressure from her family and assurances by her confessor does she consent to engage in a sexual relationship with a stranger. Lucrezia is a moral fortress assailed by its guardians (her husband, her mother, and her confessor); Oretta is a "malmaritata" resentful of a suffocating marriage and a patriarchal system that oppresses women and ignores their natural desires. In the end, unlike Lucrezia, who continues her love affair with only one man and with the understanding that they will get married one day, Oretta engages in a relationship with two young men with no other purpose than sexual pleasure. This purely capricious and wanton behaviour flies in the face of common decency and makes a mockery of the sanctity of marriage.

It is in part this libertine behaviour that separates Oretta from her predecessors and defines her as an original character. One would be hard pressed to find either in the *novellistica* or the theatre a more dissolute wife, especially when one considers that she is perversely aware that one of her lovers will also continue to enjoy her sister's favours. Another personal flaw that further underscores the originality of her character is her fear of losing her good reputation. Such a hypocritical concern, while matching that of Ambrogio, is found in none of her prototypes. Though less scrupulous than all her source models, she is the most anxious about preserving her "good" reputation. On her way to catch her husband *in flagrante amore*, she fears being recognized in her disguise and shamed in public (4.3). After having enjoyed Giulio's charms, she asks him to be careful not to make her lose in public the honour she lost in private that night with him. Also, fearing that Ambrogio has already returned home and discovered her absence, she prays God to spare her from being disgraced ("O Dio m'aiuti, ch'i' non sia vituperata," 5.1). As her fear intensifies, she begs the young men to help her for the love of God ("per l'amor di Dio," 5.2). These pious appeals and concerns for her honour accentuate the hypocrisy and sanctimony of a woman supposedly devout and honourable but actually lecherous and shameless.

The marked difference between Oretta and Lucrezia, just like that of their respective husbands, offers a sharp distinction between the imitation and its immediate source. To be sure, both *Mandragola* and *Assiuolo* denounce the socially accepted practice of unnatural marriages between old men and young women. They also conclude with an allusion to the reproductive society augured by the union of fertile young couples. But whereas Machiavelli exposes a moral world (Lucrezia) under attack by the corrupting forces of its own institutions (church and family), Cecchi paints a world mostly interested in denouncing odious customs and personal vices. The play's message is inherent in the public scorn levelled at Ambrogio's flaws and pretensions and is pointedly expressed at the end of the performance. In thanking and dismissing the spectators, the servant Giorgetto reminds them that the play teaches old men not to marry young women, and that if they make this mistake, they should refrain from all jealousy: "fate intender da parte nostra a' vecchi che vogliono tor moglie giovane, che se ne consiglino col nostro messer Ambrogio; e che se e' fanno il primo errore a torla, che non faccino il secondo a esserne gelosi" (5.8).

Scholars like Nino Borsellino accept this shopworn admonition at face value, noting that the play is devoid of any moral judgment ("libero da impicci moralistici," *Commedie* I.125). But if this is all there is to the moral of the story – that is, no morality – what are we to make of the hypocrisy and immorality branding Oretta's sanctimony and brazen promiscuity? One must go beyond the servant's stated moral if one is to appreciate the significance of the paradox informing Oretta's character. The reduction of the story to a mere lesson for old fools who marry young women raises Oretta's adultery to a just retaliation for Ambrogio's aberrant behaviour: she gave him what he deserved. More importantly, it makes her the vengeful instrument of a society bent on exposing its undesirable members and their wayward ways. Such a reading leads to a contradictory view of Oretta: a morally depraved woman on the one hand, a social "heroine" on the other. It is perhaps this paradox and all that it entails that the playwright intends to highlight through Oretta's actions. Cecchi's decision to use a character of perverted morals to expose flawed social values points to his intent to showcase a world indifferent to its own moral decadence. To the extent that the stage reflects the realities of the times, such indifference may be extended to the actual audience, who do not seem the least offended by Oretta's behaviour. Given the play's enthusiastic reception, it is safe to assume that contemporary audiences laughed at Ambrogio's foolishness and approved of Oretta's vengeful adultery or, at least, felt no sense of repulsion at her wanton conduct. From this perspective, they saw the permissive world of the stage as a true reflection of their own and laughed at their own loose morals.

Theatrical pleasure, Anne Ubersfeld points out, is never a passive reception, but is always related to situations ("une série d'activités") in which the spectators recognize affinities with their own world (330).[18] Surely, the playwright knew his times, what his audiences were likely to recognize and appreciate, and what would arouse their laughter or offend their sense of decorum. Undoubtedly, in Ambrogio's pedantry, stinginess, unnatural marriage, jealousy, credulity, and erotic fancy they recognized odious practices and behavioural aberrations so offensive to their social ethos that they joined the onstage community in a punitive and corrective laughter against the old lawyer. By contrast, they did not seem troubled by Oretta's distorted sense of honour and piety. It is dishonest of Oretta to be concerned with the preservation of the honour she continues to stain, just as it is sacrilegious of her to invoke God's mercy while committing and enjoying sin. One cannot accept Radcliff-Umstead's suggestion that Oretta, like Machiavelli's Lucrezia, appears as an "ethical pragmatist" who adjusts to a new situation

(*Carnival Comedy* 92). For, while she is indeed a pragmatist, there is nothing ethical about her vices and unchecked lewdness. If contemporary audiences did not find her behaviour offensive to their sense of decorum it is likely because they had grown accustomed to seeing such moral perversion in real life. Matteo Palmieri's view that it was most abominable ("sommo vituperio") for a wife to lie with another man had already lost its moral force.[19] Mid-sixteenth-century Florence was hardly scandalized by the extramarital affairs in which the ruling Medici family indulged. Not only were Grand Duke Cosimo and his children involved in adulterous relationships, but they also made little effort to keep them out of the public eye.[20] Bastiano Arditi complained in his *Diario* that by 1574, the year of Cosimo's death, Florence had become a cradle of crime and corruption.[21] Commenting on the comic theatre of the *cinquecento*, Vincenzo De Amicis noted that spectators preferred licentious comedies and that the best plays were usually the immoral ones because they reflected better the customs of the day.[22]

Contemporary audiences saw in *Assiuolo* a fictional reproduction of their own world, which, as Eugenio Camerini first pointed out, was more lustrous than noble, more worldly than cultured.[23] Fortunato Rizzi, in the first and most comprehensive study of Cecchi's works, concurred with the prevailing view that the playwright's indulgence towards the obscene reflected the moral degradation of the times.[24] Other scholars have since endorsed the notion that Cecchi's theatre, like most of the comic plays of the century, reflected a society increasingly complacent about its shallow moral values.[25] From this perspective, the true meaning of the play lies not in the mere condemnation of old men in love and unnatural marriage, as expressed at the end of the representation, but in the indictment of the moral permissiveness of the times. The play's focus is on the incongruity of the spectators' disapproval of Ambrogio's vices and their indifference towards Oretta's promiscuous adultery. This rather puzzling reception tends to reflect the ethos of a society that, while seemingly critical of relatively minor vices such as miserliness, pedantry, excessive jealousy, and bizarre erotic fantasies, appears not at all repulsed by the lascivious behaviour of a married woman. Stressing the link between words and deeds, fiction and reality, Prologue in Lodovico Dolce's *Ragazzo* points out that to reflect the customs of the times, one must make use of deeds and words that are lascivious: "a voler bene esprimere i costumi d'oggidí, bisognerebbe che le parole e gli atti interi fossero lascivia."

There is no question, then, that Cecchi, in imitating characters and plot elements from Boccaccio, Machiavelli, and classical Roman comedy, managed to create a truly original play and bring on stage a reflection of his own world. The humour and the social commentary of *Assiuolo* earned it the enthusiastic reception of contemporary audiences. They surely enjoyed the stage spectacle and the salacious language, with all its witticisms and obscene connotations. They also derived great gratification from their ability to recognize the play's sources and the playwright's creativity in fashioning them into a new and modern context. Undoubtedly, they saw Ambrogio as an original character, albeit of many inherited traits. For them, his many flaws not only distinguished him from his source counterparts but also made him a telling instrument for satirizing unnatural marriages between sterile old men and fertile young women. They also appreciated how Cecchi modelled Oretta after Boccaccio's and Machiavelli's characters and how, by departing from the sources' moral standards, he gave her a life and a personality of her own. Her loose morals set her apart from her predecessors and, at the same time, contributed to the representation of a world totally different from that of either Boccaccio or Machiavelli. In the end, *Assiuolo* is a true reflection of Cicero's alleged notion of comedy in that it spoke to the spectators of their own society by imitating their lives, mirroring their costumes, and reflecting their daily realities.[26] Therein lies Cecchi's creative stagecraft and the confirmation that imitation can lead to originality.

Chapter Five

Groto's *Emilia*: Fiction Meets Reality

Luigi Groto (1541–85), the blind man from Adria, a city in the Veneto region, made his reputation as a dramatist with *Adriana* (1578). The play has enjoyed considerable critical attention and has been included in several collections of Renaissance tragedies. His earlier tragedy *Dalila* (1572), though reprinted, is yet to be edited, and scholars mention it only to make passing references to its plot. Although Groto considered himself more suited to writing tragedies because of his gloomy outlook on life, due mostly to his blindness, he wrote three comedies: *Emilia* (1579), *Il Thesoro* (1580), and *Alteria* (1584).[1] All three plays remain largely unknown and are accessible only in early printings, which are marred with errors and typographical inconsistencies. Some of the pages are so darkened with ink splashes that it is difficult, at times, to make out words and entire lines. The few scholars who have examined them agree that *Emilia* is "Groto's best comedy" (Herrick, *Italian Comedy* 156). This favourable view notwithstanding, some critics lament the work's lack of originality, noting that it is too close an imitation of Plautus's *Epidicus*. Sanesi, in particular, though observing that it is more amusing and livelier than the other two comedies, concludes that it is less original. But, he is quick to point out that it must have been quite successful with contemporary audiences both for its liveliness and for its modern setting.[2] The observation is somewhat paradoxical because it implies that imitations are not original, while conceding that they can be modern and relevant. The following pages deal with this ambiguity by focusing on Groto's ability to blend the old with the new, the comic with the grim. The combination allows us a critical insight into the unique imitative process that arises from a plot based on the interlacement of contemporary war atrocities with a loose adaptation of an ancient comedy.

Dedicated to the "Illustrissimo Sig. Giovanni da Lecce Cavalliere & Procurator di San Marco," *Emilia* takes its name from the learned Emilia Casalini, a close relative of the author.[3] It was first performed in Hadria on 1 March 1579 to mark the grand opening of the local theatre built under the sponsorship of the city's governor, Lorenzo Rimondo.[4] We have no record of the number of spectators in attendance, but there is no reason to doubt Groto's claim that the play was recited before a large audience and that the actors performed with great distinction, winning acclaim for themselves, the play, and the author.[5] He was told, he states in his dedicatory letter, that the enthusiastic reception led some actors to assemble their individual parts into an integral text and went on to perform it on their own in other cities. After learning that some *recitanti* were altering the text to suit their acting preferences, he decided to have it printed in order to prevent the spread of corrupted copies.[6] Admittedly, the rush to print a manuscript for fear of distortions or theft was a Renaissance commonplace. In some instances, expressing this "fear," real or alleged, was a way of boasting about the work's popularity.[7] However, in this case there is reason to believe that the play was indeed popular with contemporary Venetian audiences because, among other things, it spoke about their city's heroic stand against the Turks during the battle for Cyprus in 1570–1. The mere mention of Bragadin's tenacious defence of Famagusta and his harrowing death must have stirred strong feelings of pride and woe in the hearts of the Venetians.

But if, on the one hand, the historical context earned the play a favourable reception, on the other hand, it risked dating it, prompting literary critics to consider it provincial and irrelevant to future and diverse audiences. This view and the perception that the play, being an imitation, lacks originality are perhaps the reasons for the dearth of editorial interest and critical attention given to it. The neglect is unfortunate, for, as we shall see, it is exactly the masterful mix of the hardship of a recent war with an ancient comic plot that makes *Emilia* not only Groto's best comedy but also worthy of inclusion in the anthologies of Italian Renaissance comedies. The blending is most creative because it rests on the ambiguity between the genre's pretence of realistic representation and the playwright's attempt to undermine it. The intended result is to cause the spectators to view with scepticism what they see and hear on stage, while, at the same time, they are confronted with realistic reminders of their painful past. The ensuing discussion examines the extent to which the factual background historicizes the dramatic action, and whether the thematic and dramaturgical innovations justify the playwright's claim of originality – whether the label "comedia nova," appearing on the text's frontispiece, is just the conventional way of describing a play being performed for the first time or a valid assertion of truly new stagecraft. In the end, it will become clear whether the work's initial popularity was due solely to its appeal to Venetian patriotism or to literary and theatrical qualities not yet brought to light.

From the Sources to the Adaptation

The adaptation follows closely Plautus's tale of the Athenian Periphanes, who is finally reunited with his long-lost daughter and her mother, a mistress he had in Epidaurus. The play's action begins as Periphanes' son, Stratippocles, returns from a victorious war, bringing with him his newly found love, Telestis. The girl is a Theban captive whose freedom he must buy. The situation poses a serious problem for the family slave Epidicus, who, following his young master's instructions before going off to war, had already purchased for him his inamorata Acropolistis. The conniving servant had convinced his old master Periphanes to buy the girl's freedom and welcome her home. He had deluded the anxious father into believing she was his long-lost daughter. Now, Epidicus must reach deep into his bag of tricks to find the money to pay for Telestis's freedom. He tells Periphanes of a rumour that Stratippocles, upon his return from Thebes, intends to buy the freedom of an old flame of his, an Athenian courtesan. He persuades the old man to foil his son's disgraceful plan by purchasing the courtesan's freedom before Stratippocles can marry her and compromise the family name. The investment should yield quite a profit, he assures the old man, for there is a certain captain interested in the courtesan and willing to pay a high price for her freedom. The scheme works and Periphanes shells out the cash for the purchase.

Pursuing his plan, Epidicus gives the money to Stratippocles, who can now buy his Theban slave's freedom. As for the supposed purchase of the courtesan, the servant, remembering that his old master wished to hire a musician to celebrate his son's safe return, brings home a music-girl, instructing her to pretend to be the courtesan Acropolistis. The plot begins to unravel when the *miles* interested in buying his beloved Acropolistis unmasks the music-girl as an impostor and refuses to pay for her freedom. A befuddled Periphanes begins to suspect that he has been tricked. His suspicion grows to certainty when Philippa, his quondam mistress, shows up in town looking for her long-lost daughter.

Periphanes recognizes the woman right away and assures her that their daughter is in the house. But when he brings out the true Acropolistis, the girl he believed to be his daughter Telestis, Philippa baulks, insisting that she is not her daughter. Periphanes, realizing that he has been soundly duped, begins to rage against the deceitful slave. The final denouement unfolds as Stratippocles learns that Telestis is actually his half-sister and Periphanes' and Philippa's daughter. The play concludes with Stratippocles marrying Acropolistis, and with Epidicus winning his freedom because his tricks led to such a happy conclusion.

Groto does not acknowledge his source, an omission quite unusual among Renaissance playwrights. But there is no question that *Emilia* closely follows Plautus's story. While the imitation's characters have different names and are more numerous – and in some cases more complex – the action's events are largely the same as those dramatized in the original play. At times, even the language is strikingly similar to that of the Latin version. For instance, the old widower Polidoro, like his Plautine counterpart Periphanes, is hesitant to marry his onetime mistress, Lucida, for fear of offending his son's sensibilities ("temea solo di offendere il figlio," 5.8).[8] The expression bears an obvious resemblance to Periphanes' "revereor filium" (2.1).[9] Also, the chance encounter between Polidoro and his former mistress is strikingly similar to that of the source in both its suspenseful tone and its word choice. Upon seeing each other, the two cannot believe their own eyes and wonder aloud:

> POL. Mi par colei ch'io hebbi in Cipri, Lucida mia, di cui generai la mia figlia unica.
> LUC. Mi par colui, che m'hebbe in Cipri, Polidoro, di cui partorii la nostra figlia (5.5).

> [POL. She looks like the woman I had in Cyprus, my Lucida, from whom I had my only daughter.
> LUC. He looks like the man who had me in Cyprus, Polidoro, by whom I had our daughter].

In the Latin version:

> PE. Certo east *** [fragment missing from the text] quam in Epidauro pauperculam memini comprimere.
> PH. plane hicine est qui mihi in Epidauro primus pudicitiam pepulit.
> PE. quae meo compressu peperit filiam quam domi nunc habeo (4.1).

[PE. Certainly she is the poor woman I remember sleeping with in Epidaurus.
PH. Clearly, this is the man who first took my virginity in Epidaurus.
PE. [the woman] who gave birth to the daughter I have now in the house].[10]

When Polidoro finally asks Lucida to jog his memory as to whether he knew her from somewhere, Lucida's question, "voi volete ch'io sia *interprete de la memoria* [vostra]?" ("do you want me to be the interpreter of your memory") is almost a translation of Philippa's reply to Periphanes: "quia tuae *memoriae interpretari* me aequom censes ("why do you expect me to *interpret* your memory," 4.1). Both mothers react in the same way and with a similar olfactory metaphor when they dismiss the music-girl as an impostor. Lucida's "Altro *odore* han le dame, altro le lepori" ("one thing is the smell of ladies, another that of hares," 5.5) parallels Philippa's "aliter catuli longe *olent*, aliter sues" ("one thing is the smell of puppies, another that of pigs," 4.2 [my italics]).

It is likely that contemporary audiences had no difficulty recognizing Plautus's text (partorii → peperit; interprete de la memoria → memoriae interpretari; odore → olent) and that they took pride in their ability to identify the classical source. But, as Groto himself knew, they expected to see more than just a reference to antiquity. They wanted to see a modern representation that not only rivalled the ancient source but also entertained them and spoke of their times. The most obviously contemporary aspects of the play, besides the language and the costumes, are the spatial and temporal settings. The story is set in modern Constantinople, where Venetian merchants continued to live even after the 1571 battle of Lepanto. The stage events are rooted in the Turks' conquest of Cyprus, especially the pillage and killings that followed the 1570 surrender of Nicosia. Upon entering the city, the Ottoman forces massacred thousands of Greek and Venetian citizens, including the island's governor, Nicolò Dandolo. Stage characters returning from the war tell stories of Venetian heroism and Turkish brutality, including the rape and/or seizure of young men and women destined for the slave markets in Constantinople. Lucida, for instance, recalls how Lala Mustapha's troops rampaging through the city broke into her house, took all her jewellery, and then stripped her young daughter from her clutching arms (4.4).

Here fact meets fiction, as the tales rise from the shadows of historical events that marked the fall of Cyprus. To a certain extent, Groto adapted the same backdrop as that of the Plautine source in that it, too, is set against a war. In both versions, the war does not simply date the story, it also serves as the source of its central episode: while away at war, a young man falls in love with a slave who turns out to be his half-sister. This simple case of mistaken identity engenders the spinning of the plays' plots. But the parallel between the historical backdrops ends here. In Plautus, the war is a mere pretext to jump-start the narrative; in Groto, it has a significant emotional impact both on the characters and on the audience. *Epidicus* does not feature reports of heroic deeds or bloody battles, and none of its characters appears remotely interested in the war. No one asks young Stratippocles about his war experience. It is as if he were returning from a hunting trip. Only old Periphanes makes a passing reference to the war as he plans to celebrate his son's safe return (2.2). If the war was so irrelevant for the Grecian stage community, one need not wonder how insignificant it must have been for Plautus's Roman audiences. The war was too alien and too distant, both in time and place, to have a particular meaning for Romans. For them, it was merely a narrative pretext for the development of the plot and practically devoid of any emotional appeal.

Unlike the Roman source, *Emilia* is cast against a war background that involves the stage community and evokes painful memories in the spectators. The fall of Nicosia is a subject of concern and discussion among the characters, who are eager to know what is happening on the island: "É bello stare in Cipri?" asks Chrisoforo rather sarcastically upon meeting the servant Tropio, just back from the war (2.3). And young Neofilo, in conversation with his friend Polipo, also just back from Cyprus, is curious about the fate of Famagusta: "Che si giudica di Famagosta?" (2.4). Undoubtedly, Polipo's prediction of the inevitable fall of Famagusta resonated deeply in the hearts and minds of Venetian audiences, who still remembered with humiliation and rage the barbaric treatment meted out to their co-nationals living on the island.[11] How could they have forgotten the gruesome death of Famagusta's famed defender Marcantonio Bragadin? After being tortured and paraded through the city's streets, he was flayed alive, and his stuffed skin was sent to the Sultan as a war trophy.[12] Sanesi, speaking of the impact the mere mention of the war might have had on contemporary audiences, observes that all references to Cyprus must certainly have wiped the smile from the spectators' lips and, igniting in them a burning flame of enthusiasm, made them shudder with proud and dignified emotion.[13]

This stirring of strong emotions in the hearts of the spectators represents a definite departure from the original source. The war is not just a device to cast the story in modern times but also an effective way to discourse with the spectators by recalling memories both proud and painful. But if, on the one hand, this intimate appeal to the audience distinguishes the imitation from its source, on the other hand, it has led literary critics to conclude that it tends to limit its relevance mostly to Venetian spectators. This view needs to be re-evaluated because it overlooks the growing Renaissance demand for a modern theatre based on recent and memorable events. In Machiavelli's *Mandragola,* Prologue tells the audience that the story takes place in contemporary Florence and that its characters are living Florentines. Cecchi's *Assiuolo* is supposedly based on an event that happened recently in Pisa, with specific reference to the 1532 Spanish occupation of Florence. In Grazzini's *Il frate,* Prologue informs the audience that the story happened in Florence during the 1539 siege of the city. Lest we brand most Renaissance plays as parochial, we must view the contemporary setting in *Emilia* not as a limitation of its appeal but as a common topos of Renaissance theatre meant to create a bridge between the real world of the audience and the fictional world of the stage.

The playwright's intent to establish a dialogue between the stage and the audience is also borne out by the length of the play and its large cast. With more than 3,000 lines, the adaptation is more than four times longer than its Latin source (733 lines). Also, the addition of four extra roles brings the total number of characters to seventeen. This expansion accounts both for thematic novelties and for the expectations of contemporary audiences to be entertained for an entire evening, at times well into the early morning hours. Pointedly, *Emilia*'s Prologue, in taking his leave of the spectators, tells them that he will see them tomorrow morning ("domattina").[14] Though the text does not give specific indications about the length of the performance, it is reasonable to assume that, just like most Renaissance stage representations, it was interspersed with diversions, including songs between acts and intermezzi featuring dances and/or short skits. The choreography and the overall quality of a particular performance usually reflected the importance of the occasion – whether a stately wedding, an official state visit, or simply an evening of fun during the carnival season. But whatever the occasion, the author's primary goal was to engage and entertain his audience.

It is with these expectations in mind that Groto, like many of his fellow playwrights, alters the source material, adds new characters, and weaves subplots that were sure to intrigue and delight the spectators. True to the theatrical spirit of the times, *Emilia* concludes in the euphoria of multiple recognition scenes and weddings – four, to be exact: Polipo-Flavia, Neofilo-Emilia, Polidoro-Lucida, and Chrisoforo-Catella. This is indeed a chaotic and happy ending quite different from that of the Plautine source, which concludes with Stratippocles' wedding and Epidicus's delight in his newly gained freedom. For the additional weddings, Groto introduces Neofilo and Flavia: the first he models after Stratippocles' friend Chaeribulus, the latter after the music-girl. Neofilo is a drastic alteration of the debt-ridden Chaeribulus, who, unable to lend money to his friend, helps him to hide the Theban captive Telestis. The role of his Italian counterpart is more complex and versatile. He is in love with Polipo's young captive, and is torn between his love for the girl and his sense of loyalty towards his friend. When it turns out that the captive is actually Polipo's half-sister, Emilia, he is free to marry her, adding to the play's happy ending. Besides his commonplace role in this staple subplot, Neofilo is instrumental in bridging the gap between the fictional world of the stage and the reality of the Cyprian war. It is in answer to his questions that Polipo talks (to the audience) about the fall of Nicosia, the burning of a Turkish ship by a Venetian lady, and the heroic stand of Famagusta's defenders.

Flavia, too, differs considerably from her Latin counterpart. Unlike Acropolistis, who appears on stage only once (4.2), primarily to be unmasked as an impostor, Flavia has several long scenes, including a lengthy and maudlin soliloquy where she expresses her undying love for Polipo. On the formal level, her role serves to censure the affected mannerisms of courtiers and Spaniards. It also helps to link the dramatic action to the antefactum – that is, Polidoro's past, especially his love affair with the woman he left in Epidaurus. When Chrisoforo instructs her how to pass for the old man's daughter, Emilia, she and the audience learn about the times and the place of Polidoro's youthful indiscretions and his longing to be reunited with his long-lost mistress and daughter. Also, Flavia's exaggerated expression of gratitude towards Chrisoforo for having purchased her freedom prompts the servant's admonition to leave all those hyperboles to the "Spagnuoli and Cortegiani." These two groups were commonly known both on stage and in real life for their pandering and pretence. Unlike her source model, who is a "music-girl," Flavia is finally recognized as the daughter of Polidoro's old friend and neighbour, the rich merchant Fronesio. Father and daughter were separated when she was a child, following the pillage and burning of their city. Admittedly, the recognition theme and the ensuing wedding is a shopworn topos in Renaissance comedy, which many playwrights, Groto included, did not hesitate to shun as trite and anachronistic.[15] However, in *Emilia*, against the backdrop of the recent devastation wrought on Cyprus and the ensuing dispersion of entire families, the theme is cogent and relevant.

The most obvious and significant alteration of the Plautine play is the transferral of the dramatic action from ancient Athens to modern Constantinople. Both plays represent to their respective audiences a world different from their own: the Romans behold the world of ancient Athens, the Venetians that of Muslim Constantinople. But unlike the Latin source, the Italian adaptation dramatizes a story that speaks directly to its audience of their own culture. As noted earlier, Plautus's representation is cast against a background of a war that is loosely linked to Athens, barely recalled on stage, and of little interest to the average Roman. *Emilia*'s action is much more pertinent to the audience, as it takes place in contemporary Constantinople where many Venetian merchants were still living. Several of the play's events are connected with the fall of Cyprus, an episode fresh in the hearts and minds of the spectators. The location is first given in the play's bill and is variously confirmed throughout the play with assertions such as "this is Constantinople" or "here in Constantinople." Also, the characters identify themselves, in one form or another, as Turks. Chrisoforo reminds his old master Polidoro that Nicosia was taken by "our people" and refers to Polidoro, Arpago, and himself as "we Turks" (1.1). He boasts to Arpago that Polidoro believes him just as "we Turks believe in the Koran" (1.3). Young Polipo talks about his experiences as a Turkish veteran of the war. His orderly, Tropio, wishes to forget the hardships of war he experienced while fighting alongside his master (2.3). Neofilo admits that the Turks conquered Nicosia because of *our* sheer number and not because of *our* military ability (my italics). He also mentions that he fought under the Turkish flag (2.4). The braggart Captain Fracassa boasts that the Sultan personally begged him to enlist in the war (3.6).

These and similar assertions may lead one to conclude that the play is about the Turks' daily realities in Constantinople; but a close look reveals that the stage reflects current aspects of Venetian culture and society. And it could not be otherwise, for the representation of an Arab world would hardly be of interest to Venetian spectators and would ultimately undermine the author's intent to engage them. A hint that the representation is about Venice is given by the play's courtesan Erifila as she inveighs against the actors who refuse to perform in the play she was hoping to see "tonight." In expressing her disillusionment, she points out that the performance was sponsored by foreigners living in Constantinople (3.4). Though she does not identify the sponsors, it is reasonable to assume that she refers to the spectators, that is, Venetian merchants wishing to see a play about themselves and their world. It should not come as a surprise – the audience certainly was not surprised – that there should be so many Venetians in Constantinople, for Venice had established a significant presence in the city following the Fourth Crusade at the beginning of the thirteenth century.[16]

One might be justifiably confused about the actual location of the play's action simply because there are no specific references to landmarks, such as buildings or streets, that might tie the story exclusively to the Muslim city.[17] The Arab authenticity of the stage world is further diminished by the Italian-sounding names of several "Turkish" characters in the play. Lascari, old Polidoro's last name, was and continues to be a popular Italian name, especially in the Veneto region. An equally popular Italian name is that of the slave merchant Barbaro. Chrisoforo refers to himself as "Chrisoforo da Grafignana," an area in northern Italy. Fracassa, the Italian synonym of havoc, became a staple character in the commedia dell'arte. The servant Vespa (wasp) is obviously Italian, as are the names of the young maidens Catella, Menica, and Rustica. As several of these names were actually commonplace in the comedy and the *novellistica* of the Italian Renaissance, Groto's audiences were likely to identify them as Italians and wonder whether the representation was indeed a reflection of life in Constantinople, as they were told.

The Stage Pretence of Realism Undermined

The Italian dimension of the play's world certainly undermines the author's own claim that the stage action takes place in Constantinople and that the characters are Turks. It also puzzles the spectators as they behold a spectacle that could be Italian as well as Turkish. Their confusion intensifies as they hear Turkish characters express themselves in ways inconsistent with their social status and/or Arab identity. Porters and servants often speak in Latin, flaunt their knowledge of classical mythology, and refer to Italian literary authors and characters with the ease of a scholar versed in Renaissance comedy. For instance, the porter Rigo recalls that for the wedding they have cooked fourteen birds ("salvis iure calculo," 4.2). Chrisoforo, asked how he is going to avoid the beating the old master is sure to give him, replies "Dominus providebit" (5.5). He goes on to flaunt his erudition by mentioning ancient writers, such as Pliny, Solomon, and Aristotle. He also mentions mythological figures, including Danae, Jupiter, Venus, and Helen of Troy. For a Turkish servant, he is surprisingly aware that Bologna is the renowned source of wisdom because of its famed university (1.5). Reflecting on the punishment he is about to receive, he acknowledges that nobody can save him from Polidoro's anger, not even "the man of science, as they say in Italy" (5.2). Old man Polidoro, too, seems unusually educated for a Turkish cattleman. He not only mentions ancient and mythological figures such as Ptolemy and Jason, he is also familiar with Italian authors and some of the characters in their works, ranging from Boccaccio's Fra Alberigo to Ariosto's Mandricardo. Even the Persian Lucida speaks of ancient generals such Scipio and Alexander. Also, the characters' frequent references to women as female cows ("vacche") is peculiar to Italian literary tradition, from Dante to Ariosto, Aretino, Cellini, and Della Porta.

The ambiguous mixture of Italian and supposedly Arab characters suggests that *Emilia* is intrinsically Venetian and only loosely and playfully arabesque. The ambiguity and its inherent amusement arise in part from the shifting sense of reality implied in the paradox of the Turks' praise of their Venetian enemies. In recalling events of the Cyprian war, some Turkish characters speak highly of the heroic resistance the Venetians put up against the overwhelming Ottoman forces. The most outspoken admirer of the Venetians' valiant stand is Polipo, a Turkish soldier just back from the war. With respect to the plot, Polipo's role is similar to that of his Latin counterpart, Stratippocles: a young man who goes to war leaving behind his love interest only to return home with a newly found lady love. To his surprise, the young woman, a presumed slave whose freedom must first be bought, turns out to be his half-sister. But, unlike Stratippocles, who never mentions the war, Polipo has the added role of reflecting and commenting on his war experience. Thus, when his young friend Neofilo prods him about the fall of Nicosia, he opines that the Turks would have failed had they not outnumbered the Venetians ten to one. As for Famagusta, he believes that the city, its weak fortifications notwithstanding, is so valiantly defended that it could only be taken by treason or a long siege. In his view, the brave Venetians will not surrender as long as they have bread, cannon balls, and powder ("pan, palle, e polvere," 2.4). He has the highest regard for the city's defenders, singling out the leaders Bragadin and Baglione for their great wisdom and military prowess. He also admires the courage and resolve of the Venetian woman who set fire to a Turkish ship. He calls her a noble lady of generous spirit, magnanimous ideals, and pure mind ("di generoso spirito, di magnanimi / pensieri, e d'una mente pudicissima," 2.4).

It is reasonable to assume that so much praise confounded Venetian audiences, who were likely to question why their avowed enemies were so in awe of Venetian valour and patriotism. As they behold a world populated by characters who identify themselves as Turks but appear to be Italian in their names and culture, they cannot but question the playwright's intent and his stagecraft. In reality, the confusion arising from the play's numerous inconsistencies is not a structural flaw but the most innovative aspect of the author's stagecraft. Groto intends to create an atmosphere of uncertainty whereby the world of the stage is and is not what it appears to be. The attempt to foster such a sense of competing realities first surfaces in the prologue, where a rebellious and irreverent Prologue warns the spectators that the representation is nothing but fiction, a mere game. He cautions them not to be fooled by appearances, pointing out that the characters claiming to be women are actually men in disguise and that those alleging to be old men are, in fact, young men pretending to be old.[18] In addition, he continues, the action takes place in Hadria, and not in Constantinople as the author wants them to believe. Disgusted at the pretence that the story about to be dramatized is real, he tears the script to pieces, takes off his stage clothes, and tells the audience that the representation is not real as the actors want them to think: "questa commedia / é finta ed essi per vera ve la narrano."[19]

Prologue, the character, is an addition to the Plautine source, which strangely does not include a prologue, a rather common feature in Roman theatre. Just like their ancient counterparts, Renaissance playwrights used Prologue mostly to state their poetics, defend themselves against envious detractors, give a short synopsis of the plot, and plead with the spectators for their attention and approval. *Emilia*'s Prologue is unique in that he subverts his traditional role by telling the spectators not to believe what they hear or see, for the whole spectacle is a sham. He considers laughable ("baie da ridere") the premise that the city represented on stage is Constantinople and that all the characters are Turks. If that were the case, he warns tongue in cheek, the ladies in the audience risked being kidnapped by the sultan, who is always looking for beautiful women. And what of the author's assertion that the action takes places during the fall of Nicosia, a decade ago? This, too, is laughable, he raves, for, if the playwright had the power to make the past come alive, people would pay him handsomely for the opportunity to relive their youth. In his unrelenting attempt to discredit the stage as a mirror of reality, he reminds the audience that the play's author is totally blind and cannot, therefore, shed light ("lume") on the intricacies of the plot. He concludes his bantering by telling the public that in the morning, when the performance is over, they will find themselves not in Constantinople, as the playwright claims, but in Hadria. He exits the stage with the greeting "a rivederci in Hadria domattina."

The attempt to undermine the established function of theatre as an image of reality is also sustained throughout the text by characters who refer to events in the play as material for a *comedia.* In some cases, they allude to the play itself as a performance (their own) that they wish to see. The courtesan Erifila, for instance, upon entering the stage, recalls how eagerly she has been looking forward to seeing "tonight's comedy." But she fears that the representation may not take place because some young actors refuse to perform unless their young sweethearts are in the audience to applaud them. After criticizing sanctimonious parents for forbidding their daughters to attend theatrical performances, she expresses her frustration with those young performers who decline to go on stage (4.3). If the spectators have any doubt about what comedy Erifila is referring to, they need only hear Captain Fracassa's comment about the play's "eyeless" author. Upon realizing that the girl Polidoro is trying to sell him is not his beloved Flavia, Fracassa insists that he would recognize his lady love anytime, anywhere, unless he were blind, like the author of the play being performed tonight ("l'autor della Comedia, che si recita / questa sera," 3.7). Neofilo, having heard the story of how old Polidoro rewarded Chrisoforo by marrying him to the young maid Catella, comments that there is plenty of material there for a "comedia" (5.8).

Taken at face value, these metatheatrical references together with Prologue's histrionic dismissal of the play's claim of realistic representation would undermine the notion of theatre as *speculum vitae.* It would also thwart the playwright's goal to hold the spectators' attention and speak to them of their world. But, seen in the context of the entire play, their true function is to help create an atmosphere of pretence and entertaining ambiguity that allows for the safe transgression of social decorum and for the light treatment of serious topics. The various allusions to the Turks' cruelties against the Venetians living in Cyprus would hardly be considered appropriate for a comic representation were they not cast in a fictional and somewhat ambiguous context. The torture and mayhem that marked the fall of Famagusta, recalled through the mention of Bragadin and Dandolo, are indeed the subject of tragedy. It is not surprising that these events became the actual source of several tragedies in the last decades of the sixteenth century.[20] The reminder that *Emilia* is the reflection of a world that is and is not what it appears to be tends to make the recollection of these atrocities less painful and more suitable for the comic stage. One might say that the atmosphere of ambiguity not only provides a light context for sombre themes but also helps to protect the spectators from unpleasant memories that are still fresh in their minds.

It is mostly for this purpose that Groto introduces the blowhard Fracassa, the *miles gloriosus* whose hyperbolic claims of military feats tend to minimize the brutality of war and move the audience to laughter. Fracassa is not a new character but an alteration of *Epidicus*'s *Miles*. In both the Latin and the Italian versions, the characters have the same narrative roles: they make the old men in the respective plays realize that they have been duped. The girl they each purchased is not the slave their devious servants represented them as. But the role of Plautus's soldier, though important to the development of the plot, is not particularly significant to the representation: he appears briefly on stage (one short scene), has relatively few lines, and has no actual name other than the generic title of Miles. He is hardly the source of laughter normally associated with the role, as he is not given much opportunity to brag about his risible martial deeds. No sooner does he begin to boast about glorious military feats than old man Periphanes dismisses it all as mere child's play and reminds him that he is standing before a true war hero. "You would run home with your tail between your legs," Periphanes warns him, "if you heard of my exploits" ("si audias / meas púgnas," 3.4). If this admonition prevents Miles from developing into a typically ridiculous braggart, it is because he is by and large a serious character. He has sincere feelings for the girl and an uncharacteristically biting wit. His wish to purchase the young slave arises from true love and not from a need to boast about the "conquest" of yet another woman, as most of his stage counterparts are wont to do. Also, after it becomes clear that the girl Periphanes was trying to sell him is not his beloved Acropolistis and that the old man had been duped, Miles goes away determined to look for her, wherever she may be: "Ego illàm requiram, iam ubi ubi est – bellator, vale" (3.4). The parting shot "bellator" (warrior) referring to Periphanes is clearly meant in a sarcastic way, as it forces a humiliating contrast between the duped old man and the self-styled war hero. The farewell may simply be read as: goodbye, you old fool, so much for your *púgnas*.

Unlike the subdued and rather serious Roman soldier, Fracassa is a ridiculously pretentious character who brags about his warlike feats and his escapes from women craving his manhood. Dramaturgically, the primary purpose of his role is to enliven a story that might otherwise be too serious for comedy. Undoubtedly, he moves the audience to laughter with his bizarre boasts. He claims that his famous sword, Lupa, is more frightening than Astolfo's horn, and that with a mere punch he can easily send his enemies to the infernal kingdom of Styx ("regni stigÿ," 3.6). To make sure that the audience appreciates this aspect of Fracassa's role, Groto assigns to Vespa, Fracassa's servant, the role of ridiculing his master. Unlike his Plautine counterpart, who has no proper name, is addressed only once, and never utters a word, Vespa has a sustained speaking part. He never misses the opportunity to call attention to his master's foolishness. For instance, when the captain crows over the legions of women who constantly chase after him, Vespa quips that they do so with long sticks to beat him up (3.6). Also, as the blowhard tells Polidoro that with the threat of his famed sword he has often chased dozens of frightened men, Vespa jokes that the captain was the one being chased and that he was usually first in the retreat (3.6). And when he boasts that with a thrust of his sword he could slice a mountain in half, Vespa deadpans, "sure, a mountain of ricotta" (5.4). Finally, the self-proclaimed idol of women, forgetful of his professed love for his beloved Flavia, winds up taking his pleasure with the prostitute Erifila and is even willing to share her bed with one of her regular clients.

Fracassa's role is not limited to simply entertaining the audience, for his claims, though ridiculously exaggerated, serve to link the fiction of the stage with the unpleasant reality of war. He brags that the reason he left his beloved Flavia behind is because the Sultan begged him to join the "noble war" against Cyprus. And, when Polidoro asks if the island has been sacked, he replies in the affirmative and gloats that he was the first to breach the Venetians defences. As for negotiating a price for Flavia's freedom, money is not an obstacle because he is confident that there will soon be another rich country to plunder. After all, he proclaims, there is never a shortage of wars ("le guerre bollono," 3.6). If these allusions to war stir the spectators' memories of Venice's defeat, their bombastic tone tends to reduce their poignant reality by casting them in the extravagantly fanciful world of a notorious windbag. It is within this world of paradoxes, of fiction versus reality, that the playwright subtly expresses his aversion to warfare. The world is so awash with wars, he seems to say, that they actually spill or boil over ("bollono"). Underscoring this repugnance, Polidoro laments the havoc wrought on Nicosia ("ruina crudelissima"), especially the death of so many Turkish soldiers and the dreadful possibility that his long-lost daughter may have perished in the fight (1.1). The servant Tropio, though promising to tell heroic tales of war, recalls the misery and the constant fears he experienced during the assault on the island ("il patir tanto, le spesse e terribili paure," 2.3).

Just as Fracassa allows for the humorous recollection of painful memories, Arpago, Chrisoforo, and Erifila provide a critical commentary on dress and entertainment. Although the social milieu of the stage remains somewhat ambiguous, it is very likely that their comments about social matters were of particular interest to Venetian audiences. Surely, it did not take long for the spectators to recognize that Arpago's repeated complaints about the cost of a woman's clothes and toiletries were actually directed at their taste and preferences. Arpago is a new character whose main role is to sell the young "slave" Flavia to Chrisoforo. The addition of this slave merchant allows Groto to begin the dramatic action with the purchase of the girl's freedom and, at the same time, to offer a scathing criticism of Venetian haute couture. His remarks are purportedly those of a businessman who bemoans the heavy expense of keeping his female slaves properly attired for the market. He complains to Chrisoforo that women, in doing their toilette, use more implements than a doctor or a pharmacist. After declaiming a long list of women's expensive beauty gadgets such as combs, mirrors, sponges, scissors, boxes, needles, and ampoules, he mocks their obsession with coiffures and perfumes. He even finds fault with the latest fad that encourages women to flaunt their partially exposed breasts ("scoprano le mammelle," 1.8). Chrisoforo concurs with the merchant's disapproval, adding that many women wear not one but several dresses in order to accentuate their hips.[21] Clearly, for these complaints to resonate with a Venetian audience, the costumes and the fashions they revile were more likely to be seen in Venice than in a Muslim city such as Constantinople.

To be sure, *Epidicus*, too, features a long and amusing list of women's array of beauty accessories, but the author's intent and the impact on the audience are totally different. As Epidicus schemes to trick Periphanes into buying Acropolistis's freedom, he warns the old man that Stratippocles is about to fall for a courtesan whose expensive taste will likely sap the family fortune. In stressing the young man's vulnerability to the seductive art of the courtesan, the slave goes on to emphasize that women tend to lure men by wearing costly and suggestive clothes: "thin-woven, closely textured, azure-linen, / lined, bordered, saffron, buttercup, shift or shiftless" ("tunicam rallam, tunicam spissam, linteolum caesicium / indusiatam, patagiatam, caltulam aut crocotulam," 2.2). In the end, he concludes, women can go through their lovers' fortune in no time. Besides the comic effect stemming from the repetitive sound of the accusative *am/um*, the list is meant to underscore for Periphanes the tempting nature of women and the high cost of their expensive taste. But, whereas this view of women is specifically meant as a threat to Periphanes' purse, Arpago's perspective is that of a merchant worried about the costly maintenance of his merchandise in a society driven by an ever-demanding high fashion. Such a business concern undoubtedly resonated with the mercantile culture of Venetian society.

Erifila: A Venetian Courtesan

This portrait of Venetian society grows fuller and more complete through the role of the courtesan Erifila. Though not a new character, she is considerably different from her Plautine model, Fidicina, the music-girl Epidicus was supposed to hire to celebrate Stratippocles' safe return from the war. Fidicina is the unwitting instrument of the slave's scheme to bamboozle Periphanes into believing that she is the courtesan he had agreed to buy and sell to the *miles*. The sale is meant to prevent Stratippocles from marrying the courtesan and ostensibly yield a big profit besides. Through a brief appearance, she reveals her true identity, which confirms the soldier's suspicions that she is an impostor and that Periphanes has been had. Groto alters the character by turning her into an actual courtesan and giving her a more active role in the development of the plot and in the representation of contemporary society. She appears in three long scenes, mostly plotting with Chrisoforo how to trick old Polidoro out of his money. To engage her help, the devious servant leads her to believe that his old master is in love with her and is willing to shower her with cash and gifts. This freshly added episode allows the playwright to inject laughter into the story, as it exploits the comedic nature of the time-honoured topos of the *amator senex*. Notably, when Erifila expresses her reluctance to sleep with Polidoro because he is a decrepit old man without teeth, Chrisoforo quips that the lack of teeth should suit her fine, as the old geezer will not be able to bite her ("non vi potrà mordere," 3.4).

A significant aspect of her role is to provide a glimpse into the life of contemporary courtesans and, paradoxically, a moral insight into the permissive habits and mores of the times. Her allusions to the love tales in Ariosto, Boiardo, Tristano, Amadis di Gaula, and Palmerin d'Oliva distinguish her as a learned lady of pleasure, a type commonly found in Renaissance Venice. Although she goes to Polidoro's house to render him her services, she is an independent courtesan with her own establishment ("Botega") and a retinue of maids to escort her around town. When the meeting with the old man goes sour, she is resentful that a courtesan of her standing should have to return home all alone without her attendants ("m'incresce che io andrò sola," 3.7). She also claims to enjoy the protection of rich and powerful clients who shower her with gifts. This prompts Chrisoforo to underscore the decline of the old aristocracy by pointing out that she stood to make more money with a rich merchant like Polidoro than with all her blazoned but impoverished "gintilhuomini."[22] To be sure, she is more than a mere prompter or cue for Chrisoforo's views on society, for she often voices her own criticism of contemporary morals. She inveighs against seemingly prudish parents who forbid their young daughters to go to the theatre for fear that they might be exposed to unseemly acts or language. Yet, she continues, they often allow their girls to read "adult" love stories and meet secretly with their beaus. When Chrisoforo warns her to be discreet in seducing grandpa Polidoro because he has a daughter of marriageable age in the house, she quickly agrees with him and proceeds to lash out at licentious parents who do whatever they please in front of their children:

> Le madri e i padri già non si riguardano
> A questi tempi di far in presentia
> De figli tutto quel che viene in animo
> Lor di fare [...]. (3.4)
>
> [Mothers and fathers are no longer careful, / these days, about what they do in the presence / of their children.]

It is fair to assume that the spectators viewed Erifila's righteous indignation as a realistic comment on their own society. But, once again, their certainty is suspended in the ambiguity issuing from the irony in which the indignation is cast. The incongruity between the courtesan's sermon and her immoral profession is bound to cause the audience to wonder how seriously to take her moral outrage. The discrepancy is consistent with the playwright's intent to represent a world where fact and fiction meet against a backdrop of laughter, irreverence, scepticism, and subversion. Be it the memories of the Cyprian war or the criticism of contemporary mores, they are always cast in an atmosphere of ambivalence, burlesque, and inconsistency. In this sense, the representation is both instructive and entertaining, as the spectators laugh while the author reminds them of their painful past and/or exposes the permissiveness of their society. Chrisoforo is both funny and obscene when he tells the young maiden Rustica that he wished he were the ladle she was scrubbing so that she would hold him by his "handle." When the girl tells him that she has to go home because she has to put the "meat in the pot," the servant lewdly offers to put it in there for her ("verrò io [...] a porvela," 1.7). Arpago, fretting over the high cost of women's fashion, notes that his ladies need two mirrors to do their hair, one for the front and one for the back. The sly Chrisoforo seizes the opportunity to colour the merchant's comment with sexual connotations by artfully mistaking the mirrors for male organs. He wonders aloud why women would want one in the front and another in the back. When the slave merchant complains, again, that the latest fashion requires dresses with a bustle or tail ("coda") in the back, Chrisoforo remarks obscenely that in his view it would make more sense for women to place it in the front so that they can adjust it with their own hands ("accomodarsela / Di propria mano," 1.8).[23]

The comic atmosphere arising from obscene allusions, double entendres, and fantastic claims of martial and virile exploits stands in marked contrast to the original source, where the comic element is limited mostly to the slave's schemes and tricks. Plautus's language is surprisingly clean by the genre's standards, and there is no clear intent to cast the world of the stage as a reflection of the times. Epidicus's bashing of women's expensive taste for clothes and the ease with which they might go through a lover's fortune is a recurrent topos in comedy, but in this case does not rise to social commentary. On this issue, the difference between source and adaptation may best be seen in the roles of their respective tricksters, Epidicus and Chrisoforo. Both characters are equally accomplished liars and master deceivers; they fool their respective old masters, spin plots and subplots, and guide the story to a happy conclusion. But, whereas the Plautine slave remains largely a commonplace trickster, his Italian counterpart is given a larger and more significant role both as a source of laughter and often as the mouthpiece of the playwright's views. His lewd remarks, whether in reference to women or old men in love, are clearly meant to arouse laughter among the spectators and, while they laugh, to remind them of their society's shortcomings. When he is not the direct source of ridicule or social criticism, he is often the cause of it, as his words and deeds tend to prompt other characters to recall the Cyprian war, to comment on social behaviour, and/or provoke laughter.

In *Emilia*, laughter is the opiate that lulls the minds of the spectators and desensitizes them to the unsettling memories of war and to the criticism of their social mores and decorum. In *Epidicus*, instead, in the absence of significant social issues concerning the world of Roman audiences, laughter remains an end in itself, a mindless entertainment. The first is a comedy meant to teach and delight, the latter is basically a farce meant to amuse. And here lies the difference between the two works. Plautus stages a situation that, detached from any specific cultural or historical moment, is for all time and for all people. The theme of devious servants scheming to trick their old masters was as much a staple of ancient comedy as it was of Renaissance comic theatre. Groto, too, relies on the old topos of the trickster servant. But, unlike the Roman model, *Emilia*'s servant is the linchpin of a narrative inextricably linked to a specific historical moment and highly relevant to Venetian audiences. The event's historical significance and temporal proximity to the audience is not a mere stagecraft device intended to lend modern status and verisimilitude to the representation. Nor is it limited to predisposing the audience to recognize the world of the stage as a reflection of their own society. It is a familiar setting meant to help create an atmosphere of tension between fiction and reality, serious and comic, theatre and meta-theatre. It is meant to entertain the spectators while moving them to reflect on their past and their present.

From this perspective, Groto distinguishes himself not only from his Latin source but also from fellow Renaissance playwrights. Throughout the *cinquecento*, leading literary critics and dramatists, in their endeavour to go beyond the example of the ancients and create their own Italian theatre, insisted that stage events be set in recent times and familiar environs. The proximity not only legitimized the claim of modernity, it also served to ground the fictional world of the stage in contemporary settings, thus providing the verisimilitude necessary to involve the audience. Groto turned this very notion on its head, as he cast the action in a realistic setting and then proceeded to subvert it or, in the words of Marina Calore, "per poi negare ad essa [...] qualunque fondamento" (307). As a result, the spectators are never sure whether the stage reflects the Arab world of Constantinople or that of contemporary Venice. Nor can they tell if the female characters on stage are real women or young males in disguise, or whether old men are actually young men pretending to be old. And finally, how much credence can they lend to a blind author? Should they be sceptical, as both Prologue and Fracassa suggest, of the playwright's ability to shed light on the world he purports to see and stage before them?

Suspended in ambiguity and lulled by hearty laughter, the spectators are unwittingly drawn into a world that, though arabesque in appearance, is mostly Venetian. The playwright's task was not an easy one, for it is quite a theatrical challenge to turn disturbing memories of war into a topic of comedy. His success is due in part to his ability to exploit the comic effect of commonplace themes and situations such as the braggart soldier, the *amator senex*, and the devious and bawdy servant. But his creative stagecraft lies mostly in his daring decision to prompt, and simultaneously undermine, the spectators' belief in the premise that the stage mirrors reality. In the end, his achievement is a true theatrical tour-de-force, as he manages to entertain his spectators while forcing them to confront their own social flaws and their proud, if painful, past. In this sense, the Italian imitation owes little to its Latin source. Groto does not merely expand *Epidicus*; he turns it into a modern play. *Emilia* is not a "travestimento" or disguise of its Roman source but "a nuova comedia," original both in form and content – original in introducing the theme of war into a comedy and in Groto's bold new way of engaging theatre audiences.

Chapter Six

Gli duoi fratelli rivali: Della Porta Adapts Bandello's Prose Narrative to the Stage

Giambattista Della Porta (1535?–1615) was a true Renaissance man, interested in a wide variety of subjects including magic, science, and dramatic literature. Born to an aristocratic family from Vico Equense on the Sorrentine peninsula, he received an excellent education, mostly from the renowned scholars who frequented his father's household. He caught the attention of the European learned community with the publication of his *Magiae naturalis* (1558–84), a compendium of scientific experiments and speculations ranging from agriculture to astrology, cryptography, demonology, divination, medicine, optics, occult philosophy, and transmutation of metals. The study was an immediate success and was soon translated into Italian, French, German, and English. It earned him the esteem and goodwill of prelates and princes, including the Emperor Rudolph II, Philip II of Spain, the Medici of Tuscany, the Gonzaga of Mantua, and Cardinal Luigi d'Este, under whose patronage he lived for many years. Della Porta's preoccupation with the secrets of nature, particularly the occult and demonology, led the Neapolitan populace to bestow on him the monikers of "diviner" and "magician" (*indovino* and *mago*). It also attracted the attention of Rome's Inquisition, which forced him to disband his Academia Secretorum Naturae and, for a time, prohibited further publication of his writings. It was perhaps his reputation as a *mago* that ultimately caused future scholars to pay little attention to his scientific contributions, including his work on optics and the telescope. But if his theories and experiments failed to win the interest of the scientific community, who regarded him as a mere "interesting curiosity" (Clubb, *Giambattista* ix), his dramatic works earned him a lasting place in the history of the Italian theatre.[1]

Ironically, Della Porta himself downplayed the importance of his theatrical work, calling it a youthful pastime or "scherzi della sua fanciullezza" (*Gli duoi fratelli*, prologue).[2] The claim is rather modest, for not only did he write plays throughout his adult life, he was also a prolific playwright, second only to fellow Florentine dramatist Giovanmaria Cecchi. He wrote more than twenty plays and a treatise on the art of comedy, *Arte da Comporre Comedie*. His seventeen extant dramas include fourteen comedies, one tragicomedy, one tragedy, and one liturgical play. Regarding his comedies, the consensus is that if the "masterpieces of Machiavelli and Bruno are excepted, Della Porta's are the best Italian comedies before Goldoni" (Clubb, *Giambattista* xvi).[3] There has always been some interest in his theatre, but it was only in the second half of the twentieth century that his work attracted book-length critical studies and caught the attention of the academic community. Louise Clubb's *Giambattista Della Porta, Dramatist* (1965) and Raffaele Sirri's *L'attività teatrale di G.B. Della Porta* (1968) became and continue to be the points of reference for all scholarly discourse on Della Porta's theatre. For both critics, his comedies in particular exemplify the transition from the Renaissance literary theatre to the spectacle of the commedia dell'arte. But there is more to this playwright's stagecraft, most notably his creative ability to adapt old plot material to the aesthetic and thematic demands of his times. Although samples of his imitative ingenuity can be found in most of his plays, which owe much to the theatre of Plautus and Terence, it can best be seen in *Gli duoi fratelli rivali* (1590), perhaps his best comedy or, as Sirri argues, "his most complex and ambitious work" ("il lavoro più complesso e ambizioso," *L'attività* 105).[4]

The Plot

The play, translated as *The Two Rival Brothers* by Louise Clubb (1980), is an exemplary adaptation of a prose narrative to the stage. It allows an insightful appraisal of the dramatist's notion of imitation and his keen sense of theatre, as well as a close look at the dialectical confrontation between the old world of the source and the living realities informing the imitation. The plot is derived from Bandello's tale of Timbreo and Girondo, two young friends in the service of King Peter of Aragon, and their love for Fenicia, the daughter of an impoverished Sicilian gentleman, Lionato de' Lionati (*Novelle* 1.22). The story takes place in Messina, where King Peter established a temporary court following his 1284 defeat of Charles II of Naples. It begins with Timbreo's courtship of Fenicia followed by their official engagement to be married. Girondo, also in love with the girl, decides to derail the engagement by leading his friend to believe that Fenicia entertains a secret lover two to three times a week. Through a messenger, he informs him that the lover will be visiting the girl that same evening and that he should come and see for himself. To set up the deception, Girondo instructs one of his servants to dress like a "gentleman" and go with the messenger behind the girl's house by the garden. The two, followed by a young man carrying a long ladder, arrive at the designated balcony and the "gentleman" climbs through the window. Timbreo, watching from across the street, needs to see no more to call off the engagement. The dishonour brought on the Lionati family affects Fenicia so deeply that she faints and remains unresponsive for such a long time that people begin to believe that she is dead.

Although the young lady does not die, the family allows the rumour of her death to circulate around town and even holds a fake burial ceremony. When she recovers from the near-fatal shock, her father decides to send her away to his brother's villa outside Messina, where she can live under a different name and eventually be married honourably. Girondo, having learned of Fenicia's "death," is so ridden with guilt that he takes Timbreo to the chapel where she is allegedly buried, tells him about the deception, and, putting his dagger in his friend's hand, begs him to take his revenge. Accepting Girondo's sincere contrition, Timbreo suggests that they go to Lionato and tell him the truth. The old gentleman accepts the apology on the condition that Timbreo marry the woman Lionato would some day choose for him. After about a year, the Sicilian invites the two noblemen to his brother's house and proposes that Timbreo marry lady "Lucilla," the name Fenicia adopted after her "death." On that same occasion, Girondo asks for, and is given, permission to marry Fenicia's younger sister. Upon hearing the story, King Peter honours the newlyweds with a public display of affection. Not only do he and his royal following meet the young couples at the city gates, they also escort them to the palace for a royal reception. In addition, he endows them with very generous dowries, and awards the impoverished Lionato a remunerative administrative position.

In adapting the narrative, the playwright made alterations required by the genre's formal unities and modified some elements to reflect contemporary realities but left the story line largely unchanged. Closely following the source, the play dramatizes the story of two young Spanish brothers, Don Flaminio and Don Ignazio Mendoza, both in love with the young and beautiful Carizia, the daughter of a noble but impoverished Salernitan, Eufranone Della Porta. Don Flaminio, distressed to learn that his brother has asked for the young lady's hand, proceeds to foil the engagement. With the help of the parasite Leccardo, he informs his brother that the girl is not as chaste as she appears, that she and her younger sister support the family through prostitution, and that he personally has been with her many times (3.7). For proof, he suggests that Don Ignazio watch the girl's house that evening, while he, Don Flamino, pays her his usual visit. As the night approaches, he tells his brother to stand across the street whence he can see for himself clients entering the house. In the meantime, Leccardo convinces Eufranone's libertine maidservant, Chiaretta, to disguise herself as Carizia's sister, stand flirtatiously by the door, and receive captain Martebellonio, the play's *miles gloriosus*.

Don Ignazio, seeing with his own eyes how quickly Carizia's "sister" receives the soldier, and believing that Carizia will receive other men with the same ease, immediately decides to call off the engagement. The ensuing dishonour and grief are such that the girl faints and is believed dead, like her counterpart in the source. When Don Flaminio hears of the girl's "death," he is overcome with remorse and tells the truth to his distraught brother. The two then call on the girl's father to express their sincerest apologies. To make sure that the family's honour is fully restored, Eufranone demands that the apology be made in public before the boys' uncle, Don Rodorigo, the region's Spanish viceroy. As Don Rodorigo tries to figure out how best to resolve the issue, and as the brothers are threatening each other with swords drawn, Polisena, the girl's mother, rushes onto the scene and reveals that her daughter is actually alive. Everyone is happy to hear the good news, especially Don Ignazio, who can now marry his inamorata. As for Don Flaminio, he will wed Carizia's younger sister. Don Rodorigo approves of the weddings and, aware of Eufranone's limited resources, presents the newlyweds with generous dowries. The play ends with everyone going to the reception at Don Rodorigo's palace.

Though the similarities between prose narrative and stage dramatization allow for the immediate identification of the source, the imitation stages a fictional world totally different from that of the original version. In re-presenting the story, the dramatist changes the names of the characters, adds servants and parasites, and transfers the action from medieval Messina to Renaissance Salerno. The time of the tale is moved up from the 1284 Spanish victory over the Angevins to the 1503 Spanish defeat of the French and conquest of Naples. The historical setting is given in the antefactum, where Don Ignazio mentions that he and his brother were among the "adventurous gentlemen" who came to Italy with the great Ferrante di Corduba (1.1). The reference is to Gonzalo Fernandez de Cordova, also known as "el Gran Capitán," who in 1503 routed the French near the Garigliano river and brought the kingdom of Naples under Spanish rule.[5] Against this historical backdrop, the Bandellian friends Girondo and Timbreo become the brothers Don Flaminio and Don Ignazio. Also, with the transfer of the action to Salerno, the playwright replaces the Sicilian Lionato de' Lionati with the equally impoverished nobleman Eufranone Della Porta, a fictional member of the playwright's own family. He also substitutes King Peter's role with that of the viceroy. The addition of servants, parasites, and other minor characters serves to lift the sombre mood of the story and turn it into a comedy.

With these alterations, Della Porta turned a medieval narrative of love, deceit, grief, and royal prestige into a fictional world that contemporary audiences were likely to see as a reflection of their own times. Undoubtedly, they were well acquainted with the socio-political context informing the stage action and with the names of some of the characters. They surely saw in Don Rodorigo the reflection of the actual Spanish viceroy who ruled the Neapolitan region in the name of the king of Spain. The rival brothers reminded them of the thousands of Spanish soldiers, government officials, and entrepreneurs who moved into the area after Spain ousted the French. Most certainly, they recognized in Eufranone the Della Porta clan that for centuries had filled important administrative and ecclesiastical positions in the area. Against this contemporary setting, the author proceeded to transform Bandello's novella into a stage action by adopting the Aristotelian unities. With regard to the unity of action, he makes very few changes, preferring to follow the source's linear plot quite closely. He omits the fake burial but retains the rumour of the girl's "death." The omission does away with the need to send the girl away to another city, making it unnecessary for the two brothers to travel there for the final denouement. It also dispenses with the rivals' visit to the chapel where Fenicia was presumably buried. The playwright also leaves out the royal festivities in the streets but concludes with a banquet, as in the source.

Though these modifications are primarily intended to facilitate the re-presentation, they have important dramaturgical and thematic effects that enrich the audience's theatrical experience. The exclusion of the chapel episode, for instance, not only helps to simplify the plot, but also responds to staging considerations and, more importantly, to the comic nature of the genre. It would be impractical to represent on the open stage an episode meant to take place inside a church and, inherently, out of sight of the audience. At best, a messenger might be used to describe the event, causing the spectators to complement the narration with their own imagination. But a verbal or virtual representation, typical of prose narrative, would rob the viewers of the sensory experience normally associated with the actual, theatrical performance. They would not see or hear the young men's grieving before the girl's presumed tomb, but simply hear about it. Also, a burial with all its funereal imagery, albeit a fictional one, is inconsistent with the lively atmosphere of the comic stage and would, therefore, frustrate its basic function to entertain. Indeed, the cheerless picture of grieving young men kneeling before the candle-lit tomb of their beloved would have a sobering effect on the spectators and seriously undermine their predisposition to enjoy the play.

The omission also promotes the unity of place in that it dispenses with the need to transfer the action to another location. In the prose source, the action moves from Lionato's house to the chapel to his brother's villa and finally to the city outskirts, where the royal party meets the newlyweds. In the play, all the action happens in the city square between Eufranone's house and Don Rodorigo's palace. The concentration of the main events in one place is essential to the stage representation, for it would be unrealistic to have the characters travel to the villa (three miles out of town), formalize the weddings, and return to town (on stage) all within the twenty-four hours in which the action is presumed to develop. The temporal incongruity would subvert the notion of verisimilitude, a fundamental requirement enabling the spectators to suspend their disbelief and allow themselves to be drawn into the fictional world of the representation. To maintain the theatrical unities, Della Porta modified the wedding reception by simply altering the sequence of events. Unlike the source, where the action moves to the royal palace for the festivities, the imitation ends on the city square, whence Leccardo bids the audience to go home. The play is over, the parasite tells the spectators, and he is on his way to the viceroy's residence for the sumptuous banquet in honour of the newlyweds.

The unity of place helps to frame the action within the twenty-four-hour period by omitting the girl's long stay at the villa. The omission is warranted not only by the formal unities of action and time but also by other dramaturgical considerations. In the source, a year goes by between

Fenicia's presumed death and the concluding nuptials. The long sojourn supports the claim that the girl had grown so exceptionally beautiful that Timbreo failed to recognize her at first. The suspense arising from the ensuing recognition scene allows the narrator to stir the readers' anxiety and direct their emotional response. If the readers' do not question the likelihood that the girl's physical appearance could have changed so fast and so much, it is not because they are gullible but because they apprehend the episode intellectually. The very nature of this apprehension causes them to cast the entire story in the limitless world of their imagination, wherein they lose awareness of all the temporal and spatial markers that frame it. For this same reason, the recognition scene would not be dramaturgically viable in the play. The spectators, unlike the readers, apprehend the story sensorially and are naturally inclined to believe only that which is realistic. It is more than likely that they would refuse to believe that Don Ignazio could not recognize his beloved Carizia after just a year of being apart.

Having thus transformed the prose narrative into a stage representation, Della Porta proceeds to add some characters and make minor modifications in others. Beginning with the young rivals, he alters their relationship, casting them as brothers rather than just friends. Although their roles are practically the same as those of their Bandellian counterparts, the change in the relationship points to the playwright's intent to place unusual emphasis on the power of love. In the original version, love prevails over friendship, as it causes the enamoured Girondo to betray Timbreo. However, friendship soon reclaims its relevance when Timbreo accepts his friend's apology and the two reconcile their differences. In the play, the force of love proves much stronger as it pits brother against brother. The rift reaches a dangerous breaking point when the siblings come close to killing one another. That the rivalry is a measure or marker of the power of love may be seen in the way Bandello's story differs from a similar episode in *Orlando Furioso* 5. In Ariosto's poem, a likely source of Bandello's tale, the rival knights do not know each other, and therefore the deception practised on the true lover is but a reprehensible deed to be avenged on the villain. The focus of the story, then, is not so much on love but on the chivalric valour Rinaldo displays in slaying the deceitful knight. In Bandello's version, the emphasis shifts to the duelling forces of love and friendship. In the play, love is so strong that it causes brothers to deceive one another and threaten each other's life.

Admittedly, the siblings have always been rivals in everything, from their studies to fencing to love affairs. But this time is different. Don

Ignazio warns that if Don Flaminio should steal Carizia from him, it would spark so much hatred between the two of them that they would kill one other ("ci ammazzeremmo," 1.1). The notion that love can undo even the strongest of blood ties is especially evident in the last act, where the brothers, quarrelling over the right to marry the younger sister of the "dead" Carizia, draw their swords and are about to spill blood. Undoubtedly, the seriousness of the threat and the theatricality of the scene add to the dramatization of the power of love. The stage commotion, the brothers' attempts to strike at one another, and the efforts of other characters to keep them apart create suspense. They also cause the spectators to reflect on the emotions that set brother against brother. The tension rises both on the stage and in the hall as the contenders, blinded by their animosity, pay no heed to Carizia's mother, who has just erupted onto the scene. Dishevelled and eager to speak, she frantically tries to stop the fighting in order to give them the happy news. But only after repeated pleas for the brothers to come to their senses can she reveal that her daughter is alive. The festive ending notwithstanding, the audience is left with the indelible impression that the power of love brought the brothers to the verge of bloodshed.

In adopting the topos of rival lovers, the author not only chooses to cast them as brothers but also stresses their Spanish identity. Unlike the Bandellian rivals, who are described as valorous knights in King Peter's court, the play's antagonists are the viceroy's nephews. This alteration, albeit minor, helps to bring the fictional world of the stage closer to the audience's times in that it reflects Spain's presence in their region. It was likely that many spectators were Spaniards or of Spanish descent, given that Spain had occupied the Neapolitan area for almost a century by the time of the play's first performance. It is not too speculative to assume that after such a lengthy stay many of them had blended with the local population, their Spanish names notwithstanding. Interestingly, the playwright seems cautiously ambivalent about his attitude towards the Spanish presence in the territory. On the one hand, he has the brothers and the viceroy speak perfect Italian, though they have been in the country no more than a couple of years (1.1). It is rather odd that they never use Spanish expressions in their speech. In *cinquecento* comedies, including some of Della Porta's other plays,[6] it was common for Spanish characters to speak in their native language, or at least mix Spanish with Italian. To be sure, these characters are mostly bragging soldiers and, inherently, a shopworn source of ridicule. On the other hand, as wlll become clear, there are indications in the play that suggest a strong resentment against Spanish rule. With regard to this sort of ambivalence, some scholars, recalling that Della Porta had written several plays for the court, argue that he was either a "double dealer, or felt none of the antipathy toward the Spanish so often perceived elsewhere" (Beecher and Ferraro, *The Sister* 45).[7]

The Source's King versus the Play's Viceroy

The parallel between the play's contemporary setting and the source's historical events would not have been lost on the audience, who presumably knew of King Peter's defeat of the Angevins. They were also familiar with Fernández de Córdoba's conquest of the kingdom of Naples after he vanquished the French forces at Cerignola and the Garigliano River. While the parallel underscores Spain's centuries-long presence in the region, there is a major difference between the political implications reflected in the historical backdrop of the two stories. In the source, the king himself represents the Spanish presence in Italy; in the play, the role is entrusted to a viceroy. Although they both stand for Spanish power and authority, the first is a liberator, the latter an occupying ruler. The king's magnanimous deeds raise him to the level of an ideal, almost mythical embodiment of benevolent princeship. The viceroy's actions, in contrast, keep him rooted in the realities of everyday life. They are both generous, as they shower the newlyweds with very liberal dowries. But, whereas King Peter's liberality enhances his reputation as the most munificent of princes, one whose queen is no less "magnifica, generosa e liberale" (1.291), Don Rodorigo's generosity is meant to benefit his own family. The king's largess confirms his famed propensity for bestowing honours and riches upon worthy subjects. The viceroy's liberality issues mainly from his wish to see the prosperous perpetuation of his bloodline, of which the two brothers are the only survivors ("per non esservi altro germe nel nostro sangue," 5.4).

Don Rodorigo's protectiveness towards his family is especially apparent in his reluctance to punish Don Flaminio for having slandered the Della Porta family and caused Carizia's "death." When Eufranone demands immediate justice, Don Rodorigo refuses to proceed against his own blood (5.1). When the frustrated Salernitan points out that the ruler's family should not be above the law, the viceroy brings forth all sorts of idle reasons, including the specious argument that punishing his nephew would not bring back Carizia. In his view, the youth's crime is excusable because of his youth. He also argues that the girl's honour has already been vindicated by the arrest of Leccardo, and promises that the parasite will be sentenced to death for his complicity in the affair. It is ironic that he has no qualms about executing a man for mere complicity in a crime but refuses to prosecute the actual "criminal." As the aggrieved father presses for swift and impartial justice, the viceroy warns that when the accused is a person of noble birth – such as his nephew – the law must proceed with caution ("con piú riguardo," 5.1). The audience must have found this argument rather perplexing, for the consideration Don Rodorigo wishes to accord his nephew is at the expense of one of their own, the equally highborn Carizia. Sadly, the longer he dances around his duty to apply the law promptly, the more widely will the rumour of the girl's dishonesty spread, and the darker will be the stain on her family name.

The intention of Don Rodorigo's slow approach to justice is clearly to shield his nephew from prosecution while looking for a suitable way to restore the Salernitan's honour. Although in the end he finds a happy and honourable solution by suggesting that his nephew marry Eufranone's "surviving" daughter, his reluctance to pass judgment against his own "sangue" reveals the despotic nature of his rule. It also calls into question Louise Clubb's view that he "is by no means disposed to tamper with justice by favoring his kin" (*The Two Rival Brothers* 27). Actually, he alone determines how and when the law is applied. He makes sure that the wheels of justice move slowly, or not at all, especially when dealing with persons of "high regard," such as family members and other Spaniards within the viceregency. One should not underestimate the audience's awareness of the political overtones informing the viceroy's view of the law as a convenient and flexible instrument of power. Undoubtedly, they recognized their own sentiments in Eufranone's insistence that if Don Rodorigo could not bring himself to enforce the law against his own nephew, he should not be a ruler. The old Salernitan reminds the viceroy that those who cannot "govern" their own emotions should leave the governing to others ("lasci di reggere e comandar agli altri," 5.1). It is likely that the expectation that princes apply the law even-handedly resonated with a Salernitan audience that was likely to resent the lordly presence of the Spanish occupiers.[8]

In this context, it is relevant that whereas the source's king honoured the newlyweds with a grand reception at the royal palace, the viceroy's festivities include his promise to empty the local prisons of all debtors. The first is presented only in his royal munificence, the latter in his role as a legislator whose decisions affect the lives of his unfortunate subjects. The contrast between king and viceroy is also apparent in the spatial opposition between Messina and Salerno. The first was a merry place celebrating its deliverance from Angevin rule and rejoicing in King Peter's munificence, the latter a woeful place of filled prisons and foreign rulers. To be sure, the reference to local jails is a commonplace in the comic theatre of the Italian Renaissance and is not always indicative of a repressive judicial system. For most characters, especially servants and parasites, the allusion to prisons or the gallows stands as a fearful deterrent against unlawful behaviour. However, in this case it tends to underscore Eufranone's allusion to an autocratic and self-serving foreign rule. The parasite Leccardo, when asked to help Don Flaminio to trick Don Ignazio, instantly refuses to get involved in such "arrant knavery," citing his fear of the law. The young gentleman reassures him that there is nothing to fear because his uncle is the lord of Salerno. But such assurance is hardly comforting to the parasite. He is quick to point out that, unlike persons of high regard, common folk are often caught in the web of the law. He tells the young grandee that in his view the gallows is only for the wretched. Justice, he opines, is like a spider web where "small flies like me get stuck and die, and lords like you are big birds that tear it and carry it away" (3.2).

Eufranone versus Lionato

Eufranone's role in helping to cast the viceroy as a ruler who views the law as a convenient and flexible instrument of power distinguishes him considerably from his source counterpart, Lionato. Although Della Porta retained the original character, he altered the role so radically that their similarity lies mostly in their socio-economic status: they are both from noble families who lost their possessions and status because of their ill-fated political affiliations.[9] They are also similar in that they are the respective fathers of the young ladies falsely accused of loose morals. But even in these roles they are different. Lionato is a tender and loving father ("lagrimoso padre") who refuses to believe the infamous allegations against his daughter.[10] In defence of her honour, he repeatedly invokes the family traditions in which she was raised (1.272). His Salernitan counterpart is a self-styled harsh and inhuman father ("rigido e inumano," 5.3) who accepts at face value the false accusations. Unlike the Sicilian Lionato, who defends his daughter's honour, Eufranone is so overcome with rage against his "wicked" daughter that he attempts to kill her. When she faints and is believed dead, he orders that she be buried immediately. Also, whereas Lionato rejoices upon discovering that his child is actually alive, Eufranone is somewhat indifferent or, at least, slow to show his emotions. Only after several exchanges between his wife and Don Ignazio does he express his happiness. He is cheerful now because, he says, the wonderful news settles the dispute between the brothers, makes their uncle happy, and delights the whole city (5.3).

Such a qualified reaction underscores Eufranone's scale of priorities, whereby paternal love features much below family honour. His rush to bury the girl and his perceived "dishonour" accentuate the contrast between his (lack of) concern for his child's life and his intense fear of sullying the family name. This is especially apparent when, having learned of his "dead" daughter's innocence, he erupts into an uncontrollable wailing, invoking the girl's name and blaming himself for having caused her "death." Granting the sincerity of his sorrow, in the end it is the question of honour that matters to him the most. He winds down his lengthy lamentations and *mea culpas* by wondering whether he should grieve over the loss of his daughter or that of his honour. He rationalizes his presumed misfortune with the crudely realistic conclusion that, while the girl is dead and there is nothing that can be done about it, the stain on the family reputation could endure forever:

> Ah, for which of your deaths shall I weep first, that of your body or that of your honor? For that of your body I need not weep much, for being born mortal and daughter of mortal man, you could not have escaped death; but I shall weep for the death of your good name, for being born the daughter of a man of honor, by your innocent death you have dishonored yourself and your family. (4.7)

Don Flaminio underscores this quasi-obsession with family honour by noting that the old Salernitan is intransigent about his reputation ("tenace del suo onore e buona riputazione," 3.1). This is not to say that honour is more important to him than it is to Lionato, for they both wear proudly the nobility of their respective lineage, the only capital they have left. What distinguishes Eufranone is his intense apprehension for the loss of his good name and the way he tries to restore it. Unlike Lionato, who was so sure of his honour that he refused to believe the shameful allegations against his daughter, Eufranone no sooner hears the charges than he is ready, dagger in hand and "foaming at the mouth like a wild boar," to kill his daughter (4.5). This fierce reaction contrasts sharply with Lionato's calm and self-assured demeanour. The Sicilian moves to protect his good reputation by sending the girl away to be raised under a presumed name. When the sorrowful Timbreo comes to apologize for having caused her "death," he seizes the opportunity to restore the family honour by extracting from the young man the promise that he will marry only the woman that he, Lionato, will choose for him. Of course, that woman will be the "dead" Fenicia. Unlike Lionato, the impulsive Eufranone wastes no time in appealing to the law for the immediate and public vindication of his good name.

Such a reaction may be seen as the manifestation of a deep-seated insecurity symptomatic of a socio-political environment more volatile than the world in which Bandello cast the original story. Lionato's unshakable belief in his noble ancestry not only buoyed him calmly through the crisis but also pointed to his certainty that in the end his honour would remain intact. This self-assurance tends to underscore the trust in the socio-political stability King Peter's victory brought to Sicily. With the liberated island returned to its traditions, the illustrious families of Sicily were reinstated in their socio-economic standing and prestige. It was the king himself who restored Lionato to his noble status by assigning him to an important post in the local administration ("un ufficio in Messina molto onorevole," 1.291). From this perspective, Eufranone's recourse to the law and his insistence that it be fairly and immediately applied points to a lack of trust in the existing political system. Indeed, Don Rodorigo's and Don Flaminio's cavalier view of the law reflects the lordly rule of the Spanish occupiers and the political instability that characterized the city of Salerno throughout the sixteenth century. Owned in succession by the Colonna, Orsini, Sanseverino, Grimaldi, and, towards the end of the century, under the direct rule of the Spanish monarchy, Salerno lived in constant socio-political uncertainty. Speaking of the volatility pervading the Neapolitan area in general, the historian Rosario Villari notes that the great unrest of 1585 revealed that behind the popular uprising there loomed a new urge for independence and new reasons for opposition to the Spanish crown.[11] It is perhaps in the context of this anxiety that we must view Eufranone's excessive concern for his honour – his only remaining asset – and his suspicion of the viceroy's commitment to immediate and impartial justice.

The Women

To a certain degree and in various ways, the differences between Lionato's character and Eufranone's extend to their respective wives and daughters. In the source, the role of the mother is limited to readying Fenicia's body for burial and to the discovery that the girl is actually alive. She has no speaking part and is never referred to by name but only as "the mother" or "the wife." She is a mere verbal construct, coming alive only through the words of the narrator and other characters who describe her actions and comment on her grief. But though she is seldom mentioned in the story, the reader is left with the impression that she is always present in all family activities, albeit in the background. In the adaptation, however, the mother is assigned a larger role, both within the family and in the final denouement of the plot. Unlike her Bandellian counterpart, she is given a name, Polisena, and is an actual character seen and heard on stage several times. Besides being a grieving mother, she is also a courageous woman who does not hesitate to defend her daughter against Eufranone's deadly fury. Leccardo tells how, upon seeing her crazed husband with dagger in hand threatening to strike Carizia, she stepped into his path and pushed him back (4.5).

Her courage does not arise from a motherly instinct alone, for she exhibits as much disregard for her own safety when she stops the duel between the two brothers. Although the siblings believe that Carizia is dead, their rivalry is very much alive. They continue to compete against each other, this time over the right to marry Eufranone's younger daughter, Callidora. Don Ignazio, blaming Don Flaminio for the cruel deception that ultimately led to Carizia's "death," will not be deprived of the opportunity to marry her younger sister and is determined to kill his brother or die in the attempt. The quarrel turns ominous when the two contenders, ignoring their uncle's pleas to come to their senses, draw their swords. While both Don Rodrigo and Eufranone watch helplessly, Polisena rushes onto the scene and, demanding to be heard, enjoins the brothers to lay down their weapons. When they refuse, she places herself between them, and dares them to strike her: "I stand between the two, and one may not strike the other unless he strikes me and the sword, passing through my body, opens the way to the other's blood" (5.3). Only then, do they lower their swords and learn that Carizia is actually alive. Now each can marry his respective girl.

Polisena's daring intervention not only distinguishes her from her docile Sicilian counterpart, it also elevates her role to one normally played by men. The courage she displays in placing herself in front of the enraged Eufranone and again between the duelling brothers is seldom associated with the "weaker" sex. If her bold stand against her husband remains an abstraction in the mind of the spectators, in that it took place off stage, her dauntless action on stage leaves no doubt about her instinctual readiness to face danger. Dramaturgically, one can only imagine the theatrical effect on the spectators as they behold a woman stepping bravely between drawn swords, while Don Rodorigo and Eufranone, unable to stop the fight, stand by embarrassed in their authority and masculinity. In the eyes of the audience, she puts both men to shame. It is significant that neither man says a word while Polisena, after pleading in vain with the quarrelling siblings, steps between them to stop the fight. Only in the following scene, after she has reconciled the brothers by announcing that Carizia is alive, do they speak. The father expresses his joy at the happy news, though not immediately; the viceroy is delighted that the ominous duel, of which he was a helpless "spettatore," turned into such a festive conclusion (5.4).

Polisena's role is significant also from a narrative standpoint, in part because her disclosure that Carizia is alive brings the plot to its felicitous resolution. Indeed, the joyful news reverses the course of a potential tragedy that threatened the very spirit and definition of comedy. This function, too, distinguishes her from the Bandellian source, where the concluding weddings are negotiated by men only: Lionato, the two rival-friends, and other "gentiluomini" (1.284). The women's presence is largely ceremonial, although the narrator uses Fenicia's aunt as a narrative device to prompt Timbreo's description of the events that led to the final outcome. Interestingly, as in the case of the mother, the aunt is referred to not by name but simply as "the aunt," underscoring the lack of importance the narrator places on this character. In the play, the same character, albeit somewhat modified, is given a name – Angiola – a speaking part, and a more prominent role in the story. Not only does she serve to stress the theme of Eufranone's impoverished nobility, she is also the go-between who facilitates the onstage meeting between Carizia and Don Ignazio. She reminds the Spanish grandee, and thus the audience, that Carizia, though poor in gold, is rich in honour ("ricca d'onore"). Her concern for the family name is so paramount that, even though the young man assures her of his noble intentions, she fears that he may be proposing an "infamous affair under the cover of an honorable offer of marriage" ("un infame amore, sotto una onorata richiesta di nozze," 2.2).

The prominence accorded to women in the play is also underscored by Carizia's role. Unlike her Bandellian model, whose actions in the narrative are mostly described or referred to by other characters, Carizia has an active presence on stage with a significant speaking part. The source's Fenicia speaks only twice: once to say she wished she were dead, following her fainting spell; the other to respond to Timbreo's question whether she accepts him as her husband. In this last instance, she speaks only to express her readiness to do whatever her father tells her to do ("io sono qui presta a far tutto quello che da messer Lionato mi sarà detto," 1.284). Carizia appears on stage twice, first to talk to Don Ignazio (2.3) and, at the end, to show everyone that she is indeed alive (5.4). Her meeting with the young suitor is particularly significant because it provides her with the opportunity to see him up close and talk to him directly about his intent to marry her. In her second appearance, she brings the plot to its conclusion as she addresses everyone on stage, forgives those who doubted her chastity, and thanks Don Rodorigo for his generous dowry.

For the audience, Carizia's presence on stage puts a human face on the force behind the passions and the actions that distinguish the play's characters. No longer merely an abstraction, as her Sicilian equivalent was, she lends concreteness to the love fuelling the brothers' rivalry and to her parents' despair. In flesh and bone, she can more easily direct the spectators' emotions to her grief and, at the same time, allow them to appreciate her noble and independent spirit. They see and hear her talking to Don Ignazio, as she probes the sincerity of his love and reminds him that her honour is her sole dowry. Only after she is convinced of his true affection for her does she accept his marriage proposal and look forward to a happy life with him (2.3). Significantly, it is she, and not her father, who chooses the man she is to marry. Such freedom sets her in sharp contrast with the source character, Fenicia, who simply accepts the husband her father has chosen for her. When told that she has been promised in marriage to Timbreo, Fenicia accepts her father's decision without knowing what the young man looks like or whether he truly loves her. She sees him for the first time just before the wedding when she is asked to accept him in her life.

Carizia's decision to accept a marriage proposal without first obtaining her father's approval not only underscores her independent character, it also enters the debate on the status of women in Renaissance society. The choice of a woman's husband was normally the prerogative of her father or, in his absence, other male relatives. This is exactly what happens in the Bandellian narrative, where Lionato tells his daughter to marry the man of his choice. The girl's immediate consent suggests that such arrangements were the prevailing practice and testifies to the cultural legitimacy of patriarchal authority. In the play, Carizia undermines this tradition as she arrogates to herself a role normally reserved to the male head of the family. Her boldness must have resonated profoundly with contemporary female audiences who were governed by the oppressive misogyny of the times. They were likely to see the contrast between Carizia's independence and Fenicia's submissiveness as Della Porta's intent to join the debate on the *querelle des femmes* that was engaging men and women of letters throughout Renaissance Europe. They undoubtedly saw from this same perspective the contrast between Polisena's assertive role and her quasi-absent Bandellian prototype. The first exhibits qualities normally associated with men, showing that women can be just as daring and resolute; the latter is but a verbal construct always in the background, a silent reminder of women's dismal place in the family and in society.

Despite the playwright's clear intent to call attention to the question of women's status, he never explicitly states his views on the subject. But, whether he was an advocate of increased female autonomy is not the point here. What is significant is that he chooses to dramatize an issue he knows will arouse the interest of his audiences and win their approval. Female spectators, in particular, could not help but appreciate his awareness of, and sensitivity to, their social condition and the need to debate and redress it. In this sense, the play brings to the fore issues that concerned contemporary audiences and were likely to engage them both emotionally and intellectually.

New Characters and the Comic Element

The playwright also knew that the audience's expectations were not limited just to the dramatization of prevailing social concerns, for they expected to be entertained as well. Accordingly, he added new characters, including braggarts and servants, whose function is to help advance the action and, more importantly, to provide comic relief to a story with all the makings of a tragedy. With their usual bags of tricks, deceits, and disguises, they create events that influence the action and weave them into the plot. Don Flaminio's lackey and confidant, Panimbolo, for instance, conceives the devious plan to smear Carizia's reputation by making her appear to be a debauched woman (3.1). The parasite Leccardo sets Panimbolo's scheme in motion by convincing the maid Chiaretta to pose as Carizia's sister and receive the braggart Captain Martebellonio for the evening. Not only does he escort the captain into the house, he also comes out to tell Don Flaminio (for Don

Ignazio to hear) to be patient, as Carizia will receive him as soon as she is done talking to her father. The ruse is meant to "show" Don Ignazio that Carizia and her sister are loose women. The trick works, and the young lover, repelled by what he has witnessed, immediately calls off the engagement, giving rise to subsequent events in the plot.

These stock types are also instrumental in helping the audience to connect various narrative strands by simply reporting onstage what other characters have done or are planning to do. Don Flaminio, hoping to keep his brother away from Carizia, wants him to believe that he is negotiating a marriage deal for him with the Count of Tricarico. The spectators have no reason to doubt the veracity of such a claim until Simbolo, Don Ignazio's servant, discovers that no such negotiations are taking place. He appears on stage to inform his master that Don Flaminio is in effect planning to deceive him. Also, the audience learns about Carizia's "death" through Leccardo, who describes the event as he saw it in Eufranone's house. Although the spectators hear loud noises and bloodcurdling screams coming out of the house, they have no idea what is taking place inside. They learn what has happened only when the parasite comes onto the stage and details for Don Flaminio how the dagger-wielding father attempted to kill his daughter, while friends and relatives tried to stop him (4.5). From a theatrical standpoint, the episode is not suitable for representation on the comic stage, for the violent commotion would cause great apprehension among spectators who came to enjoy a comedy.

Without minimizing these characters' role in the development of the plot, it must be stressed that their main function is to lift the sombre mood of the story. The spectacle they provide issues primarily from the histrionic speech and engrossing metaphors that inform their petty complaints and bombastic claims. For example, Leccardo's report of Carizia's "death" could easily darken the festive atmosphere both on stage and among the audience. But he wards off the gloomy effect of the news by describing the dying girl as having a face whiter than ricotta, cheeks of cherry-red wine, and lips more crimson than prosciutto (4.4). He goes on to portray her as an appetizing piglet. She died, he says, like a lamb with her mouth barely open, like a suckling pig roasting on the fire ("com' un porchetto che s'arroste al foco," 4.5). Thus, just as the spectators' eyes are about to well up with tears of grief, the glutton Leccardo begins to colour his description of the sad event with a list of tasty dishes. The playwright uses the same device when the police arrest the parasite for his involvement in the girl's "death."

On his way to prison, he trivializes the threat of the gallows by making fun of the actual hanging. When the policemen, hurrying him along, explain that the hangman will want to string him up right away, while the crime is still fresh or piping hot ("caldo, caldo"), he retorts, "what am I, a dish of macaroni?" But, since he must hang, he jokes, he would appreciate if they put a piece of chicken liver in his throat so that when the noose tightened around his neck, the juices would trickle down his hungry stomach. He continues to make light of his impending execution by asking to be buried in a wine cellar so that the pleasant scent will resuscitate him (4.8). Clearly, these banal references to food and drink not only serve to distract Leccardo from the thought of death but also prevent the audience from falling into a dark mood.

Stock types, such as braggarts and parasites, were expected by theatrical tradition to be a source of laughter and ridicule. Their grandiose visions of sumptuous feasts, bombastic claims of military feats, and yarns of sexual prowess were sure to provoke laughter. Undoubtedly, the spectators were diverted by Martebellonio's hyperbolic pretences, ranging from his slaying of Death to his lifting the world from Atlas's back to his holding up the "entire world like a melon" (1.4). They were equally amused by Leccardo's gargantuan appetite for tasty dishes. Their boisterous claims and farfetched metaphors become especially comical when other characters react to them and highlight the drollery. One can only imagine the laughter in the hall as Chiaretta and Martebellonio, following their amorous encounter, engage in a rapid exchange of remarks decrying each other's disappointing sexual performance:

MARTEBELLONIO. See now what strange encounters occur to my fanciful brain: thinking to make my hound run a bit after a lovely beast, it has met with a foul one.

CHIARETTA: A fine hound to be sure, that having had the chase afoot all night was too sluggish to lift his head.

MARTEBELLONIO. My hound has more sense than I, for he knows the beast by its smell, and neither for prodding nor whipping would he ever push on.

CHIARETTA. Go and ply another trade, for you know nothing about chasing women.

MARTEBELLONIO. You opened up too big a mouth, which would have swallowed up hound and master whole.

CHIARETTA. There was nothing else to do, pitted against a hound so weak-spined.

MARTEBELLONIO. I can't prick with my sword as you can with your tongue; but it's well for you that you are a worthless little female, or I'd run you clean through with one thrust.

CHIARETTA. I'm not afraid of your thrusts, for your sword bends at the point. (4.3)

Another purely theatrical exchange may be seen in the lengthy, verbal contest between Leccardo and Martebellonio. Here, the parasite ridicules the braggadocio's feats with his own tales of battles over food. At one point in the exchange, the captain tells how he fought and slew Lady Death. As for her weapon of choice, he recalls, Death decided to play ball to the death:

LECCARDO. Why not fight with her scythe?

MARTEBELLONIO. Because she well knew the power of my Dorindana. For our playing field we designated the whole world: she went to the east, I to the west.

After a drawn-out and fantastic description of how the blustering talker killed Death, Leccardo proposes to recount his own victorious fight against hunger:

> Hunger once was a live person, lean and thin, barely skin and bones, and she used to go about with Famine, and Plague and War. […] We challenged each other: the field of combat was a lake of rich broth, swimming with capons, chickens, suckling pigs, calves and whole beeves. Into this we plunged to fight with our teeth.

The soldier challenges the veracity of the glutton's tale and calls him a liar, prompting the other to return the insult. They continue the verbal skirmish in much the same hyperbolic manner with which they started it (1.4).

Throughout the play, most farcical scenes like these issue not from comical situations but from the characters' own histrionic nature. Their verbal *virtuosismo* exists chiefly for its own sake and is divorced from the story's literary component. Their repartee tends to intrude upon the text in that its sole function is to provide the spectacle or comic relief the audience expects from a comedy. Raffaele Sirri calls these humorous moments "prefabricated asides" inserted in the text (*Teatro* 3.15). In his view, the intrusion tends to underscore the looming demise of the erudite comedy and the ascendancy of the commedia dell'arte.[12] The transition from literary theatre to pure spectacle, accomplished in large part through the histrionics and boorishness of *zanni,* mostly servants and parasites, is already discernible in the middle of the century with the ever-growing popularity of the comedia *improvvisata,* which later became known as the commedia dell'arte. As Grazzini satirizes, the public grew so fond of improvised performances that it did not wish to see any other type of comedy. He wryly laments the demise of the learned comedy by noting that the *zanni* were so in demand that scholarly playwrights, such as Buonanni, Cecchi, and Cini, might as well go hang themselves ("possono ire a impiccarsi," *Rime burlesche* CII). Be that as it may, Della Porta needed to introduce entertaining characters in order to morph a quasi-tragic story into a "comic" stage presentation. In this I believe he succeeded, for these characters help to alleviate the theatrical gravity of a plot woven with dangerous deceits, violent episodes, and bloody threats. The argument that the comic elements fail to dissolve the play's "atmosfera tragica" (Pullini 310) not only has no textual basis but also tends to underestimate the cheerful impact these characters' ubiquity, verbal sparring, and hilarious claims are likely to have on the audience.

One should not assume that these characters exist only in a theatrical context, for many of them mirror the social milieu of the wretched poor in the Neapolitan area. Chantal Blanché, recalling Sirri and paraphrasing Davico Bonino, points out that Della Porta's stage servants and parasites, introduced as *marioli* (or scoundrels), are "borrowed from the Neapolitan social reality [and] are the burlesque representation of the shady world of the streets" ("empruntés à la realité sociale napolitaine [et] sont la representation burlesque du monde interlope des rues," 128).[13] Pointedly, Leccardo's repeated allusions to hunger and the gallows or "forca," though spoken in jest, are a reflection of contemporary life – the life of the streets, of course. Speaking of this glutton's complaints, Raffaele Sirri observes that the widespread crime, hunger, ribaldry, and hangings in the second half of sixteenth-century Naples are well represented in Della Porta's theatre, albeit mediated by the coarse humour of its comic characters (*L'attività* 166). Also, the reality evoked by the frequent mention of the word *forca* was bound to resonate with the spectators, who had likely read, heard, or remembered that in the 1550s the Spanish viceroy of Naples executed 18,000 people in his failed attempt to stamp out the area's rampant criminality.[14] A fitting testimony bridging the fiction of the stage and the reality of life may be found in Paolo Pacelli's poem celebrating the Duke of Ossuna's departure from Naples. The poet wishes the hated viceroy a *safe* voyage to his native Spain, never again to return and oppress the people of Naples as he had done during his rule:

> Che ci habbia in tanti modi assassinati,
> E lasciati di fame anche morire,
> Che ci habbia fatto a' Turchi rifuggire
> Da' suoi capestri, e da' ferri infocati.
>
> ....
>
> ...di te peggiore
> Non ci fu mai, né ci verrà in eterno
> Venghi da' Turchi, o venghi dall'Inferno. (*Diurnali* 43–4)

> [You have killed us with your noose,
> With red-irons and like abuse,
> Who've left us hungry here to die
> Or frightened to the Turk to fly.
>
> ...
>
> For worse than you we'll never find,
> Mid devils, Turks or all mankind!] (James Newell, trans., pp 31–2)

The allusion to contemporary realities and the comic backdrop in which they are cast underscore the imitation's creative departure from its source. The theatrical world of *Gli duoi fratelli rivali* contrasts sharply with the nostalgic *illud tempus* of the Bandellian prose narrative. Bandello celebrated the munificence of kings and the chivalrous world of honour and loyalty; Della Porta morphed that world into a realistic setting his audiences were sure to recognize as their own. The stage showed them their Salerno and even dramatized the "story" of actual Salernitan families (Della Porta). It also reminded them that the law could be bent to the will of the occupying authorities (Don Rodorigo / Don Flaminio) and that there is no justice for the wretched and the powerless (Leccardo). It is reasonable to assume that the spectators viewed Leccardo's imprisonment and the allusion to the jailed debtors as a commentary on the hunger and ribaldry that continued to plague their society. Surely, they appreciated how Della Porta turned the subservient, nameless, and practically absent women of the source into independent and courageous individuals. Young women choose their own husbands (Carizia), and older ones brave men's reckless machismo (Polisena). Unlike their prose models, left largely in the background, these women emerge as fictional protagonists in the ongoing struggle to assert a woman's right to think and act according to her own will. Their example joins the growing debate on the question of womanhood, an issue that was sure to resonate with women spectators in particular. In this sense, the world Della Porta represents to his audiences is a reflection of their aesthetic preferences and living realities. Hence the play's independence from the source, its relevance to contemporary audiences, and its undeniable originality.

Chapter Seven

Orbecche: Giraldi's Imitation of His Own Prose Narrative

The choice of Giraldi's *Orbecche* as the focus of the ensuing discussion is particularly appropriate for two reasons. First, the play inaugurates a new era for the tragic genre; second, it is a unique example of a playwright adapting one of his own short stories for the stage. It was the first *tragedia regolare*, written according to the neoclassical rules, to be represented on a modern stage (1541). The performance revived a long-lost theatrical tradition and met with great success both with theatre audiences and with fellow playwrights.[1] It encouraged the writing of tragedies in the manner of Seneca – that is, divided into acts and with plenty of blood and gore. The Senecan horrors it adopted made it a model for future tragedies in Italy and other European countries. Its author, Giovan Battista Giraldi Cinthio or Cinzio (1504–73), was a university professor at his native Ferrara and, for almost two decades, private secretary to Ercole II d'Este. He was an assiduous tragedian and an accomplished theatre theorist, having written nine tragedies and a treatise on theatre, *Discorso sulle Comedie e sulle Tragedie*. He was best known for his *Hecatommithi* or *Ecatommiti* [one-hundred tales], a collection of short stories reminiscent of Boccaccio's *Decameron* and published in 1565. The work was soon translated into French (1583) and Spanish (1590). George Whetstone and other sixteenth-century English writers translated a number of stories into English. The collection became a rich source of plot materials for many successful plays, including Shakespeare's *Measure for Measure* and *Othello*. It was also the source of *Orbecche*, which Giraldi based on the second story of the second Deca (*Ecatommiti* 2.2).[2]

With *Orbecche*, Giraldi treated Renaissance audiences to a cruel and bloody spectacle never seen before on the Italian stage: human limbs on a tray, agonizing screams, blood streaming onto the stage, and a violent suicide in plain view. It was a bold move, for so much bloodshed went against the theatrical poetics of the time. Most playwrights generally adhered to the decorous example of Greek tragedy and the advice of Aristotle and Horace. The latter, in particular, thought that it was distasteful and unrealistic ("incredulus odi") to stage episodes in which humans were literally dismembered.[3] Though there is no question that the Ferrarese playwright drew inspiration from Seneca's *Thyestes*, the most memorable example of staged atrocities, Seneca was not his primary source. He took the play's plot, characters, and gruesome details directly from his own prose narrative and turned them into a cohesive and powerful stage representation. The application of the Aristotelian unities helped to portray a fictional world that, though rooted in ancient mythology, spoke to contemporary audiences of their own realities. They surely appreciated the dramatization of cultural issues, such as the ongoing debates on princeship and womanhood, and, in all likelihood, approved of the formal innovations. They undoubtedly viewed the stage atrocities as a daring challenge to traditional aesthetic preferences. The following discussion centres on the theatre adaptation of the prose source, with particular attention to Giraldi's stagecraft and the changes that make the theatrical imitation original.

The Plot

Briefly, the novella tells how young Oronte came to the royal court in the city of Susa, Persia. Once admitted to the court, his administrative and military skills earned him King Sulmone's favour and trust. Soon the young courtier, in reality the illegitimate and abandoned son of a queen, fell in love with the king's daughter, Orbecche. They eventually decided to get married, but, fearing Sulmone's disapproval and proverbial wrath, were careful to keep their plan a secret. Their happiness turned to despair when the king revealed his intention to arrange a marriage between Orbecche and Prince Selino, the heir-apparent of a neighbouring kingdom. The dilemma prompted the couple to flee the country. Thus, while Sulmone was away putting down a revolt somewhere in the kingdom, they escaped to Armenia, where for the next nine years they and their two children lived under the protection of King Settin. Sulmone, enraged by the betrayal, swore bloody vengeance on the young couple and demanded their immediate extradition. But Settin refused to honour the request on the grounds that the newlyweds' crime was but a sin of love ("peccato d'amore"). Undeterred,

Sulmone turned to deception and sent his counsellor Maleche with false promises of forgiveness to convince the couple to return home. Soon after their return, he murdered Oronte and the children, decapitating the first and dismembering the others. He then presented Orbecche with their body parts on silver platters. Though the gruesome sight was more than the young wife and mother could bear, she bravely mastered her grief and feigned acceptance of her father's forgiveness. As they embraced, she stabbed him with the same knife he had used to slaughter the children and then proceeded to cut off his head. Finally, emotionally drained and overcome with grief, she killed herself.

The stage adaptation follows the source rather closely, except for minor character alterations and some structural modifications required by the transformation of the genre. The action takes place in front of Sulmone's palace, where all the characters come to dramatize their roles. The killings take place inside the dungeon of the tower rising on one side of the palace. Presumably, the massive structure dominates the scenic space, but the scene layout is not altogether clear. The numerous spatial cues pointing to the palace give no indication as to its precise location within the scene. It is plausible that the set consists of imposing buildings adorned with columns and statues lining a wide street that recedes in perspective towards the city in the background, as illustrated in Serlio's set for the tragedy. Another likely layout might consist of a regal palace with a main entrance and two small doors on each side. The façade, much like ancient stage sets on which Palladio based the design of his Teatro Olimpico (1585), would face the hall. This alternative plan is to be preferred for two reasons. First, its frontal perspective makes it much easier for the audience to see the infamous tower where the murders take place. Second, since all the characters work and live in the palace, additional buildings would stand idle and empty, casting a lifeless shadow on the stage.

The representation begins with the prologue, which, though common in comedy, is a novelty in the tragic genre.[4] The actual play opens with the goddess Nemesis calling on the infernal Furies to bring grief and bloodshed on the House of Sulmone. Their scourge is reinforced by the ghost of Sulmone's wife, who has risen from the depths of hell to savour her imminent revenge upon her murderous husband and her "treacherous" daughter. Blaming Orbecche for Sulmone's discovery of her incestuous affair with her own son, she happily predicts that both daughter and father will soon bathe in their own blood. The playwright chooses to begin the action with the king's decision to arrange a political marriage between Orbecche and Prince Selino. Orbecche and Oronte, worried that their four-year-old secret marriage will soon come to light, ask the wise Malecche to plead their case with the king. Unlike their source counterparts, they never contemplate fleeing the country. The old counsellor finds Sulmone already aware of the betrayal and fails to sway him from his resolve to punish the young lovers. Sulmone dismisses Malecche's argument that to forgive is a princely virtue, insisting that a ruler must be strong and resolute, lest he should appear weak and vulnerable. Accordingly, he lures Oronte and the children into the dungeon inside the palace tower and butchers them. Thus, unlike the novella, the play's action issues from a single plot, takes place in one location, and spans only the last day of the victims' lives.

This implementation of the Aristotelian unities entails significant alterations to the original story. The choice to locate the entire action in Sulmone's court tends to alter the way the spectators perceive the story. In the source, the narrative is anchored in the contrast between Armenia and Persia: the former peaceful, the latter plunged in revolts. In the first, the voice of reason and understanding of King Settin prevails. In the other, there is only the cruel and despotic will of Sulmone. In Armenia the young couple and their children were safe and happy; in Persia they meet their bloody death. This opposition between good and evil underscores the enmity between the two rulers, for they have long been great enemies ("capital nimico," 1863). Also, it highlights their contrasting notions of kingship: one benevolent and forgiving, the other cruel and merciless. The first is a humanist prince, the latter a bloody tyrant. The reader apprehends the narrative, framed within these two extremes, by associating Armenia with good values and happy events and Persia with violence and death. The reader's perception of the story is largely cerebral in that it arises from a dispassionate comparison of two diverging views, especially with regard to love, family, and political power.

In the adaptation, the spectators' experience is mostly emotional, since they apprehend the story as a live dramatization of the conflict between good and evil, right and wrong. They are bound to be intimately close to an action they perceive sensorially, that is, by hearing and seeing the characters expressing their predicaments. This mode of apprehension is particularly effective, as the audience is exposed only to the gut-wrenching events that take place in and around the accursed palace. It is not difficult to imagine their anxiety upon hearing the messenger's detailed description of Sulmone's sadistic dismemberment of his victims. Distressing as it might be for them to hear, it is but a preamble to the wanton butchery they are about to see with their own eyes on the open stage. The spectators watch in horror as, in what is perhaps the most gruesome scene ever represented on the tragic stage of the Italian Renaissance, a royal servant uncovers Oronte's head and hands and the children's body parts for Orbecche to behold. They also hear with trepidation Sulmone's cries for help and see his blood streaming out of the palace door as his crazed daughter hacks him to pieces. They hear her last despairing words as she kills herself on stage, right in front of them. Such a concentration of ghastly deeds allows the playwright to impress upon the spectators only the evil aspects of the narrative, drawing them into the victims' world of despair and predisposing them to a profound cathartic experience.

The unity of place, then, emerges as the optical angle from which the playwright directs the audience to view the story and its novelties. One of the most obvious alterations is in the theme of marriage. In the source, the narrator dwells on the length and strength of the couple's union and on their willingness to defy convention for the sake of love. Orbecche vows to defy her father if he tries to force her to give up Oronte and marry a man of her father's choosing. Without hesitation she declares herself willing and ready to risk his wrath and forgo her claim to the throne (1861). The couple's decision to flee the kingdom issues as much from their fear of the king's revenge as from their wish to preserve their happy life together. In Armenia they lived happily with their two children for nine long years. In the adaptation, the emphasis on their love is drastically reduced. Their marriage lasts only four years (2.1.423) and is mentioned not so much to celebrate it as to establish the basis for the plot, most notably the king's revenge. It is but a narrative expedient meant in large part to provide the context for the two most important themes of the play: the question of women's position or *querelle des femmes*, and Sulmone's tyrannical notion of kingship.

Orbecche and the Question of Women's Position

In the source, there is hardly any reference to society's dismal view of women and the misogynist culture oppressing them. Though the narrator expresses his sympathy for Orbecche and her grief, he does not mention the status of women as inferior humans. In the play, the theme is of major relevance, as the young heroine repeatedly deplores her fate, noting that nothing makes her more unhappy than being a woman ("l'esser donna"). In a lengthy soliloquy of more than one hundred lines, she ruefully points out that women are more wretched and less free than any other "animal" on earth and that they are despised by all, including their own fathers. She also denounces their lack of the most basic freedoms, lamenting that women are severely punished if they attempt to act according to their own free will. Faced with her father's decision to force her into a political marriage, she denounces the custom that favours gold-laden husbands over husbands of gold (2.3.872–921). She complains that oppressive male power denies women the right and the ability to think and act freely:

> Com'a perpetuo carcere dannate,
> Sotto l'arbitrio altrui sempre viviamo
> Con continovo Timor, né pur ne lece
> Volger un occhio in parte ove non voglia
> Chi di noi cura tiene. (2.3.900–4)

> [As if damned in eternal prison, / we live always under male control and / in constant fear. We are not permitted / to direct our stare at something or someone without the consent of / those who control us.]

This dismal portrait of woman's condition is not a trite literary commonplace, for the ancient tradition it evokes, from Medea to Sofonisba to Cleopatra, tends to underscore the timeless and universal misogyny that continues to treat women as inferior beings.

Far from being a mere rhetorical device or an expression of self-pity, Orbecche's dejection is a strong indictment of the misogynist notions that stirred the Renaissance debate on the question of women. For the spectators, the issue was not a mere intellectual debate but a vivid reminder of their own cultural realities. Many women in the audience would surely have endorsed Nannina de' Medici's complaint: "Don't be born a woman, if you want your way."[5] Who among the spectators, mostly learned members of the upper class, had not heard of the tragic end of Giovanna of Aragon, Duchess of Amalfi? Married at the young age of twelve and widowed by the time she was nineteen, she chose to marry her steward, thus tarnishing the family name. Her brothers hunted her and finally had her murdered, sparing neither the children nor the husband (1510). Almost a century later, John Webster adapted the macabre episode for his acclaimed *The Tragedy of the Dutchesse of Malfy* (1613). Most spectators would soon hear about the 1546 tragic death of the poetess Isabella Morra at the hands of her own brothers. Outraged by her (platonic?) relationship with the poet Diego Sandoval De Castro, they killed her, her teacher (the go-between), and eventually Sandoval himself.[6] The episode, reminiscent of Boccaccio's tale of Isabetta, who died of grief after her brothers killed her lover (*Dec.* 4.5), was a reflection of the general attitude of the times as portrayed in treatises on female virtues and housewifery. Some Renaissance authors recommended, among other things, that a good wife follow her husband like a shadow, smile when he smiles, and appear sad when he is sad. Others wished that men could have a family without having to take a wife, for, as one writer puts it, it is far better to live without one ("viverne senza").[7] It is reported that Marsilio Ficino used to say that women should be used like "chamber pots, hidden away once a man has pissed in them."[8]

In the context of the Renaissance debate on women, the play's Orbecche is not just the voice of the aggrieved weaker sex but also the symbol of strong womanhood. In some instances, she is quite capable of rising to the level of men in both decisiveness and violence. Her murder of Sulmone is particularly illustrative of her "manly" ability, especially if viewed against the source. In the prose version, Orbecche kills her father in a rather trance-like, methodical way. In the play, she attacks him with all the fury and cruelty normally attributed to men. In the novella, she pulls the knife out of her older boy's body and pretends to hand it to Sulmone, asking him to kill her. When the king tries to embrace her as a sign of his love and forgiveness, she drives the knife into his chest. Then, as an afterthought, she proceeds to avenge the death of her second child by pulling the knife out of his corpse and plunging it into the king's throat. After a long, wailing monologue, she completes her revenge by cutting off the king's head and offering it to her dead husband. At the end, having gathered the corpses of her loved ones, she lies over them and kills herself with the same knife with which she severed her father's head. Although she characterizes the bloody deed as a "vendetta," the focus of the scene is not so much on a mother's revenge as on the profound pathos of a mother's grief. Her visceral moaning, her wild hugging and kissing, now of her husband, now of her children, her gentle gathering of their lifeless bodies and lying over them as she is dying are outward manifestations of unbearable and numbing grief.

Interestingly, though the characters vent their anger, express their grief, and appeal for mercy, the narrator maintains a mostly neutral tone, leaving the readers to their own emotional reactions. He concludes the story by simply noting that members of the court, upon discovering the bodies, buried Sulmone in the royal crypt, and placed the others in a single sepulchre. His last comment is that both the cruel king and the daring lovers received the punishment they deserved ("degno castigo," 1866). In the play, on the other hand, there is a clear intent to predispose the audience to abhor the tyrant and pity the victims. In describing the atrocities he witnessed in the dungeon, Messenger portrays the king as a heartless and bloodthirsty man, referring to him as cruel, evil, monster, and traitor. By contrast, he characterizes the victims as innocent, pitiable souls ("innocenti [...] poverelli [...] miserelli," 4.1.2139–78). This characterization causes the stage audience, namely Coro, to inveigh against the king, calling him a venomous serpent and bloodthirsty lion. Coro is so moved by the narrative that he wonders whether Sulmone's heart was that of a ferocious tiger and whether a more weird or wicked story had ever been told (4.1.2281–3002). Adding to Coro's disapproval, Semichoro, who witnesses Sulmone's murder, notes that the king's death was well deserved and that poor Orbecche is in such agony that it is a miracle she is still alive. Also, Sulmone's remains, far from being buried in the dignified manner of the source, are ordered thrown to the wolves and vultures. Thus, whereas in the prose original the narrator's attitude towards the king is by and large neutral or indifferent, in the play, the stage audience expresses abhorrence towards the cruel tyrant. Their reaction is bound to stir the spectators' passions and direct their emotional response.

To be sure, the stage Orbecche is as grief-stricken as her source counterpart; however, she is much more vengeful and displays more savagery in murdering her father. Semichoro, looking into the palace from just outside the main entrance, is shocked to see how furiously she hacks Sulmone's body. In describing the scene taking place out of sight of the audience, he tells how Orbecche, holding the two knives she pulled from her dead children, approaches her father and unexpectedly stabs him in the chest with one knife and cut his throat with the other. Then, in a wild frenzy, she cuts off his hands and head. She moves about like a tiger bewailing her slaughtered cubs and looks around fiercely like one who has lost her mind ("forsennata"). Semichoro declares that he never imagined there could be so much violence in a human being, especially in "una donna" (5.2.2846). Finally, at a loss for words to describe her destructive rage, he warns that there is nothing more fearful than a woman driven by grief and love:

> Né vento, né fuoco, né altra forza,
> É tanto da temer, quanto una donna
> Che si veggia privar del suo marito
> E sia dal duolo a un tempo e d'Amor spinta. (5.2.2849–52)

[Neither wind nor fire nor any other force / is to be feared as much as a woman / who sees herself deprived of her husband / and is driven at once by grief and love.]

The spectators do not wait long to see for themselves evidence of Orbecche's bloody vengeance. They behold her coming out of the palace carrying her father's hands and head still dripping with blood. Turning to the silver trays still holding Oronte's and the children's limbs, she offers them the king's body parts as a token of their avenged deaths. She then stabs herself to death before a horrified audience.

Semichoro's astonishment before so much fury in a female character undoubtedly vexed the playwright's potential detractors. Such a violent woman did not display the propriety of behaviour of which Aristotle speaks when discussing the qualities befitting tragic characters. Acknowledging that "there is such a thing as manly character," Aristotle warns that "it is not fitting for a woman to be manly or clever" (*The Poetics* 3.15.29). For some literary critics of Giraldi's times, Orbecche's frenzy must have seemed too much of a male trait to reflect the prevailing notion of womanhood. Just like Alberti and Castiglione before them, they believed that women, unlike men, do not possess warrior-like qualities, but passions, piety, and domestic sweetness. The characterization of Orbecche's actions as "manly," then, was an indictment of Giraldi's challenge to traditional views of woman. Anticipating such criticism, Giraldi had Lady Tragedy herself defend the play's representation of women as wise and strong. Addressing the reader, *La Tragedia a chi legge*, appended to the text, insists that once free of all prejudice, people will find that in prudence and wisdom women can rival any wise man:

[....] 'n prudenza e senno /
(Rimossa che ne sia la invidia altrui) /
Agguagliar puote ogni saggio uom del mondo." (3221–3)

[in prudence and wisdom / (void of all envy) / [a woman] can equal any wise man.]

With regard to Orbecche's violence against her father, *Tragedia* admonishes against harsh judgment. She warns that wise people should know the resolve that "despair and suffering might cause in a woman's heart" ("Che può desperazione e grave doglia / In cor di donna," 3230–1). With this portrayal of women both as victims of a misogynist culture and as dauntless individuals, Giraldi forces a public dialogue about society's view of women. In this sense, Orbecche is uniquely original and culturally relevant. She not only rises above the grief-stricken character of the source, she also emerges as a dramatic voice in a debate that was of major concern in Renaissance Italy.[9]

Sulmone versus Malecche: The Debate on Kingly Prerogatives

Just as the unity of place allows for the alteration of Orbecche's character, the compression of the gruesome events into a twenty-four-hour period helps to transform Sulmone from a mere vengeful tyrant to a bloodthirsty and sadistic killer. Ostensibly, his role is essentially the same as that of his prose counterpart. Like his prototype, he murdered his incestuous wife and son, slaughtered Oronte and the children, and killed many others. But there is a marked difference both in the degree of his brutality and in his rationalization of his violent behaviour. In the source, he is introduced as a vengeful king who killed his depraved ("scelerata") wife because she was engaged "dishonestly" with her son (1859). The qualifying attributes "depraved" and "dishonest" tend to attenuate his violent reaction, as they imply a moral condemnation of the wife's behaviour and a justification of the murders: the king was compelled to give the victims what they deserved. But as the story unfolds, there is no doubt that he is a ruthless killer. He murders Oronte by placing a hood over his head and choking him to death with his bare hands. He cuts off the young man's head and then has the body thrown in the same pit where he had discarded all the victims he had killed in the past. A few days later, when the children have returned from Armenia, he simply slaughters them as one would slaughter "innocent lambs" (1865). He then places on silver platters Oronte's head and the boys' bodies, with the knives still stuck in their throats, and, with fiendish satisfaction, presents them to Orbecche, telling her that it is the wedding gift she deserves (1865). The gesture completes Sulmone's portrait as a brutal and vengeful individual and raises him to the level of the mythical Atreus, his Senecan counterpart.

In the play, where time limits require the entire action to take place in one day, Sulmone butchers his victims all at the same time. Also unlike in the source, where he simply exacts his revenge, in the adaptation he acts with unspeakable, sadistic savagery. According to the messenger's account, he made Oronte and the children watch each other's mutilation before he killed them. In addition, unlike his prose counterpart, he cut off

Oronte's hands while he was still alive and mockingly offered them to him. Then, falling on the children like a lion falls on its "bloodied prey," the messenger recalls for the stage audience, he slaughtered them and threw them at the feet of their dying father. All covered with blood, he then severed Oronte's head and ordered that the body be thrown to the dogs and vultures. Then, noticing that one of the boys was still alive, he finished him off by stabbing him repeatedly in the chest. The messenger recalls that throughout the ordeal the king enjoyed the ghastly bloodshed, at times laughing, at times deriding the agonized victims (4.1). This tendency to take pleasure in his victims' suffering is also apparent in his treatment of his daughter. In the source, he spares her life because he intends to give her in marriage to a worthy husband ("a marito degno"); in the play, he does not kill her because he wants to cause her cruel and intolerable pain ("crudele e intollerabil doglia," 3.2.1703).

The new emphasis on gore and savagery is undoubtedly meant to heighten the play's dramatic tension in order to horrify the spectators and blur the distinction between the real world and that of the stage. The playwright succeeded in his intent, for we are told that during the play's 1541 performance, a lady spectator (a friend of the actor playing Oronte) fainted upon seeing the victims' limbs on the silver platters. But the intensification of violence goes beyond the formal purpose of frightening the audience, for it points to a significant change in Sulmone's character from a vengeful king to a depraved and savage killer. The thematic implications of this change may be observed in his rationalization and use of violence. In the prose version, he kills mostly to satisfy his wounded ego. The narrator notes that when Sulmone heard of the couple's secret marriage and escape, he swore immediate vengeance ("tutto alla vendetta si dispose," 1862). The readers have no doubt to what extent he might carry his vengeance, for they already know of his propensity for bloodshed. In the very first line of the narrative, they learn that he is a cruel and fearless king who murdered his wife and son upon finding them embracing under incestuous sheets.

The stage Sulmone, unlike his prose or Senecan parallel, views revenge not just as an end in itself but as a political imperative. In his opinion, Oronte must die because he betrayed a king's trust. The children must also be dispatched, for they could easily become a living reminder of the royal shame and a potential threat to the legitimacy of the crown (3.3.1684–9). Ironically, even Oronte believes that Sulmone's past use of violence was due to political necessity. When Orbecche tries to convince him that her father is actually a bloodthirsty killer and thus not to be trusted, he tries to defend the king's history of violence. He argues that Sulmone had no other choice but to murder his wife and son because incest is too "grave" a crime for a king to forgive. Orbecche counters that if reasons of state sanction the killing of unfaithful wives, nothing justifies the senseless murders of so many other innocent people. There was no reason for him to murder his own brother, a most decent and kind man, she adds. Oronte again attributes Sulmone's fratricide to political necessity, arguing that the killing was the result of a power struggle between the brothers. In the end, he concludes philosophically, the thirst for power is often more powerful than piety or brotherly love (2.3.752–65).

Oronte's defence of Sulmone's bloody deeds is particularly significant, albeit naïve, because it encourages the audience to view the king not just as a vengeful man, as in the novella, but also as a prince who uses force for reasons of state. After all, his argument goes, the king murdered his wife and son to uphold the dignity of the crown, and killed his brother to solidify his control of the kingdom. Plausible as this justification may be, it stands in sharp contrast to Orbecche's foreboding, causing the spectators to wonder whether Sulmone's violence is an end in itself rather than a political necessity. The king insists that he must punish Oronte because he is guilty of *laesae majestatis*, a crime no ruler can afford to condone. Friends and foes would consider him the most "vile" among kings if he failed to avenge a slight to the prestige of the crown (3.3.1661–5). He must exact not just a simple vengeance but a punishment appropriate to the outrage ("[...] simil fosse / La vendetta a l'oltraggio," 5.1.2513) so that it may serve as a warning to others who might be tempted to test his royal resolve. He tells his henchmen that with the bloody display of Oronte's murder he intends to show other courtiers and the world what happens to those who dare to challenge his authority:

Gli altri che 'n corte son sol per costui
Potranno avere innanzi esempio tale
Che sapran per qual via debbano inviarsi
Per fuggir così crudo e fiero intoppo. (5.1.2445–8)

[The others who are at court through him / will have before them such an example / that they will know which way they must behave / in order to avoid so cruel and fierce a fate.]

From these words, it is clear that Sulmone sees the use of violence as a rhetorical projection of royal power. For him, the gruesome killing is a show of force meant to enhance his reputation as a ruler able and ready to defend his kingdom. In one of his long soliloquies, he refers to the murders as an opportunity to display his will power ("dimostrare il poter nostro al mondo," 3.3.1680). To do otherwise, he believes, would make him appear weak and vulnerable. In the world of power and politics, appearance is of paramount importance and, as Machiavelli points out, a prince must be careful to cultivate it. Sulmone seems to follow this precept rather closely, especially in his decision to murder his victims all at once. In *Prince* 8, Machiavelli advises that a prince who must engage in acts of violence should do them all at once so that "being tasted less, they offend less" ("assaporandosi meno, offendino meno," *Opere* 80). To do them over an extended period of time, he warns, would earn him the reputation of a bloodthirsty ruler.

Sulmone's Machiavellianism comes into sharper focus when contrasted with Malecche's humanist notion of kingship. In the novella, Malecche is introduced as the king's old cousin and trusted adviser. Because of his special affection for Orbecche, he tries in vain to convince the king to forgive the girl and turn his hatred into fatherly love (1864). As a royal emissary, he travels to Armenia to seek the couple's extradition to Persia. Not suspecting the king's sinister intent, he persuades the trusting couple to return home. In the play, though his role remains largely unchanged, his character acquires a political dimension that places him in sharp ideological contrast with Sulmone. His firm and oft-expressed belief that rulers should be humane, just, and forgiving recalls the liberal views of King Settin of Armenia. In the novella, Settin contrasts his liberal and compassionate notion of government with Sulmone's penchant for revenge and bloodshed, and is particularly contemptuous of his foe's unwillingness to see the young couple's marriage as a simple sin of love rather than an act of treason. His strong disapproval of Sulmone's tyrannical rule explains, at least in part, their sworn enmity ("crudeli inimicizie," 1862).

The playwright chooses not to feature Settin in the stage adaptation but retains the king's liberal views by attributing them to Malecche. This new aspect of the counsellor's role results largely from the formal need to adhere to the Aristotelian unities. The concentration of the action at Sulmone's court requires the omission of faraway Armenia and the events that took place there. Indeed, considering the great distance separating the two kingdoms, Settin's presence in the play would be in violation of the unities of time and place. But the novelty inherent in the omission of the Armenian king's character and in the alteration of Malecche's role is not a mere formal requisite. It serves to dramatize the question of kingship. In the prose version, the issue is expressed mostly through Settin's liberal views of government and his disapproval of his nemesis' penchant for violence. In the play, it grows out of Sulmone's arguments for the use of force against Malecche's insistence that a benevolent prince is far better than a despotic one. The contrast turns into a veritable debate with well-defined notions of the princely qualities a ruler should exhibit for the effective government of the state.

When Sulmone resolves to punish Oronte for his treacherous deed, Malecche counsels clemency, noting that to forgive becomes a noble lord ("il perdonare è da Signor gentile," 3.2.1172). He exhorts his cousin to follow the celebrated example of King Pisistratus, who chose to pardon the young man who dishonoured the crown by forcibly kissing the princess, his daughter (3.2.1306). In a tone reminiscent of Castiglione's courtier, he argues that true princely virtues are not vengeance and brutal force but compassion, prudence, and piety ("senno, valor, pietà, clemenzia," 3.2.1257). Sulmone counters this humanist notion of kingship with the Machiavellian belief that a ruling prince must avoid being perceived as irresolute and weak. In his view, kings would be considered the most abject among men if they left unpunished crimes against the crown. Not only must he avenge the stain on his honour, he must do it in a "royal" fashion, that is, a manner worthy of a true king ("di me degna esser Re vero"). Thus, just as he trusted Oronte and was betrayed by him, now Oronte, in a classic Dantean contrappasso, trusts him and that trust leads him to his death ("Che la fé istessa lo conduca a morte," 5.1.2455–2515). In this sense, his murder of Oronte is not as personal or instinctive as that of his prose counterpart but rather the calculated deed of a tyrant intent on projecting his fearsome resolve.

Malecche insists that compassion not cruelty – forgiveness not revenge – enhances royal prestige and endears a ruler to his subjects. Sulmone counters that a prince who seeks to be loved by his subjects risks total ruin. In a tone reminiscent of Machiavelli's argument on whether a prince should be feared or loved (*Prince* 17), he points out that it is actually better to be feared. He also believes that it is not unusual for subjects to hate their lord. In his view, hate and power share the same relationship, just like two siblings born from the same womb. Embracing Machiavelli's precept, he warns that rulers who avoid being feared ultimately lose the state:

> Abbiami in odio pur, pur che mi teman
> Tutti i sudditi miei. Nati ad un parto

Son, come due fratelli, il regno e l'odio,
E chi non cerca esser temuto, cerca
Lasciare il regno tosto e venir servo. (5.1.2482–6)

[Let my subjects hate me as long as they fear me. / Like twin brothers, hatred and royal rule / were born from the same birth. / And he who does not wish to be feared / will lose the kingdom and become a slave.]

Pointedly, fear should be born not out of a ruler's constant use of violence but out of the sporadic and public demonstration of it. As in Machiavelli's example of how Cesare Borgia had Remirro de Orco quartered and displayed in the town square for the people to behold and beware (*Prince* 7), Sulmone produces the bloody limbs of his victims for the world to see. The gruesome show, he believes, will reaffirm his fearsome reputation and keep his subjects in great awe and fear of him. Such a belief is not a mere theoretical assumption, for not only does it draw from Cesare's notorious deed, it also informs similar decisions by other Renaissance rulers. Surely contemporary audiences recalled other displays of violence, such as those ordered by Cesare's father, Alexander VI. Soon after becoming pope, Alexander ordered the hanging of known murderers and stipulated that their bodies be left as a "rotting example on the gallows" lining the bridge leading to Castel Sant'Antagelo (Strahem 69). The Grand Duke of Toscany, Cosimo I, mandated that the corpse of Giovanni di Menco Catasta, a rebel from the city of Lucca, be left hanging in plain view as an "example to others."[10] Whether grounded on fact or fiction, practice or theory, the emphasis on the "example to others" is not in the degree or frequency of the use of force but in the rhetorical threat of it. Recalling the notion of *imitatio Dei*, a commonplace simile in the tragic theatre, Sulmone likens the fearful effect of his display of violence to God's use of thunderbolts. Though thunderbolts kill only occasionally, their potential threat never fails to remind humans of God's ire and power. In his own words,

Un Re dovrebbe esser terribil sempre,
E lo dimostra chiaro il Re del cielo,
Il qual, mentre serbar vuol la sua altezza,
Tien ne la man il fier fulmine ardente. (5.1.2474–7)

[A king should always appear terrible, / as demonstrated by the King of the heavens / who, wishing to maintain his dignity, / holds in his hand the fierce thunderbolt.]

The analogy is not a mere topos of tragedy, for Sulmone actually believes in the god-king correlation. At the beginning of the play, Nemesis states that she intends to punish Sulmone exactly because he thought himself equal to God ("al par de la divina altezza," 1.179). The simile is particularly relevant because it allows Sulmone to inject the element of the divine into the debate on kingship. Malecche refutes the claim of divine likeness by pointing out that, like any other humans, kings are subject to the whims of Fortune. The rich and powerful of today, he reminds his cousin-king, may be the wretched beggars of tomorrow (3.2.1360). The warning turns prophetic when the king meets his gruesome death at the hands of his own daughter. As she cuts him to pieces, his dying wish is yet another "vendetta," and his last words are a pusillanimous cry for help and mercy: "Oimè, pietade!" Unlike in the novella, where Orbecche stabs her father twice and offers his head to her dead Oronte, in the play, she carries his severed limbs out of the palace for everyone to see. Through this public display of violence, she turns on its head Sulmone's own view (Machiavelli's?) on the projection of power. The world, and thus the audience, beholds the miserable death of the once fearful tyrant, the self-proclaimed godlike king.

It is important to point out that the king's death is not just the revenge of an aggrieved victim but also the fulfilment of divine justice. From the very beginning of the play, the spectators know that the goddess Nemesis has summoned the Furies to exact God's revenge on the hubristic king. Messenger reports that the dying Oronte repeatedly pleaded with Sulmone to spare the children, reminding him that, if he did not fear human retribution, he should fear divine justice. Unable to move the hardened killer, the grieving father assures him that if the gods are watching, he should expect their harsh revenge ("aspra vendetta," 4.1.2159–2219). Also Coro, reacting to the messenger's description of the savagery he witnessed in the dungeon, inveighs against the bloody tyrant and predicts that he shall not escape the certainty of God's judgment (4.1.2430–9). Semichoro, watching Orbecche frantically slashing her father's body; judges the slaying righteous and suggests that "God could not have been more pleased by the death of so evil a tyrant" ("a Dio non s'offre vittima più grata / D'un malvagio Tiran com'era questo," 5.2.2867–8). The immediate relevance of these imprecations lies in the playwright's intent to stir and direct the spectators' emotions against the king and his fearsome behaviour. But their function is not a mere dramatic device to make theatre, for is also a conscious attempt to influence the spectators' view of kingly prerogatives. More specifically, it forces them to join the ongoing Machiavellian debate on princeship that continued to shape the political dialogue in Renaissance Europe.

Machiavellian Princeship Anchored to Religious Morality

One must be careful not to assume that Sulmone's death implies the rejection of the God-king analogy. For many spectators, the analogy was a fundamental argument in the ongoing debate on princeship and was in harmony with the current notion of the nature of political rule. With their participation, virtually of course, the issue expands to include aspects of reasons-of-state theory, a theory that stressed, among other things, the connection between royal power and the divine.[11] Counter-Reformation writers forged a political theory that, integrating humanist and Machiavellian precepts, conceived of an ideal prince as both fearsome and just, vengeful and forgiving. Giovanni Botero, in his *Della ragione di stato* (1589), reflecting the prevailing political thought of the time, argued that royal power proceeds from God. In his view, kings should observe divine law and cultivate noble qualities such as justice, munificence, and wisdom. They should also establish a reputation as fearsome rulers through the occasional and effective show of force. In this respect, Botero believes, princes would be just like God who, with his display of thunder and lightning, instils terror and fear in the hearts of mankind:

> Prudentemente severo fia colui che con poche esecuzioni ed asprezze terrà il popolo in ufficio e si farà tener per terribile, imitando in ciò Dio, il quale con tuonare spesse volte cagiona negli animi degli uomini paura e terrore senza danno; ma acciochè i tuoni non perdano il credito per non far mai colpo, tra mille tuoni saetta qualche volta, e per lo più qualche cima d'albero o giogo di monte. (Aggiunte, 2.434)

> [Prudently severe is he who, with few executions and roughness, holds his people in check and in fear of him. In this he imitates God who, by thundering frequently, stirs fear and terror in the hearts of men without actually hurting them. But in order for his thunderbolts not to lose their credit by never striking a target, once in a thousand He strikes the top of a tree or the peak of a mountain.]

Thus, not only does Botero appreciate, like Machiavelli, the importance of a fearful reputation as a rhetorical means for reducing violence, he also, like Sulmone, links a king's behaviour to divine deeds. But if the political zeitgeist endorsed the God-king analogy and the need for a king to appear fearsome, it could not accept Sulmone as the ideal representative of the emerging concept of princeship. His political morality was too rooted in excessive and sadistic violence. The rejection of his kingship, already proclaimed by the stage audience, and presumably by the playwright, is signified by his grisly death. Pointedly, the champion of an ideology grounded in bloodshed is himself the victim of bloody violence. He is dismembered in the same way and with the same knife with which he cut up his victims. And, like them, he falls victim to deception, as Orbecche leads him to believe that she has actually forgiven him. Ironically, he perishes at the hands of the one who, in his mind, is to guarantee the future of the dynasty. These ironies tend to vindicate Malecche's liberal views, upend Sulmone's notion of kingship, and bolster the spectators' approval of his demise. Undoubtedly, his death reminded contemporary audiences of Creon's belief that "the king who holds his throne with cruel sway / must fear the fearful; on its author's head will fear return" (Seneca, *Oedipus* 3.1.753–6).

The context of fear in which Creon's wisdom places Sulmone's death must not be taken as an indictment of politically motivated violence, which was generally recognized as a basic tenet of a ruler's rhetorical projection of power. It is instead a denunciation of Sulmone's predisposition to excessive cruelty. Political theorists agreed that a ruler might employ forceful means provided he did not offend society's moral and religious values. This qualified acceptance of the limited use of force, while vindicating neither Sulmone's notion of kingship nor Malecche's liberal views, tends to reconcile elements of humanist idealism with key Machiavellian precepts. The ethos arising from such a reconciliation warns tyrants that they are subject to divine laws and the whims of Fortune. Kings, just like any other humans, must fear God and be mindful of the ups and downs of life. In the absence of these restraints, rulers run the risk of going astray and, like Sulmone, ruining both themselves and the state. In this sense, the violence-ridden world of *Orbecche* emerges as an exemplum of a pernicious notion of kingship whereby unbridled despots wantonly bring suffering on their subjects. Inherently, it suggests that the political stability of a state depends largely on a cultural and religious context that justifies the ruler's actions and motives. In the words of the nurse in Torelli's *Merope* (1593), without the rule of just princes, cities and kingdoms are useless skeletons and vile shadows ("inutili cadaveri, e vili ombre," 1960–5).

The debate on kingship is not merely an abstract intellectual exercise, for its dramatization surely confirmed in the spectators' mind Prologue's reminder that they are fortunate to live happily in prosperous Ferrara and not in the distant and forlorn Susa. By the end of the play, they have experienced the cathartic cleansing brought on by the sense of fear and pity normally associated with tragic representations. Perhaps more importantly, their experience is also marked by the inevitable contrast between the miserable world of the stage and their own prosperous lives. The difference between the "here and now" of the auditorium and the "there and then" of the stage allows them to see the spectacle as the contrast between the possible world of the play and the real world of the audience. The first is violent and threatening; the second is peaceful and safe. From this perspective, the theatrical experience takes on the form of a meaningful event as it moves from the fearful reminder of how terrible life could be under an ungodly tyrant, such as Sulmone, to the comforting awareness of being governed by a most magnanimous lord, such as Duke Ercole. Lest some spectators miss the connection, Prologue cautions them that if they live safely in the great city of Ferrara, it is thanks to Duke Ercole:

> Mercé de la giustizia e del valore,
> Del consiglio matur, de la prudenza
> Del suo Signor … (Prologo 57–60)

> [Thanks to the justice, the valour, / the mature wisdom, and the prudence / of its Lord …]

It is not lost on the spectators that, though the debate is between Sulmone and Malecche, it is Orbecche who murders the tyrant and figuratively rejects his brand of kingship. Ironically, she triumphs in death, as she celebrates her revenge by killing herself. This is not an act imposed by a father or husband but a free and spontaneous act of resolve. As a woman, she was denied the freedom to choose a husband and live with him and their children. In death she claims that prerogative. Her suicide represents not the defeat of her struggle against patriarchal authority but rather the vindication of a woman's right to decide how to live or, in this case, how to die. From this perspective, she emerges as a heroic voice in the ongoing debate about women's position. With her complaints about the inferior status of women, she denounces the cultural misogyny of the time; by her daring actions, she claims the intellectual ability and the human dignity to think for herself. At the close, the spectators leave the auditorium with two gruesome scenes vividly impressed in their minds: Sulmone's murder and Orbecche's suicide. The first they see as the symbolic endorsement of the emerging reasons-of-state theory of kingship, the latter as the virtual vindication of women's autonomy.

The novelty and creative dramatization of these themes distinguish *Orbecche* from its prose source and, at the same time, account for Giraldi's theatrical genius. The distinction arises primarily from the formal changes necessary for the genre transformation and the resulting shift of emphasis from the characters' actions to their motives. The original Sulmone murdered and dismembered his victims because of his cruel and vengeful nature. Although nine years had gone by since the young couple first fled to Armenia, he savoured his bloody revenge with the same intensity as if he were still living the outrage of long ago. By contrast, the stage Sulmone, though still the cruel and vengeful self of the source, attributes his bloody deeds to reasons of state. Political imperatives, he argues, require a king to project his power and resolve through violence. The distinction is also apparent in the evolution in Orbecche's character. Though still the grieving mother of the prose narrative, she rises to champion the cause of womankind in the ever-divisive *querelle de femmes*. These changes enabled the fictional world of *Orbecche* to resonate with contemporary audiences both aesthetically and thematically. The sight of bloodshed challenged their aesthetic assumptions and expectations, while the debates engaged them emotionally and intellectually. Thus, Giraldi morphed his novella of blood and gore into a stage spectacle that, though largely faithful to the prose story, serves as an original source of entertainment and as a fresh forum for debating cultural issues.

Chapter Eight

Dolce's *Marianna*: From History to the Stage

"The difference between a poet and a historian is this: the historian relates what has happened, the poet what could happen."

(Aristotle, *The Poetics* 2.9.18)

Lodovico Dolce (1508–68) was one of the most active and encyclopedic writers of the Italian Renaissance. He wrote on gems, language, love, marriage, memory, painting, philosophy, and women. He also authored biographies, chivalric poems, and dramas. According to Ronnie Terpening, he produced "more than a hundred volumes bearing his name, whether as author, editor, translator or critic – a writer who had gained, in his own century, universal renown" (3). His prolific production notwithstanding, his literary reputation rests mostly on his theatrical works, consisting of five comedies and a great number of translations, adaptations, and modernizations or *rifacimenti* of ancient tragedies. His dramatic works assured his popularity among his contemporaries and helped to propagate tragedies modelled on Seneca and Euripides as far as England and France. His stagecraft is notably apparent in his most creative plays, the comedy *Il ragazzo* and the tragedy *Marianna*. This last is considered his masterpiece and is counted "among the best Italian tragedies of the sixteenth century" (Herrick, *Italian Tragedy* 176). The play enjoyed great success with contemporary audiences following its very first performance in1565 at the court of Ferrara. At that performance, the number of spectators grew so large that, according to the author, it actually hindered its recitation and another performance had to be scheduled a few days later.[1] In our times, though the play is featured in most anthologies of the tragic theatre of the Italian Renaissance, neither its themes nor the author's stagecraft have received sufficient critical attention. In the ensuing discussion, I intend to highlight Dolce's theatrical mastery by focusing on his creative ability to turn Josephus's story of Herod and Mariamme into a gripping stage representation. Building on the historical event, he frames a fictional world where the evils of power and jealousy lead to a tragic finale that damns both the victim and the tyrant.

Unlike most Renaissance tragedies, mostly based on mythology or ancient history with a heavy presence of pagan deities, *Marianna* is placed in a historical context that is entirely Christian. It deals mainly with the tragic end of the Jewish queen Mariamme, the wife of King Herod. The story's original source is Flavius Josephus's *Ancient History of the Jews*, mostly *Antiquities* 15 and *War of the Jews*. In Italy, the story was celebrated in Boccaccio's biographies of famous women, *De claris mulieribus*. The short narrative provides a succinct version of the queen's virtues and heroic death.[2] The collection was loosely translated into Italian as early as 1397 by Donato Da Casentino, and went on to see several more *volgarizzamenti* well into the sixteenth century.[3] It is possible that Dolce knew the story of the beautiful queen and her unbearably jealous husband from Boccaccio's work. He may also have read it in one of the circulating translations, most likely in Betussi's 1545 expanded version. But the stage adaptation features details and events not found in the *De claris* sketch or its *volgarizzamenti*. For instance, the charge of adultery against Marianna, which is central to the development of the play, is not mentioned in Boccaccio or the translations. Nor is there any mention of the king's execution of his own sons and mother-in-law. Also missing from the *volgarizzamenti* is any mention of the queen's "house arrest" in the fortress of Alexandrium, and the king's despair following her death.[4] Dolce's dramatization of these and other historical details leads to the conclusion that he must have known Josephus's actual account through Pietro Lauro's 1544 Italian translation of the Greek original.

The Historical Source

Josephus's story of Mariamme, the last queen of the Hasmonean dynasty, begins with her marriage to Herod in 37 BCE and ends with the king's death in 6 BCE. By this marriage, the commoner Herod acquired royal status. He proceeded to consolidate his power by murdering those who might contest his legitimacy, including Mariamme's brother and grandfather. Herod was madly in love with his queen. In time, he became so insanely jealous that when he left for Egypt to appear before Marc Anthony, he instructed his trusted brother-in-law, Joseph, to kill her should he not return from the mission. His reason for such an unusual order was that he could not live with the thought of another man enjoying the beauty he could no longer have. Upon learning of these murderous instructions and of Herod's brutal murders of her kin, Mariamme became ever more hostile towards her husband. Her open contempt for his humble origins eventually earned her the hatred of Herod's sister, Salome, who went so far as to insinuate that her own husband, Joseph, had had an affair with the queen. Mariamme defended her innocence vehemently but failed to dissuade Herod from murdering his own brother-in-law.

The king's obsessive jealousy tortured him so much that he grew ever more suspicious of his wife and began to see her as a threat to the throne. When he was summoned to appear before the victorious Caesar Octavian, he instructed his trusted captain, Sohemus, to take Mariamme to the nearby fortress in Alexandrium and keep her and her mother, Alexandra, under close guard. He also left orders to kill both women should he not return from the Roman camp. Upon his return, Salome and her mother, Cypros, increasingly resentful of Mariamme's haughtiness, convinced him that his love for the queen was not real. It was, they told him, the result of a love potion the queen had given him. His love for Mariamme thus shaken, Herod was easily provoked to accuse her of having engaged in an adulterous affair with Sohemus. Once again, the queen defended her honour strenuously and vented her deep hatred towards her bloodthirsty husband, telling him that she would rather die than continue to live with him. The enraged king, egged on by his mother and his sister, sentenced Sohemus to death and ordered Mariamme to stand trial. The queen's mother, fearing for her own life, sided with the king. He, in a burst of anger, had Mariamme beheaded in 29 BCE. No sooner was she dead than Herod was seized by an unbearable sense of guilt and fell into a paroxysm of grief: he kept on calling her name as if she were alive, and eventually went into the desert to cry out his despair. He was finally shaken from his anguish when he learned of a plot against him. Once again his old self, he quickly moved to foil the conspiracy, arresting and putting to death the principal instigators, including Mariamme's mother. In 6 BCE, the year he died, he had his own sons, Alexander and Aristobulus, executed on the suspicion that they, too, were plotting against him.

Dolce followed Josephus's historical narrative closely, though he made some changes, mostly for dramatic effect and to comply with the unities of theatre. He retained the location of the action, kept the same characters, and gave reasonably accurate accounts of their deeds. The challenge before him was to stage events that happened at various times during a thirty-year period. He proceeded to turn the story into a stage representation by rearranging the chronology of certain events and by locating the action in a single place. With regard to the unity of place, he located the action at the fortress or Castello in Alexandrium, just outside Jerusalem. Though the scenic space is not clearly defined, there are enough spatial references to assume that it consists of a wide street or square with the Castello on one side, Salome's palace on the other, and a backdrop with a perspective of the city of Jerusalem in the distance. The inclusion of Salome's residence in this spatial arrangement is a departure from Josephus's account. Upon leaving to appear before Octavian, Herod decided to keep his wife away from his own family and therefore sent Salome and his mother to the fortress of Masada and Mariamme and her mother to Alexandrium. Though the alteration brings the play into compliance with the unity of place, some might question Dolce's decision to locate Salome's residence in the scenic space. After all, she is a minor character and appears on stage only once. But the relevance of the building lies not so much in Salome's role in the development of the plot but in the visual impact it has on the audience. The spectators cannot help but see it as an iconic contrast to the Castello. On one side stands the palace of the evildoers, Salome and her mother; on the opposite side rises the foreboding Castello holding the "good" Marianna, her two children, and her mother. For the audience, the two structures are the suggestive symbols of love and hate, the forces that tear apart the susceptible king and lead him to his tragic fall.

The plot is simple and straightforward: Salome leads her brother, Erode, to believe that the hateful and haughty queen schemed to have him poisoned. After the malicious charge is disproved, the action centres on the king's obsessive suspicion that his wife is engaged in an adulterous affair with his most trusted captain, Soemo. Before the end of the play, Erode has ordered the executions of Soemo, Marianna, her children, and her mother. The author deals with events leading to the dramatic action by including them in the *antefactum* that the queen and her nurse dramatize in the first act. In some cases, characters refer to past events as foreshadowings of things to come. For instance, Marianna suspects that Erode will one day murder her just as he killed her brother and grandfather ("per far di me qual del fratello e l'avo," 2.1194).[5] The linearity of the story not only conforms to the Aristotelian unity of action, it also sharpens the focus on the contrasting forces of love and hate. These passions control and direct all the king's energies and ultimately unleash his most brutal instincts against his nearest and dearest. Dolce skilfully cuts through the source's long narrative of the couple's troubled relationship and chooses to concentrate on the king's destructive jealousy and the bloodshed it engenders. Succumbing to his tormenting demons, he condemns his wife to death and damns himself to a life of grief and despair. In this sense, he too is a tragic figure, for, try as he may, he cannot escape the ghost of his guilt.

With regard to the time frame, Dolce compresses a number of historical events into the last day of Marianna's life. He recalls episodes that happened before the queen's death and represents others that in reality took place many years afterward. In Josephus's chronology, Mariamme was executed in 29 BCE, Alexandra in 28 BCE, and the children in 6 BCE. In the stage adaptation, they are all executed on the same day. The staging of events that have yet to take place has no significant impact on the length of the play, nor does it affect the realistic dramatization of the story. Its function is mostly dramaturgical in that it tends to highlight Erode's excessive cruelty. Also, by representing multiple executions at the same time, the playwright intended to stir the spectators' emotions and draw them closer to the world of the stage. One can only imagine how horrifying it must have been for the spectators to hear the details of the executions of an elderly grandmother, a mother, and her young children. Undoubtedly, they regarded with revulsion a bloodthirsty man whose brutality placed him among the most vengeful rulers of theatre. Erode's savagery was likely to evoke in the minds of the spectators gruesome images of Seneca's Atreus, the stage prototype of all violent and sadistic rulers. Many in the audience would surely also recall Giraldi's Sulmone, the Atreus of the tragic theatre of the Italian Renaissance.

Josephus's Herod versus Dolce's Erode

The association of Erode with the cruellest tyrants of the stage does not reduce him to a mere bloodthirsty ruler, for he is much more complex than his stage counterparts. To be sure, Dolce's characterization of the Jewish king is by and large faithful to the historical model: ruthless and ambitious, insecure in his kingship and in his love, and always fearful of betrayals and conspiracies. But the stage imitation centres primarily on the king's insecurity and his emotional relationship with the queen. The result is a fictional character tortured by baleful jealousy or, in the words of Marianna, "avelenata gelosia" (1.328). Thus, unlike his historical counterpart, whose actions were often motivated by alleged attempts on his royal legitimacy, Erode comes alive through his irrational suspicions of adultery, his bloody murders, and his final grief. Josephus's Herod, too, was insanely jealous of his wife. He had his brother-in-law, Joseph, and Sohemus executed on suspicion that they had been too "intimate" with the queen. But his use of violence against members of the Hasmonean dynasty was mainly motivated by his constant fear of being overthrown. In 35 BCE, he killed Mariamme's seventeen-year-old brother out of fear that the popular prince might some day attempt to reclaim the throne of his ancestors. Josephus writes that Herod, perceiving the people's admiration for the prince as a threat to his crown, "resolved to complete what he had intended against the young man" and had him murdered (*Antiquities* 15.3.3).[6] Four years later, a similar suspicion led him to murder Mariamme's grandfather, Hycarnus II. He accused the old man of consorting with the enemy and had him strangled (*Ant.* 15.6.3).

Just before Mariamme's trial in 29 BCE, Herod had Sohemus executed on the suspicion that he had been involved in a love affair with the queen. However, seen in the context of the preceding events, it is clear that Herod also suspected him of treason. Upon his departure for Egypt to appear before Caesar Octavian, the king placed Mariamme and her mother under guard for fear that they, taking advantage of his absence, might "bring the multitude to a revolt, and introduce a sedition into the affairs of the kingdom." Thus, writes Josephus, he instructed his treasurer and Sohemus "that if they should hear any mischief had befallen him, they should kill them both and, as far as they were able, preserve the kingdom for his sons, and for his brother Pheroras" (*Ant.* 15.6.5). When, upon his return, he learned that Sohemus had revealed his murderous instructions to Mariamme, he immediately drew the conclusion that they had become intimate and were plotting against the crown. With regard to Alexandra, he had her killed after discovering that she had joined a conspiracy against him. Years later (6 BCE), he executed the children he had with Mariamme, Alexander and Aristobulus, because he believed their behaviour was seditious and a real threat to the throne (*War of the Jews* 1.24.3).

In the imitation, Erode is tormented by the same demons of betrayal and treason. But the reasons for his violent behaviour arise mostly from his love-hate relationship with Marianna. Such a shift from the source is expressed in part through his excessive cruelty against the queen. In the historical account, upon hearing that Sohemus had revealed his instructions to kill Mariamme, he simply ordered the captain "seized and put to death at once" (*Ant.* 15.7.4). In the stage version, he is primarily moved by jealousy as he presents Soemo's heart, head, and hands on a silver platter to Marianna, telling her to behold the limbs of the "felon" she loved so much (4.2363). His deep-seated suspicion is that the two intended to marry and "together take over and rule my kingdom" ("e 'nsieme / D'occupar in tal guisa il regno mio," 3.1898). Though the gruesome scene is reminiscent of Sulmone's dismembering of Oronte, it should not be seen as a mere theatrical allusion to Giraldi's *Orbecche.* Unlike Sulmone, who took pride in the grisly show and called it the resolve of a powerful ruler, Erode's wish is to punish his wife for her disdain of him or simply to reduce her haughtiness ("alterezza," 3.1571). The macabre incident is the expression of a fiercely jealous husband who cannot entertain the notion that another man might enjoy his wife's beauty.

When he finally allows the execution of Marianna to proceed, he orders that she must first witness the death of her children and her mother. The timing and circumstances of these killings, which in the source took place at different times and long after the queen's death, indicate the playwright's intent to accentuate Erode's wish to hurt the queen. In the historical account, Alexander and Aristobulus were killed when they were adults for allegedly scheming against the throne. In the play, they are little boys, innocent victims of Erode's vengeance. They are murdered presumably because of their defiant defence of their mother's virtues and because of the king's wild suspicion that they might have been born from Marianna's alleged affair with Soemo (4.2610–75). But his most obvious motive is to make Marianna suffer all the more. He specifically orders that she be made to watch the boys being strangled and her mother decapitated (4.2680–90). Erode's aim to cause unbearable grief to his contemptuous wife is reminiscent, albeit obliquely, of Medea's killing of her children in order to punish their father, the scornful Jason. But, unlike the crazed Medea, Erode is blinded by a fit of anger that momentarily suppresses his real love and unleashes his pent-up resentment of his haughty queen.

Anger, suspicion, and jealousy distinguish Erode from the historical Herod, who decided Mariamme's fate because of seemingly reasonable fears. In Josephus's version, Herod ordered his wife to stand trial after Salome convinced him that his excessive love was the direct result of a love potion the queen had given him. Despite the jury's guilty verdict, he elected not to carry out the death sentence and accepted instead his courtiers' advice to imprison her in one of the kingdom's fortresses. But Salome and her party argued against imprisonment on the grounds that, as long as she was alive, Mariamme could incite the populace to rebel against the king. The scenario was indeed too dangerous and too real for the king to ignore; thus, he decreed her death. In the adaptation, the calculating Herod morphs into a fictional tyrant prone to uncontrollable impulses and torn by violent passions. For him, the queen is not so much a political threat as a humiliating reminder of her disdain for his love and his plebeian pedigree. Thus, Herod's fears of betrayals and conspiracies give way to Erode's contrasting and tormenting emotions. In his own words, he feels pulled in opposite directions by the forces of love and reason:

> Che d'una parte mi ritiene amore,
> E d'altra la ragion mi volge e sprona,
> Né so ben risoluto qual di due
> Portar debba vittoria del mio core. (3.1996–9)

> [For, on the one hand, love holds me in its grip / and, on the other hand, reason stirs and leads me. / Nor do I know which of the two / will ultimately win me over.]

To mould the historical Herod into a more volatile stage ruler, the playwright introduces a new character, the royal Consigliere or counsellor. Unlike other *consiglieri* of the Renaissance tragic theatre, whose role is to counsel the tyrant in kingly virtues and political options, much like an adviser to Castiglione's or Machiavelli's prince, his role is to appeal to his king's better judgment. He advises Erode to reconsider his hastily ordered executions, noting that his stirred emotions cloud his judgment. With a clearer mind, he could see that his victims' guilt is based on mere conjecture (3.1597–1631). With regard to Soemo's alleged adultery and treason, for instance, the counsellor points out that the loyal captain had no motive to conspire against the crown. Did he not enjoy all the royal honours and privileges a courtier could possibly desire? Also, he could not have fancied a coup d'état because he was fully aware that the people would have considered him a usurper and killed him (3.1685–92). He pleads for Soemo's life, suggesting that life in prison or exile might be a more fitting punishment (3.2008–9). But his arguments do little to shake Erode's fatal resolve. Jealousy and suspicion lay such a hold on his mind that he even suspects Soemo of having fathered the two young princes, Alessandro and Aristobolo. The oddity of this fear is particularly evident when he mistakes the boys' plea for their mother's life as proof of their illegitimacy (4.2607). He is so paranoid that he considers them bastards whether or not he is their father:

E se di questo corpo usciti foste,
Ancor non crederei mi foste figli.
Onde vi tratterò come bastardi. (4.2641–4)

[And even if you were sired by me, / I would still refuse to believe that you were my children. / Thus, I will treat you as bastards.]

The true source of such blind hatred lies in his deep resentment at the loss of happiness that his suspicion of his wife's adultery has caused. He reproaches Soemo for having robbed him of the happy life he fancied with his beloved Marianna: "senza sospetto alcun, come felice" (3.1990).

Undeterred by his failure to soften Erode's bitterness against Soemo, the counsellor continues to plead with the king to allow his emotions to cool off so that he can see the baselessness of his suspicions. He first reminds him that the accusation that Marianna tried to poison him has already been proven false. He then proceeds to dispel the allegation that the queen conspired against the crown, noting that she had all the power she could possibly want. She actually stood to lose influence and prestige if she became a widow (3.1653–81). As for the alleged adultery, he insists that the queen has always been a chaste and faithful wife. She is too young and too beautiful to fancy a love relationship with the old and ugly Soemo. It is inconceivable, the old counsellor continues to argue, that she would prefer such a man to her young and vigorous husband. If she had been determined to take a lover, she surely would not have chosen old Soemo over one of the many handsome noblemen who frequent the court (3.2032–40). He begs his lordship to revoke the hasty sentence against the queen, lest he should live to regret it, just as Alexander the Great agonized over his impetuous murder of his dear friend Cleitus. Overcome by grief and guilt, Alexander tried to kill himself with the same lance he had used to kill his friend (3.1702–3). Consigliere concludes his plea by reminding Erode that his so-called justice proceeds not from sound judgment but from blinding and impetuous ire ("da l'ardor et impeto dell'ira," 3.2747).

In this emotional bewilderment lies Erode's tragic flaw. His passions make him so unstable that no sooner does he order the executions than he changes his mind and tries to revoke them. But, it is too late. When he learns that his victims have already been killed, he is so overcome with remorse that he even considers committing suicide. Only when Marianna, the source of his inner demons, is gone does he come to his senses and begin to regret his murderous actions. He realizes that his suspicion of adultery was indeed born out of jealousy, that Consigliere had duly warned him against rash and irrevocable sentences, and that he had ordered the executions out of hatred, ire, and "sdegno" (5.2921–39). He finally understands that he was misled by the venomous lies of his perfidious sister, Salome ("l'empia mia sorella," 5.3231). But he cannot undo what he has done, nor can he have back what he has forever lost. He nearly goes mad, much like his historical counterpart who, overwhelmed with grief, kept on calling out Mariamme's name and eventually went off into the desert to give way to his anguish (*Ant.* 15.7.7). He even engages in a virtual "dialogue" with his dead queen, wailing over her death and asking inconsolably,

Ahi, Marianna mia, dov'ora sei?
[...]
Ahi, Marianna mia, non mi rispondi?
[...]
Ahi, Marianna mia, dove sei gita? (5.3233–45)

[Ah, my Marianna, where are you now? [...] / Ah, my Marianna, why don't you answer me? [...] / Ah, my Marianna, where have you gone?]

Though both the stage king and the historical king grieve uncontrollably over the dead queen, there is a significant difference in the source of their sorrow. According to Josephus, the desire for Mariamme burned in Herod's heart "even more strongly than before." In vain did he try to divert his mind with feasts and parties, as his health began to deteriorate. The thought of his dead queen, Josephus notes, seemed to seize him even more, as if by "some Divine vengeance." The suspicion that the king's emotional and physical deterioration was willed by divine justice gained widespread credence among his subjects. They viewed the pestilence that visited the entire kingdom as God's punishment "for the injustice that had been done to Mariamme." The death of many friends and relatives and the burden of the blame for the people's misery affected the king so much that he wandered off into the desert like a deranged man. He became hopelessly ill, Josephus continues, and only the threat of a coup against the throne brought him back from near death (*Ant.* 15.7.7). From the historian's perspective, then, Herod's suffering was exacerbated by the apprehension that God was punishing him for the murder of his wife and the other innocent victims.

Dolce dramatized Erode's suffering by shifting the cause of his sorrow from divine vengeance to his overwhelming sense of guilt and loss. Having acted with destructive passion against his victims, he is now tortured by that same passion. He regrets his impetuosity, blames himself for listening to Salome's lies rather than to Consigliere's sound advice, and longs for the one he loved and killed. Unlike his historical counterpart, who felt no remorse for his evil deeds but only the increasingly burning desire for Mariamme, a repentant Erode suffers from a deep sense of remorse that causes him to wail with abandon and ultimately drives him to the brink of suicide. Twice does he consider killing himself just to be with his beloved Marianna. But he is forced to acknowledge that he would more likely be cast into the deepest corner of hell, far from his chaste and hallowed wife. In his own words,

> discenderei da te lontano,
> Pieno di sceleraggini a l'Inferno. (5.3252–3)
>
> [I, with all my iniquities, would descend / in Hell, far away from you.]

Future audiences will be reminded of Erode's painful plight as they hear Shakespeare's Othello express his fears that when he and Desdemona "meet at compt," her spectral "look will hurl my soul from heaven, / And fiends will snatch at it" (5.2.316–18).[7] But, unlike Othello, Erode does not end his grief by killing himself. As he must live with his tormenting sorrow, he hopes to alleviate his guilt by honouring his victims and punishing those who led him to his crimes. Accordingly, unlike his historical namesake, who kept Salome in his inner circle and eventually married her off to one of his friends, the stage king plans to punish her for having deceived him with her malicious accusations. He also intends to memorialize his victims by preserving their bodies in the royal burial grounds, always aware that his guilt will never leave him (5.3232–85).

Mariamme versus Marianna

Though Erode lives on to bemoan the painful consequences of his bloody deeds, the real victims of his irascible temper are those he has killed, especially the queen. Unquestionably, Dolce raises Marianna's anguish to a level of intensity much higher than that of her historical prototype. To be sure, the playwright adopts the source Mariamme with all her virtues and flaws. Josephus says that she was

> a woman of an excellent character, both in chastity and in greatness of soul; but she lacked moderation, and had too much of combativeness in her nature. Yet she had more than can be said in the beauty of her body and in the dignity of her bearing in the presence of others. And this was the principal source of her failure to please the king and to live with him harmoniously. For she was pampered by the king out of his love for her, and under the expectation that he could never be harsh to her, she took too much liberty with her speech. (*Ant.* 15.7.6)

For "liberty of speech," the writer likely meant her open disdain for the king's humble origins and his unquenchable thirst for power. Her contemptuous attitude not only provoked the king's anger, it also earned her the enmity of his entire family. In the end, it was the principal flaw that brought her to her tragic death.

In his characterization of the stage queen, Dolce retains most of Mariamme's royal demeanour in the face of death. However, he intensifies her suffering by making her watch, on Erode's orders, the killing of her own children and her mother. He accomplishes this change by modifying the behaviour of some source characters, rearranging the temporal sequence of certain events, and adding new elements to the plot. One of the characters he alters is that of Alexandra, Mariamme's mother. In the original version, she is described as haughty, frequently suspected of plotting against the crown, and always at her daughter's side. However, when Mariamme was tried for crimes against the king, Alexandra turned against her. Fearing for her own safety, she joined her daughter's enemies and proceeded to assault her both physically and verbally. In Josephus's view, her manner towards her daughter was so "indecent" that she accused her in public of being "wicked and ungrateful to her husband, and that her punishment came justly upon her for her insolent behavior." Her conduct was "so outrageous," the author continues, that she went so far "as to even seize Mariamme by the hair. [... She] was greatly despised by the rest for her indecent exhibition" (*Ant.* 15.7.4). The play's Alessandra exhibits none of this "indecent" behaviour and remains a loving mother all the way to the end. The playwright turns the despicable character of history into an innocent victim of Erode's fury in order to deepen Marianna's agony and raise her tragic stature.

Admittedly, Dolce's Alessandra has a limited role: she appears only once and has a minor impact on the development of the plot. Her brief appearance serves to inform the queen that Erode has learned of Soemo's alleged treason, and that mother and daughter should now fear for their lives. With compassion and reassurance, she counsels her daughter to place their shared fate in the hands of God, for there is no escaping the king's dreadful jealousy (Act 3). Gone are the source's allusions to her seditious activities that ultimately led to her execution; gone is the contemptible character who turned against her own daughter with vile words and ignoble theatrics. On the stage, she is the encouraging voice of a caring mother who stands by her daughter as they both accept the inevitability of their tragic fate. Instead of turning against her daughter in order to save her own life, she goes to her death with courage and saintly resignation. She dies with the added anguish of beholding her grieving daughter, who is made to watch as the executioner cuts off her head. For reasons of decorum, the spectators do not see the actual beheading, but they hear the details as Nunzio, a messenger, describes them to the king. She died with dignity and piety, praying God to forgive the cruel king and asking her daughter for one last kiss. But the messenger's emphasis is on Marianna's grief, on the "river of tears" rushing down her cheeks, and on their final farewell. The agonizing scene moved to tears all the people ("il popol tutto") who came to witness the sad spectacle, adds the messenger (5.3016). Coro, commenting on the messenger's account, concludes that the bloody sight was so unbearably painful that it would have moved the most savage beasts, let alone a loving daughter:

> Ma fu spettacol fiero,
> Da non poter soffrire,
> Veder innanzi gli occhi
> Colei morir col ferro,
> Ond'ella ebbe la vita. (5.3055–9)

> [But it was a fierce spectacle / that could not be endured / to see before her eyes, / killed by the steel, / the one who gave her life.]

As if watching the decapitation of her mother before her own death was not punishment enough, Erode ordered that Marianna also witness the strangling of their two children. In the source, Herod had his sons killed long after Mariamme's death and for political reasons. The playwright chooses to move up the episode and modify the young characters in order to emphasize Erode's cruelty and Marianna's suffering. In the historical version, the young men were much older, as they were killed some twenty-three years after their mother's death. In the adaptation, though of mature speech and sentiment, they are mere boys or "garzoni [...di] sì poca età," pleading desperately for their mother's life (4.2655).[8] They are killed simply for reminding their father that, if they are too young to avenge their mother's death, divine justice will exact just revenge upon him. The enraged king takes the warning as a threat to his person and repudiates them as Soemo's offspring. It is not difficult to envision the emotional impact on the spectators as they hear about the boys' moving plea for their mother's life and their valiant stand against their father. Their murder, following so noble a sentiment at such a tender age, reveals Erode as a monster who surpasses his historical counterpart in both cruelty and rage.

According to Nunzio, Marianna showed her grief through a "river of tears" flowing down her cheeks as she bade farewell to her dying mother. But she did not moan; nor did she say a word as she watched her children being strangled one after the other. Their moving words of filial love and the gruesome spectacle were so unbearably painful, the messenger recalls, that she stood motionless as if she were a painting or a marble statue. He likens her to the hubristic and arrogant Niobe, who turned to stone while bemoaning her slaughtered children (5.3143–5). In this respect, the adaptation is consistent with the historical characterization of the Jewish queen who "went to her death with a calm demeanor and without a change in the color of her face." Even in the last moments of her life, Josephus writes, she showed "the nobility of her lineage" (*Ant.* 15.7.4). But the imitation deviates from the source in the characterization of Marianna as an implacable victim crying for divine revenge. Before offering her neck to the sword of the executioner, she inveighs against her fierce husband and questions why God's punishment is so slow in coming:

> O giusto Dio, puoi sofferir la tanta
> Impietà d'un fierissimo Tiranno?
> ... Ma dove é 'l castigo
> .....
> Deh, perché tardi? (5.3175–80)

> [Just God, how can you suffer so much / impiety from so fierce a Tyrant? / ... But where is the punishment [...] / Oh, why are you so slow in coming?]

It is not unusual for a tragic hero, especially in the theatre of the Italian Renaissance, to invoke divine help and take comfort in its unfailing justice. What is interesting in Dolce's tragedy is that God is mentioned so frequently that He becomes a virtual character, a living spiritual force in the hearts and minds of the dramatis personae. Unlike in the source, where the deity is hardly a factor, in the play God has a significant, sustaining role, especially for the victims who go to their deaths trusting in His justice. But in Marianna's case, the faith that sustains her throughout her ordeal appears to fail her at the last moment. With a cry reminiscent of Christ's despair on the cross ("My God, why have you forsaken me?" Matt. 27:46; Mk. 15:33; Psalm 22:1), she impatiently questions whether there is divine justice and why it is so slow. In doubting her faith, albeit momentarily, she dies the death of the lone, despairing, tragic heroine. Unlike her mother and the children, she thinks mostly about the world she leaves behind. Her dying words are full of passion in the defence of her honour and brim with hatred towards her tormentor. In her appeal to the people – "as you can see, compassionate people" ("Ben vedi tu, popol pietoso"), and again, "everyone of you should know" ("sappi ogniun di voi") – there is the clear intent to incite them to rebel against the unjust king whose cruelty has no equal under the sun (5.3169–84). If the wheels of divine justice move slowly, let the enraged populace take up her cause.

Marianna's cry for revenge underscores further the distinction between the prose narrative and the stage imitation. The difference between the historical and fictional queens lies not in their individual character or their fateful end. They are equally disdainful of an insanely jealous and pathologically suspicious husband and are ultimately victims of his ruthlessness. The divergence is to be found mostly in the way they meet their respective deaths. Admittedly, they both die with royal dignity, but the stage queen, unlike her source, goes to her death defiant and vengeful. This difference is partly due to the great grief the fictional queen is forced to endure in watching the gruesome murders of her family. Although she witnesses the killings without ever losing her composure and courageously offers her own head to the executioner, she goes to her death still living her human passions. No longer the subdued Mariamme of history or the Jacobean Mariam of Elizabeth Cary, she dies a defiant death.[9] Erode, his cruelty notwithstanding, failed to crush her combative and disdainful spirit. From her severed head, the messenger recounts, were heard the words, "rejoice, cruel Herod; here is my end" ("Saziati, crudo Erode; ecco 'l mio fine," 5.3212).

Erode and the Theatre Audience

Thus, Dolce turns Josephus's prose account of the turbulent relationship between Herod and Mariamme into a stage dramatization meant to strongly excite the spectators' emotions. Although there is no way of knowing the extent to which *cinquecento* audiences let themselves be drawn into the action, it is reasonable to assume that the queen's suffering moved to tears even the most stoic of spectators. In the words of Coro, the queen's grief was so heart-rending that it would move to compassion even the most ferocious bears, tigers, and serpents. More specifically, Nunzio informs the king, and thus the viewing public, that the people witnessing the executions wept so intensely that he cannot find words to describe it ("non vi potrei dir sì come pianse / il popol tutto," 5.3046–8). While the messenger's vivid description is meant primarily to stir Erode's guilty conscience, it also tends to make both the stage and the hall audiences virtual spectators of the gruesome scene. In a way, it invites all those who hear his report to emulate the emotional response of the *popolo* who witnessed the executions. They, too, like the actual spectators of the queen's agony, if not induced to tears, would be more coldhearted than the wildest of beasts.

Dolce does more than simply move the spectators to fear the tyrant and pity the victim, a stirring of emotions normally expected from the tragic stage. By deviating from the historical version, he creates the unusual situation whereby the spectators pity the victim and at the same time fear and pity the terrible tyrant. While they are horrified by the details of the cruel and senseless executions, they cannot help but feel some sort of compassion for the repentant and grieving Erode. In the source, the king inspired no compassion. On the contrary, the people attributed to him the misery that visited the entire kingdom. In their view, his and their suffering issued from God's retribution for his wanton cruelties. This should not come as a surprise, since he based his murderous decisions on calculated political imperatives. Because he was fully conscious of the gravity of his deeds, he was less likely to elicit the people's sympathy. He knew what he was doing, and got what he deserved. Also, if he continued to long for Mariamme, he never voiced contrition for his crimes nor did he regret having listened to Salome's malicious advice. By contrast, in Dolce's play Erode's cruelty is somewhat attenuated by the fact that he acts under the sway of uncontrollable anger and that as soon as he realizes his error, he repents and attempts in vain to rectify it. The news that the executions had already taken place, thus preempting his attempt to revoke the sentences, plunges him into a grief so deep that, according to Coro, he could not utter a word ("non può formar parola," 5.3216–17). He goes on living a life of despair, always grieving over his crimes and his beloved Marianna: "Ah, my Marianna, I will always mourn / my grave misdeed and your death" ("Ahi, Marianna mia, piangerò sempre / Il grave mio peccato e la tua morte," 5.3285–6).

As the spectators leave the theatre with Erode's last words still echoing in their ears, it is not unreasonable to assume that they empathize with the miserable tyrant. They are likely to perceive his destructive anger and jealousy as weaknesses to which all mortals are susceptible. In the play's closing lines, Coro underlines this odious, human vulnerability as he warns against succumbing to ire, the true cause of untold human miseries:

Vedete, egri mortali,
Come l'ira é cagione
D'incomparabil mali.
Però non vi lasciate uscir di mano
Il fren de la ragione. (5.328891)

[You see, wretched mortals, / how ire is the cause / of great afflictions. / Thus, do not let out of your hands / the reins of reason.]

This view of ire as a human frailty tends to further attenuate Erode's tragic flaw, forcing the audience into an emotional swing towards the man who, having succumbed to blinding passions, lost control of his sound judgment and made the fatal error of his life.

As the object of pathos oscillates from the dead victim to the remorseful murderer, the spectators find themselves fully drawn into a rather unusual theatrical experience: they pity the victim and at the same time fear and commiserate with the grieving tyrant. The anomaly is indeed a theatrical feat on Dolce's part in that he skilfully creates a bloodthirsty character capable of inspiring terror and compassion at the same time. From this perspective, Erode differs considerably not only from Josephus's calculating and unremorseful Herod but also from the bloodthirsty and sadistic tyrants of tragedy. Admittedly, he indulges in bloody spectacles reminiscent of stage tyrants, but, unlike them, he repents and is tormented by the haunting voice of a guilty conscience. Anguish and remorse distinguish Erode mostly because, unlike his stage prototypes, he ultimately acknowledges the harm he did to others and to himself. The human qualities informing his tragic conflict are so realistic that some critics consider him "the most believable tyrant among all the Italian descendants of Seneca's Atreus, Hercules, and Nero" (Herrick, *Italian Tragedy* 177).

Different from the prose narrative source and from all stage prototypes, *Marianna*'s king owes his originality to the playwright's keen sense of dramatization. Barely altering the historical facts and simply rearranging them in time and place, he creates a drama wherein an insanely jealous husband subjects his wife to a most gruesome and painful spectacle before murdering her. Josephus's ambitious, calculating, jealous, and ruthless king is morphed into a fictional tyrant driven by jealous love and revenge. This emotional cauldron, and not the political aims and fears of his historical original, is the basis for the bloodshed that turns him into a tragic figure. In the source story, Herod seldom fell prey to his emotions. In most instances, he moved deliberately and methodically against those whom he suspected of sedition. He saw his victims – including his own children, Mariamme, and her relatives – primarily as potential political threats to his crown. Though he ordered the queen's execution because of her alleged affair with Soemo, his true fear was that she might become a destabilizing force in the kingdom as long as she was alive. Dolce's Erode, on the other hand, orders executions in the heat of passion and is ultimately the victim of his own blinding rage. Hence his tragic flaw; and hence the fall that renders his drama all too human and makes him a worthy predecessor of Shakespeare's Othello.

The alteration, redistribution, and time compression of events also tend to turn the story of a haughty queen into the hellish drama of a grieving mother. Though still disdainful of her husband and his upstart family, Marianna is portrayed not as a political threat to be eliminated but as an innocent victim of a ferociously jealous husband. Pointedly, Dolce omits Josephus's politically charged question whether she should be killed or imprisoned following her guilty verdict. Instead, he focuses on her good qualities of a faithful wife and loving mother. This tends to de-emphasize the political significance she had in the source, causing the spectators to concentrate on her suffering and on the fortitude with which she endures it. The playwright succeeds in creating a character who, while retaining her prototype's dignity in the face of her own death, sustains with composure the unbearable grief of watching the killing of her family. Heavy as the burden of her sorrow might be, it does not crush her noble and proud spirit. She dies not as a conquered victim but as a defiant heroine ever disdainful of her king's power and cruelty. This undaunted courage sets her apart from her source character and earns her a place among or above other heroines of the tragic stage of the Italian Renaissance.

Dolce's modification of source elements, besides satisfying the genre's formal requirements, serves to magnify the play's tragic conflict and to intensify the audience's cathartic experience. Admittedly, unlike the populace in the original source, the theatre public does not witness, for reasons of stage decorum, the bloody executions and the queen's anguish. It only hears Coro's moralizing comments and Nunzio's grisly and heart-rending details. However, this representation by description, a technique often used to represent what cannot or should not be shown on stage, is so graphic and stirring that it gives the spectators a virtual representation of the actual beheadings and stranglings. They can imagine the suffering and the cruelties that ultimately induce them to fear the tyrant and pity the victim. Through this same theatrical device, the playwright also recalls the wailing of those who actually saw the ghastly spectacle, prompting the spectators to partake of that sorrow and in essence guide their emotional response.

It should be recognized that the play alters the historical source only minimally and in minor ways. Most notable are the metamorphosis of the "indecent" Alexandra into a caring mother and the introduction of the new character, Consigliere. Their respective roles do not add to the story, but they do buttress the play's tragic element: Alessandra's death intensifies Marianna's grief; Consigliere's advice helps to externalize his lord's internal conflict between raging passions and sensible alternatives. With regard to Soemo, the playwright simply gives him the opportunity to defend his integrity before the king, an opportunity history had denied him. Here again, the effect of the alteration is to highlight the extent to which jealousy clouds the king's mind, preventing him from appreciating his captain's unfailing fealty. As for Erode and Marianna, Dolce does not fictionalize their personas. He simply shifts the emphasis from the impersonal perspective of history to the harrowing dramatization of their deep-seated flaws and passions: the queen's defiance and suffering, the king's jealousy and rage. The clash of their respective personalities leads to the death of the first and a life of remorse for the latter, making them both victims of their own flaws.

If Herod and Mariamme belong to a particular moment in Jewish history, Dolce's dramatization elevates them above the barriers of culture and time. Their all-too-human failings and the intense feelings that inform their actions enable them to transcend their specific culture and time and place in history. Thus, with few additions and only minor adjustments, the playwright transforms an episode of history into a human drama of grief, love, hatred, rancour, revenge, and remorse. More than a tragedy of kings and queens, *Marianna* is the tragedy of husbands and wives tortured by love and jealousy. Theirs is a drama that plays and replays on the universal stage of life. Therein lie *Marianna*'s originality and Dolce's theatrical genius.

Conclusion

All serious discussions about the Italian Renaissance theatre must begin with the classical stage of Greece and Rome. Playwrights took their inspiration from this tradition by first performing, translating, and finally imitating it. In the first phase, Italian humanists learned to appreciate the genre by studying and performing Latin plays. Their enthusiasm was soon shared by a larger section of society ever eager to attend performances or readings of classical plays in Italian translation. Audiences felt privileged to have the unique opportunity to attend stage representations of the great masters of the ancient world. Growing public interest encouraged authors to write their own plays, which they often based on plot material from the old texts. The practice led to a flurry of imitations, some of them slavish but others creative and in many ways original. A debate ensued between those calling for an original Italian theatre and those arguing that originality was a relative concept, since most things had already been said and done. For them there was nothing new under the sun ("nihil sub sole novum"). The controversy ultimately led to an understanding of originality not so much as the invention of new material but as the creative adaptation of old situations to current, living realities.

The growing consensus was that theatre should dramatize a fictional situation that spoke to contemporary audiences about themselves and their world. For the comic stage, it became acceptable to depict stories from the distant past, provided they were presented as events that took place in modern times and in familiar places. It was not unusual for playwrights to tell audiences that the story happened in a specific modern city, if not in their own. Often, they dated the plot by placing it in the context of recent cultural or historical events, such as wars or state celebrations. As for the tragic genre, it continued to draw its plot material from history and the mythical world of gods and kings. However, dramatists were quick to claim that their works were original, noting that they used old threads to weave new clothes for Lady Tragedia. Prologue in Dolce's *Medea*, for instance, informs the spectators that they are about to see an old tragedy dressed in new clothes ("con nuovi panni"). A play's originality, then, consisted in its author's poetic and theatrical ability to draw the spectators into the dramatization of themes and situations that, though borrowed from old sources, were particularly relevant to the times. Their cathartic experience issued from the representation of a fictional world that stirred realistic fears and heartfelt emotions. Whether in tragedy or comedy, playwrights imitated the classical stage with the intent to develop a theatre that was neither Greek nor Roman but their own.

The imitation of time-honoured situations such as old men in love, wily servants scamming old misers, and the demise of bloodthirsty tyrants was an accepted practice of making theatre. For comic material, playwrights relied mostly on Plautus, Terence, and even Aristophanes; for tragic stories, they looked to Aeschylus, Euripides, Sophocles, and Seneca. They also dramatized events and characters from history. Reliance on the past allowed them to claim the *auctoritas* of the ancients while rivalling them in stagecraft. The spectators took pride in their ability to recognize the classical source and in their competence to compare it with the imitation. Writers, ever eager to amaze their audiences and win their applause, did not hesitate to venture beyond the example and the poetics of the classical stage. In tragedy, in particular, they broke away from the Greek model by dividing the text into acts and scenes and by introducing a separate prologue. Seneca had already introduced some of these changes, but his example was inconsistent and rudimentary. Several of his plays were not divided into acts (*Thyestes*); others had the prologue integrated into the text (*Medea*); and yet others had no prologue at all (*Octavia*). Some playwrights went against tradition by choosing to adapt stories from fiction rather than history or myth. At times, they even dared to stage shockingly bloody scenes, challenging established Aristotelian and Horatian precepts. They also introduced tragedies with happy endings, to the acclaim of their audiences. In a deliberate rejection of Aristotle's poetics, Giraldi Cinthio defended the notion of *tragedie di lieto fine*, arguing that it was better to vex Aristotle's supporters than to displease the spectators "for whose pleasure the play is performed" ("per piacere dei quali la favola si conduce in iscena," *Discorso* 184).

Almost all playwrights produced comedies and tragedies more than twice as long as the early models in order to meet the demands of the occasion they were to help celebrate. Obviously, innovations were more common in comedy, where a less restrictive poetics accorded authors considerable flexibility. They often spoke to local audiences about their cities and social mores and wove story elements from different sources into multilayered plots. Unlike tragedy, comedy was a popular form of entertainment mostly because its histrionic nature appealed to larger audiences. Also, it was relatively inexpensive to stage and could be easily performed in convents and / or private residences. As a result, social and religious organizations as well as private individuals were eager to sponsor a motley variety of writers to display their stagecraft. With so many authors intent on creating a modern Italian theatre, the genre increasingly diverged from classical models, albeit never too far. Playwrights looked more and more to the *novellistica* for inspiration, and, in many instances, borrowed and mixed elements from both the ancient stage and the Italian *novella*.

There is no evidence to suggest that the genre developed in a systematic fashion from its rise in the early cinquecento to its demise towards the end of the century. The playwrights' individual preferences and the cultural / regional diversity informing their works preclude any attempt to determine how the erudite comedy evolved, lost its inspiration, and eventually relinquished the stage to the increasingly popular commedia dell'arte. Undoubtedly, the principal cause of its decline was its inability to keep pace with changing cultural trends and aesthetic preferences. Mid-sixteenth-century Italy felt the dogmatic sway of the Counter-Reformation, which stifled intellectual creativity by indexing books, prohibiting publications, and, in some cases, punishing daring writers. Political rulers, too, became more repressive, in part as a result of the Inquisition's demand for cooperation in enforcing church authority and in part because of the influence of Spanish rule over most of Italy. These conditions led to a culture of servility that inhibited creative freedom and encouraged intellectuals to enter the uninspiring service of the courts or the church. Thus, weary and unable to reflect upon their own reality, playwrights grew increasingly dull, re-presenting trite and conventional situations with shopworn characters. As Donald Beecher points out, "the plays were fully scripted, but they remained an assembly of identifiable parts" (*Renaissance Comedy* I.29). Anton Francesco Grazzini, commenting on the rise of improvised comedy – the early form of commedia dell'arte – imagines its characters, commonly known as *zanni*, telling audiences that neoclassical plays were so tedious that they bored not just the spectators but even the columns in the hall ("ma verrebono a noia alle colonne," *Rime* XXIX). The zanni of improvised comedy were so much in demand, he quipped, that erudite playwrights had no option but to hang themselves ("impiccarsi," *Rime* CII).

As imitation lost its creative impetus and traditional comedy became tedious, theatregoers began to prefer the lively antics and practical jokes of the roguish zanni. Audiences also favoured other escapist forms of entertainment, such as the idyllic and lyrical skits normally performed as intermezzi between acts. Grazzini wryly noted that these skits, originally introduced to embellish Comedia, became so popular that audiences tended to scoff at the representation while they waited impatiently for the "marvellous" entertainment of the intermezzi (*Rime* XX). Commenting on the general lack of interest in dramatic representations, a spectator of the1568 performance of Bombace's *Alidoro* lamented that aesthetic taste had grown so whimsical that the spectators no sooner heard the first part of a play than they looked for other, more playful forms of amusement (Ariani, *Il teatro* 2.996) A reason for this growing lack of interest was undoubtedly the genre's failure to revamp its stock characters and reflect the audience's evolving sense of entertainment. Holding fast to tradition, the comic stage continued to cast and recast characters in the same old roles until their actions and speech grew so standardized that they became predictable and consequently insipid and tiresome. Wily servants, old men in love, old misers, pedants, braggart soldiers, and parasites eventually acquired a stage life of their own. As such, they were ultimately absorbed into the masked types of the commedia dell'arte, where they morphed into the famous Arlecchino, Colombina, Tartaglia, Pantalone, Capitano, Dottore, and others.

The heavily stereotyped characters weakened the nexus between literature and spectacle that for decades had been the cornerstone of the Renaissance comic theatre. Neoclassical comedy, or *commedia regolare*, was losing its traditional structure as its comic element was becoming detached from the themes and situations it normally defined and underpinned. This rupture encouraged playwrights to promote new notions of comedy. They introduced the *comedia grave*, which combined the serious with the ridiculous, the tragic with the comic. Prologue in Sforza Oddi's *Prigione d'amore* tells the spectators that the type of comedy they are about to see is so unconventional ("stravagante") that it will cause them to cry and laugh at the same time. The new formula would gain widespread success, especially in France where years later it inspired the *comedie larmoyante*. In Italy, it helped to seal the fate of the conventional *commedia erudita*, as it uncoupled the comic element from the plot. Specifically, it undermined the classical connection between the literary and the theatrical, the story and the spectacle. Such is the case in Della Porta's *Gli duoi fratelli rivali*. Its tale has all the makings of a tragedy, though the author calls it a comedy. But there is nothing comical about an enraged father who attempts to kill his innocent daughter. Nor is it amusing to watch two brothers, swords drawn, come close to killing one another. If the play is a comedy, it is only to the extent that it features stock characters whose theatrics and verbal spats serve to distract the audience from the story's sombre themes. Its farcical scenes are, by and large, pre-constructed insets with a life of their own, meant to provide the spectacle audiences had come to expect from a comedy.

In other instances, the comic element served to turn the play's literary component on its head by undermining its traditional pretensions to realistic representation. In Groto's *Emilia*, for example, Prologue tells the audience not to believe what they are about to see, for it is all a big lie. He exposes the characters as fraudulent impersonators, noting that those claiming to be women are in fact young men, and those pretending to be old men are actually young men feigning to be old. A similar attempt to undermine the stage's credibility is found in Della Porta's *La furiosa*, where Prologue cautions the spectators not to believe what they see or hear. He declares himself embarrassed not so much by the actors' pretence as by the spectators' gullibility. Also, just as in *Gli duoi fratelli rivali*, the comic element is practically divorced from the action. The function of the comic types, then, is mostly to distract the spectators from the grim world of the stage, be it the Turkish atrocities recalled in *Emilia* or the threat of bloodshed hovering over *Gli duoi fratelli*.

Thus fractured, undermined, and repetitive, neoclassical comedy scripted its own demise. The vacuum it left was eventually filled by the increasingly popular commedia dell'arte, an art form that welcomed and exploited the histrionics, verbal virtuosity, and mannerisms of the theatrical stock types of the Renaissance stage. Based largely on the spectacle component of the traditional literature-spectacle binomial, the new commedia went on to dominate the European comic stage, especially in France and Italy. For more than a century, this form of entertainment became the choice and the expression of the times, until its mindless and crude antics drove it to its own extinction. It was with Goldoni (1707–93) that the genre regained its literature-spectacle integrity and reclaimed the comic stage of yore, albeit in a new cultural environment and in keeping with the aesthetic preferences of the day. Combining popular features of the waning commedia dell'arte with elements of Molière's stagecraft, Goldoni brought back on stage a commedia that was both literary and theatrical.

As for the tragic stage, it continued to imitate the classics and dramatize material from history, mythology, and religion. Undoubtedly, this diversified source of material inspired new generations of playwrights to produce acclaimed masterpieces. The beginning of the seventeenth century saw the biblical and historical tragedies of Federico della Valle, most notably *La reina di Scotia*, *Ester*, and *Iudit*. Carlo de' Dottori distinguished himself with his *Aristodemo* (1657), a play that Benedetto Croce called one of the major masterpieces or "capolavori" of the Italian tragic theatre (*Aristodemo*, intr.). Scipione Maffei's *Merope* (1713) received widespread acclaim both in and outside of Italy. Voltaire modelled his *Mérope* on the Italian version, and in the preface to the play's first edition he acknowledged his debt to the Italian playwright. Oliver Goldsmith called Maffei's work "the most finished tragedy in the world" (Phillimore, *The Italian Drama* 220). Towards the end of the eighteenth century, the genre found its most powerful expression in the works of Vittorio Alfieri, the greatest dramatist in the history of Italian tragedy. In his plays, he consistently dramatized his aversion to political tyranny and his fervent advocacy of freedom. No wonder he became an inspiration for the patriots of the Risorgimento, Italy's great struggle of independence. These concluding remarks would not be complete if one failed to mention that the genre embraced the *tragedia di lieto fine*, which evolved into the *melodramma*, the precursor of the operatic genre of today.

Notes

1. Imitation: The Link between Past and Present

1. Machiavelli starts *Discourses* 3.43, with this reflection: "Sogliono dire gli uomini prudenti, e non a caso né immeritamente, che chi vuole vedere quello che ha a essere, consideri quello che è stato; perché tutte le cose del mondo in ogni tempo hanno il proprio riscontro con gli antichi tempi" ("Prudent men are wont to say, not by chance or without merit, that those who wish to know what is to be should consider what has been, for all the things of the world, in every instance, have their connection with those of ancient times," *Opere* 389).
2. Accordingly, Machiavelli adds, "debbe uno uomo prudente intrare sempre per le vie battute da uomini grandi, e quelli che sono stati eccellentissimi imitare" ("a wise man must always follow the paths beaten by great men and imitate those who were most worthy," *Opere* 70).
3. For a comprehensive overview of the history of imitation, especially literary imitation, see, among others, Thomas Greene, *The Light in Troy*. On the classical theory of imitation, see George Converse Fiske, *Lucilius and Horace*, vol. 1, and J. Gannon,"Literary Imitation in Renaissance Poetic."
4. The full text of Seneca's oft-quoted metaphor is the following: "Apes, ut aiunt, debemus imitari, quae vagantur et flores ad mel faciendum idoneos carpunt, deinde quidquid attulere disponunt ac per favos digerunt et, ut Vergilius noster ait, stipant et dulci distendunt nectare cellas" ("We should follow, men say, the example of the bees, who flit about and cull the flowers that are suitable for producing honey, and then arrange and assort in their cells all that they have brought in; these bees, as our Virgil says, pack close the flowing honey, And swell their cells with nectar sweet," *Ad Lucillum epistulae morales* 2: 84.3).

5. Horace, contrasting Rome's rustic culture with the sophistication of Greek civilization writes that while Rome conquered Greece with its arms, Greece conquered rustic Rome with its arts ("Graecia capta ferum victorem cepit et artis intulit agresti Latio," *Epist.* 2.1.156).
6. Villani notes that in the late 1330s there were about five hundred young Florentines studying philosophy, but more than twice as many were studying mathematics (*Cronica* 3.12.94). Also, Aron Gurevic, focusing on the growing needs of a rapidly expanding commerce, writes that secular schools began to appear in small and big urban centres, where students learned the three Rs. Education shifted from the classical to the applied sciences, roman numerals gave way to Arabic numbers, and the zero was introduced for the first time "Gradualmente si forma la 'mentalità aritmetica' [...] l'inclinazione e il gusto per il calcolo, per la precisione, qualità non altrettanto caratteristiche del precedente periodo del Medioevo" ("Gradually an arithmetic mentality takes shape [with] an inclination and appreciation for calculus and precision, qualities not especially peculiar to the preceeding Middle Ages," 298).
7. Nancy Brown, describing the "making of books" in the late Middle Ages, quotes several copyists, usually monks, complaining about their strenuous work. One writer complained that, "these three fingers hold the pen, but the whole body aches." Another wrote, "It is excessive drudgery. It crooks your back, dims your sight, twists your stomach and sides. Pray, then, you who read this book, pray for poor Ralph" (34).
8. For an entertaining and rewarding account of Bracciolini's adventurous search of manuscripts and the impact some of these texts had on Italian humanists, see Greenblatt's *The Swerve.*
9. Garin, 32, notes that Aurispa returned in 1421. William Roscoe writes that Guarino Veronese and Francesco Filelfo visited Constantinople, and other regions of the east, with little success. Aurispa, on the other hand, was very successful and brought 238 manuscripts "amongst which were all the works of Plato, of Proclus, of Plotinus, of Lucian, of Xenophon" (1.42–3). Many other works are enumerated in one of his letters to Traversari.
10. With regard to Boccaccio's and Salutati's view of Petrarch's style, see James Hankins's "Petrarch and the Canon."
11. Noting that Cicero was not the only person who had many admirers, Petrarch recalls the evening he spent at a goldsmith's house in Bergamo and how the next day he left with "honoribus et concursu hominum pulsus" ("all sorts of honours and surrounded by a great number of supporters," *Epyst. fam.* XXI.11.13). With reference to this episode, Scaglione, 5, writes, "The visit became a street pageant and a triumph worthy of a

victorious Roman general, with officials and a throng of admiring public paying homage to him on his way to and from the house."

12. Quoted in Frazier, 17.
13. In a 1359 letter to Boccaccio, Petrarch declares that he never borrows or lifts the words of his precursors, he simply acknowledges the source and then transforms it honourably, "ut imitatione apium e multis et variis unum fiat" ("just as bees imitate by making honey from various nectars," *Epyst. fam.* XXII.2.16). For a detailed discussion of Petrarch's views on imitation, see Bosco, *Francesco Petrarca* 128–30. On the notion of imitation in the cultural and philosophical context of the Renaissance, see Ulivi, *L'imitazione nella poetica del Rinascimento.* In the Renaissance, the Senecan apian simile became a point of reference, as seen in Rucellai's *Api* (4–5); Poliziano's *Stanze* (vv 200–1); Castiglione's *Cortegiano* (1.26); Dolce's *Apologia* (2.v[r]). Castelvetro, *Poetica* (2.1.37–8) gives an informed perspective of the Renaissance concept of imitation.
14. For the debate on literary imitation among Italian humanists, see McLaughlin's *Literary Imitation,* especially pp 185–274.
15. Leonardo da Vinci writes that many pompous men of letters "vanno sgonfiati e pomposi, vestiti e ornati, non delle loro, ma delle altrui fatiche; e le mie a me medesimo non concedano; [...] non inventori, ma trombetti e recitatori delle altrui opere" ("go around full of themselves, dressed and decorated not with their own works, but those of others. They refuse to recognize and attribute to me my own works. [They are not inventors like me], but windbags and declaimers of other people's works," *Scritti,* Proemio 1).
16. For a detailed discussion, see Hans Baron, 48 *et passim*. Bruni, in his assessment of Brutus and Dante's treatment of him, paraphrases Tacitus's view that with the end of the republic, and thus the end of freedom, the brilliant minds of the past disappeared ("preclara illa ingenia, ut inquit Cornelius, abiere," *Laudatio* 19). In Tacitus's own words, "postquam bellatum apud Actium atque omnem potentiam ad unum conferri pacis interfuit, magna illa ingenia cessere" ("following the battle of Actium, and when it became critical for peace that all power be conferred on a single man, those great minds ceased to appear," *Historiae* 1.1).
17. On this issue, Jerrod E. Seigel, 10, writes that Bruni's writings should be approached as a product of a "culture which centered on rhetoric and eloquence." In his view, the proper adjective to describe Bruni's "humanism is not 'civic,' but rhetorical" (23).
18. Towards the end of the second dialogue, Donato Giannotti tells Michelangelo that he would have placed Bruto and Cassio not in the mouth of

Lucifer, as Dante did, but in the highest sphere of Paradise ("nella più honorata parte del Paradiso," 90).

19. For details, see Thomas Martin's "Michelangelo's Brutus."
20. The treatise was "rediscovered" in 1414 by the Florentine humanist Poggio Bracciolini, who found it in the Abbey of St Gallen, Switzerland. He publicized the manuscript to a receptive audience of Renaissance humanists, just as interest in the classical, cultural, and scientific heritage was growing.

    The first printed edition, an incunabula version, was published by the Veronese scholar Fra Giovanni Sulpitius in 1486 (with a second edition in 1495 or 1496). But none was illustrated. The Dominican friar Giovanni Giocondo produced the first version illustrated with woodcuts in Venice in 1511. Translations into Italian were in circulation by the 1520s, including the one with new illustrations by Cesare Cesariano.
21. Machiavelli dwells on this notion in *Discorsi* 1. Proemio, as he argues that in most emerging situations, including situations that deal with civil law, medicine, and politics, we tend to look to the examples of the ancients ("agli esempi degli antichi," *Opere* 126–7).
22. In Grazzini's *La Spiritata,* Prologue notes that in our day, actual recognition events are "impossibili e sciocchi." Also, Prologue in Luigi Groto's *Thesoro* argues that it is strange that contemporary playwrights don't know how to end a comedy without timeworn recognition scenes between relatives kidnapped during the sack of Rome, or Naples, Messina, Algiers ("sanza far, che fratelli, figli, o suoceri, / presi nel sacco di Roma, o di Napoli, / di Messina, o d'Algier si riconoscano"). Though family dispersion was, indeed, becoming a worn-out topos, there is no denying that, as Donald Beecher points out, "the Turks and their dreaded raids, especially in the south of Italy, provided the perfect mechanism for the separation of families and the loss of identities" (*Renaissance Comedy* I.25).
23. Luigina Stefani quotes from a letter Isabella wrote to her husband on 17 February 1498. The duchess asked her husband to send her some good plays because she did not like the ones she saw in Ferrara. She complains that *Bacchidi* was "longa e fastidiosa," and *Soldato glorioso* was a "fastidioso spectaculo" because of the "longheza de li versi." She liked *Asinaria* because it was not too long ("per non essere stata troppo longa," 24).
24. Reflecting on the difficulty and the need of writing creatively, Petrarch writes, "Frivolum est soli senio fidare; et qui hec invenerunt, homines erant [...] Nec nos moveat tritum illud ac vulgare, nichil novum esse vel dici posse" ("It is silly to rely only on the ancients, for the first inventors were men too [...] Nor should we concern ourselves with the trite and common view that there is nothing new to say or that remains to be said," *Epystole seniles* 2.1).

25. Aristotle never spoke of unities per se. The formulation of the so-called Aristotelian unities was developed by Renaissance critics reacting to incidental comments Aristotle makes about the time span of dramatic action. On the importance of the unities for the nascent Renaissance stage, see Russo, *La tragedia* 15.
26. Vasari, 6.442, recalls that Bastiano San Gallo used such props in his stage production of Landi's *Commondo* performed for Cosimo's wedding to Leonora of Toledo in 1539.
27. Among the things that bring "gran diletto" to the spectators, Serlio lists such things as "uno squadrone di gente, chi a piedi e chi a cavallo, le quali con alcune voci o gridi sordi, strepiti di tamburri e suono di trombe, pascono molto gli spettatori" ("a troop of people running, some on foot others on horseback, who, with the sound of voices or muffled screams and the uproar of drums and trumpets, delight the spectators," 204).
28. On this subject, John Storey, 60, observes, "The relationship between text and audience is a productive one. A text does not carry its own meaning or politics already inside of itself; no text is able to guarantee what its effects will be. People are constantly struggling, not merely to figure out what a text means, but to make it mean something that connects to their own lives, experiences, needs and desires. The same text will mean different things to different people, depending on how it is interpreted."
29. In a marginal note to his "Discorso," Giraldi underscores the teaching effectiveness of theatre over prose writings. He points out that the playwright often treats the same topics as the philosopher, but "per l'artificio ch'egli usa, giova e diletta e porge utile non pure a coloro che son capaci di conoscere i sentimenti ascosi sotto le finzioni, ma anco agli altri che non sono cosí atti alla profonda intelligenza" ("through the use of his stagecraft, he delights and teaches not only those capable of perceiving hidden meaning, but also those less intellectually gifted," 275, n48).
30. Of course, not everyone subscribed to the poetics of verisimilitude. Cervantes' Cura inveighs against the many *comedias* that in the first scene introduce a character as a teenager who in the second scene reappears as a bearded adult ("hombre barbado"). In his long tirade against unrealistic representation, the clergyman laments that in too many plays the action starts in Europe, moves to Asia, travels to Africa, and finally ends in America (*Don Quixote de la Mancha* 1.48.570).
31. "non posso, se non col la
Stampa sodisfare à tanti che ogni giorno
Da diverse parti mi ricercano di copia, la
Quale spero, quanto più sarà letta debba esser lodata."

[I cannot, if not by having it / printed, satisfy so many who every day / from various regions ask me for a copy / which, I hope, the more is read the more it will be praised.]

32. For more examples, see Donatella Riposio's *Nova comedia,* especially pp 19–28.

2. Machiavelli's *Mandragola*

1. For a detailed discussion on the date of composition, see Sergio Bertelli, and Sara Mamone.
2. Giovio's comment is cited in Mamone, 189. With reference to the 1522 Venetian performance, Sanudo wrote that there was "assaissima zente con intermedii di Zuan Pollo e altri bufoni, e la scena era si' piena di zente, che non fu fato il quinto atto, perché non si poté farlo, tanto era il gran numero di persone" ("a huge crowd. The intermezzi were performed by Zuan Pollo and other clowns. The hall was so crowded that it was not possible to go on with the entire performance," *Diarii* XXXII, Venice 1892, p. 458). For the English text of Sanudo's entire testimony, see Linda Carroll's translation in Patricia Labalme's edition of the *Diarii,* p. 492. Also with regard to the immediate success and popularity of *Mandragola,* Giovanni Manetti wrote to Machiavelli (28 February 1526) that the play was performed in Venice the same night as Plautus's *Menaechmi.* He adds that the Roman comedy, though beautiful and well recited, was considered a "cosa morta" compared to *Mandragola* (*Machiavelli:Lettere* 452).
3. According to Richard Andrews, 51, the play was printed three times during the 1520s, and by 1630 there were at least fifteen editions. As for the growing reputation of its literary quality in more recent times, Vincenzo De Amicis, *L'imitazione* 176, considered *Mandragola* the most perfect comedy in the Renaissance. He said it was the best play ever written up to that time and that, according to Voltaire, it was better than all of Aristophanes' comedies. Borsellino, *Rozzi e intronati* 72, notes that *Mandragola* inaugurates the great season of Florentine comedy.
4. See Luigi Vanossi, *Lingua e strutture* 11, and Borsellino, ed., *Commedie del Cinquecento* 88. For an extensive discussion of possible minor sources, see Ezio Raimondi, *Politica e commedia* 173–97, and Davico Bonino, *Niccolò Machiavelli. Teatro* xiv.
5. All page references to Boccaccio's *Decameron* are to Carlo Salinari's edition.
6. For the debate on verisimilitude in Renaissance Italy, see Marvin Carlson, *Theories of the Theater,* especially 39–56.

7. Carmela Pesca, 53, argues that the play would not be the same and the characters would be out of place if the action took place anywhere other than in Florence.
8. Sara Mamone, 191, writes that in the early sixteenth century "la sintesi tra visione prospettica e drammaturgia restituita troverà la strada del palcoscenico. La *Mandragola* sarà proprio uno degli episodi precoci di questa sintesi" ("the synthesis between perspective and the theatrical representation soon finds its way onto the stage. *Mandragola* is one of the earlier examples of this synthesis").
9. All references to Machiavelli's *Mandragola* are to Sices' and Atkinson's bilingual edition.
10. On the church's sanction of Lucrezia's adultery, see Di Maria, "The Ethical Premises."
11. Storey, 60, notes that spatial unity "serves to centralize the location of the action and to reduce the need for messengers to describe events that took place away from the scenic space. The use of verbal representation takes away from the stage and returns the events to a narrative form, robbing the stage of its most important function, that of representing rather than referring."
12. Richard Andrews, 53–4, believes that "what has been practiced on her is effectively rape," and that, unlike Livy's Lucretia, she "accepts her rape and succumbs." For Giulio Ferroni, 80, Lucrezia is a symbolic model of the "shrewd" ("savio") Machiavellian. Yael Manes, 33, echoing Ferroni's view, writes: "Lucrezia appears to be the perfect model of political behavior; she is the sage who is active and adaptive in the face of fortune; she is the one who truly possesses virtù in *La mandragola*." Borsellino observes that Lucrezia redeems her condition of the unhappily married woman with Machiavellian *virtù* (*Commedie* xxvi). Roberto Alonge, 258, argues that Lucrezia dupes her husband and her lover so that she can count on two husbands, not only for sexual pleasures but also for the certainty of having children or, in his words, "figliare abbondantemente."
13. Besides calling it "una notte getsemanica," Alonge, 253, writes that, like Christ, "anche Lucrezia vuole che il calice sia allontanato da lei. L'angoscia di Lucrezia per cio' che deve accadere e' la stessa angoscia del Cristo alla vigilia del Calvario" ("Lucrezia, too, wants the chalice to be moved away from her. Lucrezia's anguish for what must happen is the same anguish as that of Christ on the eve of Calvary").
14. For a discussion of this political allegory, see Antonio Sorella, 17–19.
15. Borsellino defines Ligurio as a "consigliere fraudolento piú per intima vocazione che per desiderio di un utile immediato" ("fraudulent adviser

driven more out of a natural tendency than by the desire of some immediate gain," *Commedie* xxvi).

16. In his edition of Machiavelli's *Lettere,* Gaeta notes that the Gonfalonier Soderini managed to have Machiavelli elected to head the Florentine mission to the emperor, but Soderini's political enemies succeeded in reversing the selection and sent Vettori instead (181, n16). Commenting on this episode, J.R. Hale, 102, writes that while Machiavelli was making preparations to leave for the mission "there were complaints from Soderini's opponents. Why should he [Soderini] send one of 'his' men, a departmental official, when there were young *uomini da bene,* the very group from whom future ambassadors should be chosen for training, standing idle?"
17. Viroli, 98. Also, Machiavelli's friends, such as Filippo Casavecchia and Alessandro Nasi, in their respective letters dated 30 July of that year, comforted him following his deep disillusionment and humiliation surrounding this episode.
18. In a letter to Francesco Guicciardini (16–20 October 1525), Machiavelli speaks of Nicia's simple-mindedness or " 'la simplicità' di Messer Nicia" (*Lettere* 438). Also, Prologue introduces Nicia as a lawyer schooled on "Bogusius" or Buezio (meaning Boethius), whereby the play on the word "bue" (ox) implies, as Giannetti and Ruggiero point out, "that this lawyer is both a fool (bogus) and a cuckold (wearing horns)," 73, n7.
19. On the vulgarity of Nicia's language, see Borsellino, "Per una storia" 232, and Giorgio Cavallini, *Interpretazione* 7–20.
20. Crowley, 153, reports Jacopo de Campi's detailed description of impalement as applied by the Turks during their 1453 siege of Constantinople.
21. Alonge, 243, noting that this woman raises the issue of sex and wealth, argues that she represents, with Sostrata and Nicia, a bourgeois society "alle prese con i propri desideri, che ruotano sempre intorno all'orizzonte del sesso, del piacere, del denaro" ("concerned with its desires, which tend to rotate around sex, pleasure, and money").
22. The presence of depraved clergymen within the religious community continued well after the Council of Trent called for the establishment of seminaries in order to better prepare young men for the priesthood. Dava Sobel, 129–30, writes that Suor Maria Celeste Galilei, the daughter of Galileo Galilei, complained repeatedly about the unscrupulous confessors assigned to her convent. In a letter to her father, the young nun complains that the friars go around gossiping about the nuns to the point that "our convent is considered the concubine of the whole Casentino region, whence come these confessors of ours, more suited to hunting rabbits than guiding our souls." She also charged that the confessors served only their

own interests, and that "the more they could wring out of us, the more skillful they considered themselves."

23. In *Discourses* 1.11–15, Machiavelli discusses the political instrumentation of religion and gives several examples to illustrate how ancient societies used religion according to their needs or "secondo la necessità." For a discussion of this notion, see Alberto Tenenti, "La religione di Machiavelli."
24. Victoria Khan, 204. The view of Machiavelli as "irreligious" dates back to Reginald Pole's belief that *The Prince* was written by Satan and that its teachings expressed the kingdom of the Antichrist. For a balanced view on the subject, see De Grazia's *Machiavelli in Hell*, especially 30–56.
25. Upon Cosimo's death in 1574, his son and successor, Grand Duke Francesco I, ordered Camilla cloistered in the convent of Murate and later in Santa Monica. She was allowed to leave the convent only in 1586 to attend her daughter's wedding.
26. She appears in 3.1,10,11 and 5.5,6. In general she has no more than two or three short lines in each scene.
27. Cited in O'Faolain and Martines, 181.
28. Francesca Malara, 222, comparing *Clizia* to *Mandragola*, writes that the latter represents the arduous process by which one comes to the founding of a household and the guarantee of its survival. Also, Harvey Mansfield, 28, noting that a succession problem may affect any family, writes that Machiavelli's general advice is to find a remedy regardless of its morality. *Mandragola*, he concludes, is part of Machiavelli's "campaign for a 'perpetual republic.' "

3. *Clizia*: From Stage to Stage

1. In his letter of 22 February 1525, Neri writes: "La fama della vostra commedia é volata per tutto; et non crediate che io habbia havuto queste cose per lettere di amici, ma l'ho havuto da viandanti che per tutto [sic] la strada vanno predicando le gloriose pompe e fieri ludi" ("The enthusiastic reception of your comedy has spread all over the place. Please don't think that I heard about it through letters from our friends, but from travellers who are going around town proclaiming its great choreography and entertaining situations," Machiavelli, *Lettere* 418)
2. Beatrice Corrigan, 77–8, counts at least seven Renaissance imitations of Plautus's *Casina*, including Machiavelli's *Clizia* (1525), Berardo's *La Cassina* (1530), Dolce's *Il ragazzo* (1541), Cecchi's *I rivali (1556)*, Lanci's *La Ruchetta* (1584), Della Porta's *La fantesca* (c. 1592), and the anonymous *Il capriccio*. This last one was written, she suggests, by a member of the Accademia

degli Intronati around 1566–8. In 1999, Michael Lettieri and Giulio Molinari edited *Il capriccio* and called it a very important remake ("un importantissimo rifacimento") of Plautus's *Casina* (8). As for plays that borrowed plot elements from *Casina*, one must include Bibbiena's *La Calandria*, Gelli's *L'errore*, Strozzi's *Commedia in versi*, and Giannotti's *Il vecchio amoroso*.

3. Marvin Herrick, *Italian Comedy*, 79, notes that "*Clizia* closely followed the original *Casina* of Plautus in plot and characters, even in dialogue, but Machiavelli improved upon the Roman playwright in economy and managed to make his play seem to be a slice of Florentine life." Beatrice Corrigan, 79, compares *Clizia* to its Latin source and observes that "practically no change has been made in the plot development, but by skilful light use of local color, and a summary of recent history rather in the style of *Il Principe*, Machiavelli has given a genuine Florentine flavor to a Greco-Roman comedy." Carmela Pesca, 62, while noting a sense of seriousness, which is lacking in the Latin source, calls *Clizia* a rewriting ("una riscrittura) of Plautus's *Casina*. Borsellino, *Commedie* xxvi, labels it "un ricalco umanistico della *Casina*" ("a humanistic retracing of *Casina*"). Luigi Russo, *Commedie* 159, laments that scholars dismissed it "col pretesto che essa era un'imitazione e una riduzione della *Casina* di Plauto" ("on the pretext that it was an imitation and a reduction of Plautus's *Casina*"). Richard Andrews, 55, suggests that Machiavelli's infatuation with Barbara Raffacani Salutati, who sang the madrigals in the first performance, "gives a personal twist to the plot of *Clizia*, which otherwise would appear as a reworking of Plautus' *Casina*."
4. Unless noted otherwise, all translations of *Clizia* are taken from Sices' and Atkinson's bilingual edition.
5. Plautus makes no secret of the fact that *Casina* is a close imitation of the no-longer-extant Greek comedy *Kleroumenoi* or *The Lot-Drawers* (332–20 BCE) by Diphilus of Sinope. In the words of Prologue, *Kleroumenoi* and later *Sortientes*

   were titles fit for ancient audiences
   of Greeks and Romans – hardly your condition –
   say *The Lot-Drawers, or The Used Sortition.*
   To Athens Greek Diphilus first brought it,
   then Plautus wrote it out again, for plaudits.

   Unless otherwise specified, all quotations are from James Tatum's translation.
6. For a comparison of the two versions, see Vanossi, 62–96.
7. Sices and Atkinson translate Prologue's warning to the audience "non aspettare di riconoscere o il casato o gli uomini" as "do not expect to recognize either the household or the people." Since "household" and "people"

could be construed as the same thing, I believe that it makes more sense to consider "casato" synonymous with "caseggiato" or "houses." From this perspective, I consider more appropriate Oliver Evans's translation, "don't expect to recognize the house and the people." With regard to a playwright's fear of being maligned or cited for libel, Prologue in Grazzini's *Il frate* refuses to disclose the real names of the characters "per non essere tenuto lingua trista" ("for fear of being labelled an evil tongue.")

8. Cleandro appears in nine scenes, including three soliloquies. There are thirty-four scenes in the play; Sofronia appears in twelve of them, Nicomaco in twenty, Pirro in five, and Eustachio in six.
9. Quotations from the Latin text are from Friedrich Leo's 1895 edition.
10. On the question of homosexual tendencies and behaviour in Roman comedy, see Jane M. Cody, "The *senex amator* in Plautus' *Casina*," in *Hermes*, 104, 4 (1976): 253–76.
11. Although this section of the Latin text is somewhat mutilated, and of Myrrhina's original line we only have the phrase "perlepide narrat * * *" (5.4.997), the context supports James Tatum's free translation: "He's telling it all so charmingly, just as charmingly as can be, and the joke's on him."
12. Speaking of Cleostrata's victory, Moore, 180, writes, "Like the worst stereotypes of women not sufficiently controlled by men – wives with big dowries, matronae who protested against the lex Oppia, women involved in Bacchanalia – Cleostrata gains complete power over her husband."
13. This concern for the spectator becomes commonplace in the comedy of the Italian Renaissance. See, for instance, *Gli ingannti* by the Accademici Intronati di Siena. But, whereas in the Italian comedies the concern is justified because most plays are very long, often twice as long as their Latin models, in Plautus's works, including *Casina*, there is no justification, since they tend to be relatively short.
14. Vanossi, 73, calls her "esempio di religiosità e di incorrotto senso morale." Malara, too, believes that Sofronia is truly a moral and religious woman, and not a passive bigot: "una donna moralmente e religiosamente consapevole, convinta, non una passiva bigotta" (217).
15. Faulkner, 41, argues that "we find a domestic reconstitution with the knowing wife now completely in charge." Malara, 239, notes that *Clizia*, like *Mandragola*, "si chiude su un'altra immagine di donna forte, padrona non solo del proprio destino ma del destino di tutta la sua casata" ("concludes with another image of a strong woman, mistress not only of her own destiny, but also of the entire household"). Manes, 64, observes that Sofronia "does not simply wield power; she actually obtains legitimate

auctoritas to rule the household. She replaces the paterfamilias and becomes the materfamilias."

16. For more details on the relationship between Nicomaco and Sofronia, see Di Maria's *Nicomaco and Sofronia*.
17. Ezio Raimondi, 230–3, also believes that the play concludes with an actual return to the *status quo ante* of the family hierarchy.
18. Luigi Russo writes that Machiavelli, though nearing sixty years of age, still fancied erotic fantasies. With reference to a letter Machiavelli wrote to Lorenzo dei Medici, Russo notes that Niccolò "si diltettava pur sempre che 'fusse nelle cose veneree maravigliosamente involto" ("always delighted in being involved in things that were sensual," *Commedie* 160).
19. Most readers acknowledge this onomastic instance, which Ronald Martinez aptly calls the "stitching together of portions of the author's first and last names" (123).
20. Besides Strozzi's letter, see the letters from Guicciardini (August 1525) and Jacopo di Filippo Falconetti (5 August 1526). See, also Ferroni 109.
21. Guido Davico Bonino, lxviii, expanding on the political dimensions of the parallel Nicomaco/Machiavelli, points out that following the 1522 conspiracy against Cardinal de' Medici, Machiavelli realized that "aveva netta la coscienza d'essere ormai un intellettuale tagliato fuori dalla trama attiva della politica" ("he had become an intellectual cut off from the active life of politics").
22. Sanesi, *La commedia* 217, complains that Machiavelli should not have reduced himself to a simple "imitatore o riduttore." Giuseppe Toffanin, 439, opined that the author treated Plautus's plot just as a "traduttore" would: "C'é qualche zambillo di quel suo spirito sardonico: ma é troppo chiaro che egli si riposa sulla sua trama come un traduttore" ("There are traces of his [Machiavelli's] sardonic spirit [in Clizia], but it is too obvious that he sits on the plot just like a translator"). These and similar views conditioned scholarly criticism for a long time. Only of late have scholars begun to recognize the play's merits.

4. Cecchi's *Assiuolo*: An Apian Imitation

1. For a list and a discussion of Cecchi's plays, see Fortunato Rizzi, *Le commedie osservate*.
2. Grazzini writes,

   A giudizio del popol fiorentino
   e delle donne, che più pesa e grava,
   il Cecchi ha vinto e superato il Cino,

che prima era un poeta a scaccafava;
or, come avesse spirito divino,
se ne va altero e sgonfia e sbuffa e brava,
dato avendo al Buonanni anco la stretta,
e il Lasca sguizza e Frosino sgambetta. (*Rime burlesche* XCII, p. 422)
[In the judgment of the Florentine people, / and that of the women, which weighs and / counts much more, / Cecchi has beaten and surpassed Cino / who used to be a highly acclaimed poet. / Now, as if possessing a divine quality, / he [Cecchi] goes about holding his head high, boasting and gloating, / having given Buonnami a big squeeze. / In the meantime, Lasca slips away while Frosino scampers.]

3. For Sanesi, *La commedia* 325, *Assiuolo* may not be the best comedy of the Italian Renaissance, but it is definitely "uno dei migliori frutti che il teatro comico del sec. XVI abbia prodotto in Italia." Scoti-Bertinelli, 154, called *Assiuolo* Cecchi's "testamento artistico."
4. For the critical fortunes of *Assiuolo*, see Eisenbichler's introduction to his translation of the play. Recently, the Nabu or BiblioBazaar Press reproduced in paperback Milanesi's 1923 edition of Cecchi's plays. In 1996, the Center for Reformation and Renaissance Studies published Bruno Ferraro's translation of *La stiava* (*The Slave Girl*). Donald Beecher included Eisenbichler's translation of *Assiuolo* in his 2009 collection of Renaissance comedies.
5. *Assiuolo*, prologue. All quotations are from Borsellino's edition, vol.1.
6. In the introduction to *Le cene* 1.48, one of the narrators explains that the *Centonovelle* he is carrying contains "le favole di Messer Giovanni Boccaccio, anzi di San Giovanni Boccadoro" ("the tales of Messer Giovanni Boccaccio or, I should say, Saint Giovanni Golden tongue"). Speaking of Boccaccio's popularity, Mario Baratto, 93, points out that in the first half of the *cinquecento* the *Decameron* was well known in all cultural circles, including the less literate ("divulgato in tutti gli ambienti culturali, anche medi").
7. "Chiù, chiù" is a distortion of the Spanish "Quièn es allà?" used during the 1532 Spanish occupation of Florence. Ambrogio tells Giannella that the password "Chies aglià," was used "nel '32 la notte per Firenze" (3.5).
8. For a detailed discussion of this hero concept, see Di Maria's "Structure of the Early Form of the 'Beffa,' " and "Fortune and the 'Beffa' in Bandello's *Novelle*."
9. The translation is from Eisenbichler. The original reads, "Per la gelosia mi sono tolti gli spassi di fuori, e per la vecchiezza quelli di casa" (4.3).
10. Quotations from the *Decameron* are from Salinari's edition.

11. Renaissance audiences were very familiar with Plautus's *Casina*, as most playwrights borrowed freely and openly from its characters, situations, and themes. For details, see *Clizia*, n2.
12. Incidentally, "gagliardo" (strong and spirited) was also a type of dance. Caroline Murphy, 190, reports that on 22 April 1569, Isabella de' Medici danced a "gagliardo" with the Archduke of Austria.
13. Giorgetto's prediction (4.6) recalls Ariosto's tale of the jealous painter Galasso (*Satire* 5, vv 298–328). As the story goes, the devil appeared to the painter in a dream and gave him a ring to keep on his finger as a sure guarantee against his wife's infidelity. The anecdote is an expanded version of Poggio Bracciolini's "Visione di Francesco Filelfo" (*Facezie* 132, p. 115).
14. For Nicia's homosexuality see the related discussion in chapter II. As for Giannella's homosexuality, Ambrogio declares that he would trust nobody but Giannella to guard his wife's chastity: "Chi ha bella moglie, come ho io," he opines in a short soliloquy, "bisogna che se n'abbia cura da sé, e massime in Pisa, dove sono scolari giovani spensierati [...]; e non la fidi né a serve, né a famigli [...]; quantunque io credo, che di Giannella me ne potrei fidare" ("Those who have beautiful wives, like me, must be watchful, especially in Pisa, where there are many young and care-free students [...] never entrust her to the care of maids or servants [...] although I believe I can trust Giannella," 2.1).
15. With regard to the perception that homosexuality was a threat to Florence's population growth, Richard C. Trexler, 2.34, notes that the prologue to the establishment of the Ufficiali della Notte (1432) warned that "unless homosexuality was repressed the city was threatened with godly extinction." See also my "The Ethical Premises," 32.
16. Anfrosina's wish to avoid a scandal is reminiscent of Sofronia's need to trick her husband in order to bring him back to his senses ("al segno," *Clizia*, 5.3).
17. Moschino, in his dialogue with Tribolo and Ridolfo del Grillandaio, recalls how *Mandragola* and *Assiuolo* were performed together, alternating their respective acts. Moschino believes that there had never been such a great feat and does not think one can write better comedies than these two "jewels." As for the authors, he marvels: "What great minds!" Here is a sample of the dialogue:

    "Moschino: Per la fede mia che in Fiorenza non fu fatto mai sí bel trovato: due scene, una da una parte della sala e l'altra dall'altra; due prospettive mirabili, una di mano di Francesco Salviati, l'altra del Bronzino; due comedie piacevolissime e di nuova invenzione; la Mandragola e l'Assiuolo: fatto che era il primo atto di questa, seguitava l'atto di quella, sempre accompagnandosi l'una l'altra, senza intermedii, in modo che una comedia era intermedio dell'altra. Solamente al principio cominciò la musica e al fine finí. Io non credo che si possi far meglio di queste due comediette; le sono una gioia. Il Machiavello e Giovan Maria mi posson comandare. Oh che belli intelletti! Mi piace quei passi tratti del Boccaccio sí destramente; perché, alla fine, il comporre è un filo che esce d'una matassa filata di diversi lini in piú gugliate." (I. Rag. 4, p. 29)

[I swear that in Florence there was never so beautiful a performance: two stages, one on one side of the hall and the other on the other side. Two marvellous perspectives one created by the hand of Francesco Salviati, the other by Bronzino. Two most entertaining and original comedies: *Mandragola* and *Assiuolo*. Each act of the first (comedy) was followed by the performance of one from the other, alternating one and the other, without intermezzi. In such a way that each play served as intermezzo to the other. The spectacle began and ended with music. I do not believe that one can do better than these two delightful plays: they are a jewel. Machiavelli and Giovan Maria [Cecchi] have won me over. Oh, what outstanding minds! I like those passages skilfully borrowed from Boccaccio, for, in the end, a composition is but a thread that comes out of a skein of various strands spun in needlefuls.]

18. And on p. 334, Ubersfeld writes, "L'univers fictionnel posé en face du spectateur convoque l'univers référentiel du spectateur, celui de son expérience vecué, comme de son expérience culturelle. Si le spectateur s'écrie: 'C'est comme cela, c'est cela que j'ai vu et vecu!' ce n'est pas seulement que le spectacle convoque sa mémoire, ses souvenirs, c'est un cri de joie, c'est la trace du plaisir de reconnaître justement ce qui a été vu et vecu" ("The fictional universe placed before the spectator evoques the referential world of his lived experience as well as that of his cultural experience. If the spectator exclaims: 'It's just like that, it's that [world] which I have seen and lived,' it is not only that the spectacle stirs his memory, his memories, for it is also an exclamation of joy. It is a sign of the pleasure one derives from recognizing that which he has truly seen and lived").
19. In his *Della vita civile* (c. 1438), Palmieri also advised that a woman should not only be chaste but should avoid any appearance of unchastity (Palmieri 133).
20. On the Medici's indifference to public opinion regarding their extramarital affairs, see Caroline Murphy's well-documented historical account of Isabella's life. Speaking of Isabella's adulterous relationship with her husband's cousin Troilo Orsini, Murphy observes that the affair, though

clandestine, was not a secret, and that "word spread to even the darkest corners that the line of influence in Florence ran from Troilo to Isabella" (176).

21. Arditi, 57, laments that Florence had become a city full of assassins and that "ogni notte si sentiva feriti e morti e altri vari e brutti casi" ("every night there were instances of people being wounded or murdered and many other criminal activities"). From April 1574 to July 1575, he adds, 186 people were killed or wounded.
22. De Amicis, 94, writes that "il gusto del secolo prediligeva le commedie licenziose [...] le commedie più originali e migliori sotto l'aspetto letterario sono le più immorali, appunto perché più fedelmente ci rappresentano i costumi contemporanei" ("the taste of the times preferred licentious comedies [....] The best and most original comedies from the literary point of view are the immoral ones exactly because they represent faithfully contemporary customs").
23. Camerini, *Nuovi profili* 3.25, observes that "quando la società é splendida più che gentile, raffinata più che veramente civile, la commedia corre alle arti più grossolane e indecenti, e lusinga le tendenze più basse e brutali dell'umana natura" ("when a society is more splendid than cultured, more superficially refined than truly civil, comedy descends to the most gross and indecent means. It also tends to appeal to the lowest and crudest tendencies of human nature")
24. Rizzi, 112, writes: "l'indugio sull'osceno da parte del Cecchi rivela quanto fosse avvilito a que' tempi il senso morale nel pubblico e nella società" ("Cecchi's indulgence with the obscene reveals how debased was society's sense of morality").
25. Terpening, 66, notes that the immorality of many Renaissance comedies "illustrates the life of the times," in that "they are a reflection of a century that delighted in scandal."
26. Donatus, 1.22.5, commenting on the role of comedy, writes: "comoediam esse Cicero ait imitationen vitae, speculum consuetudinis, imaginem veritatis" ("comedy is, says Cicero, imitation of life, mirror of costumes, and image of truth"). Actually, Cicero never said this, he simply mentioned the role of comedy in chastising wicked agitators and seditionsists, ("populares hominess improbos, in re publica seditiosos," *De republica* 4.X).

5. Groto's *Emilia*: Fiction Meets Reality

1. These dates are on Groto's dedicatory letters prefaced to the respective texts.
2. Sanesi, *La commedia* 265, writes that "*l'Emilia*, quantunque derivi dall'*Epidicus* di Plauto, di cui riproduce con più amplio svolgimento la favola, e sia per ciò, nell'invenzione, meno originale di esse le superi

entrambe per ricchezza di facezie, per ingegnosità di burle e per vivacità di dialogo" ("though *Emilia* derives from Plautus's *Epidicus*, of which it reproduces the story rather loosely, and is therefore less original than the other two, it surpasses them both for its numerous gags, ingenious jokes, and vivacious dialogue"). Daniela Coletto, 366, speaking of Groto's comic language, notes that *Emilia* is perhaps the best of the other two comedies, and if it is not the best, it is certainly "quella che risponde ai canoni, più ricorrenti e accettabili, di organicità, di unità, di relativa armonia" ("the one that best reflects the prevailing norms of unity and harmony").

3. Giovanni Benvenuti, 127, notes that Emilia Casalini, Groto's relative, was a noble woman of great intellectual talent ("di raro talento"), known especially for her knowledge of Greek and Latin. On this subject, see also Giuseppe Groto, 122.
4. The title page of the 1579 Ziletti printing states that *Emilia* was performed in Hadria, on 1 March 1579, under the government of his most illustrious lordship Lorenzo Rimondo. This corresponds to the date Groto gives in his dedicatory letter dated 16 August 1579. In the same letter, he proudly writes that Lord Rimondo "mi commise, che io formassi una Comedia, la qual fosse la prima ad apparir nel Theatro, che si veniva tutta via apparecchiando" ("commissioned me to write a Comedy that would be the first to be performed in the Theatre being built at the time").
5. In Groto's words, the play was performed "con gran frequenza di Popolo, e con molta Gloria de recitanti, che honoraron se stessi, l'opra, & l'Autore" ("in front of a large audience and with much acclaim for the actors, who did great honour to themselves and the author," Dedicatory letter).
6. Regarding the spreading of distorted versions of the manuscript, he recalls that many actors came to him and "protestarono, che io mi risolvessi con qualche mia correttione à stamparla prima, ch'eglino ne desser fuori à penna le copie, che per avventura mal corrette si spargerebbono" ("insisted that I make the necessary corrections and have it printed before they [the actors] divulged their versions full of errors," Dedicatory letter).
7. Ariosto, for instance, in his prose version of the *Cassaria* complained that his original text had fallen prey to unscrupulous printers who mangled it ("laceraronla") and sold it in shops and public markets. Also, Lelio Gavardo Asolano, in dedicating the 1590 performance of Sforza Oddi's *Prigione d'amore* to Galeazzo Paleotto, wrote that so many people were asking for a copy of the play that he could only satisfy the demand by having the text mass printed: "only through printed copies can I satisfy the many requests of those that from various areas are asking for a copy: the more it is read, the more it is appreciated." For the Italian text, see chapter I, n31.

8. All quotations are from the 1579 Ziletti edition.
9. For the Latin version of *Epidicus*, I cite from F. Leo's edition (The Latin Library, http://www.thelatinlibrary.com/).
10. I use Constance Carrier's translation from the Slavitt and Bovie edition.
11. Hopkins, 82, writes that following the fall of Nicosia (September 1570), the Turks went on a rampage that resulted in the "massacre of between 16,000 and 20,000 inhabitants, and the sacking and pillaging of all the houses and businesses left untouched by the siege. Only attractive young men and women were spared from the slaughter, and they were sent to the slave markets in Constantinople." After the defeat of Lepanto (October 1571), Hopkins continues, the Sultan "gave vent to his awesome temper, demanding that every Spaniard and Venetian [...] in Constantinople be arrested and executed within the next two days." Fortunately, Selim was persuaded to rescind his orders (168).
12. Ibid., 98–9. The commander of the Ottoman forces, Lala Mustapha, had Bragadin "flayed alive, his skin stuffed and further subjected to abasements, such as being hanged from the yardarm" of a ship. Ottoman soldiers were encouraged to throw garbage and excrement at the chained Bragadin and pull his hairs from his beard. Mustapha himself came out "to spit on the Venetian, and to empty his chamber pot over the old man's head." Some believe that Bragadin's flaying might have inspired Titian's *The Flaying of Marsyas* (1575). Turkish cruelty had a long and notorious history, especially during Mehmet's sultanate. Roger Crowley, 341, writes that upon the fall of Negroponte (1470), the bloodthirsty Mehmet not only put to the sword hundreds of locals, including women and children, he also had the Venetian *bailo*, Paolo Erizzo, "sandwiched between planks and sawn in half." To be sure, war atrocities were not practised only by the Turks. Crowley, 370, tells that in 1500 when Benedetto Pesaro, the Republic's captain-general of the sea, captured the Turkish pirate Erichi, "he roasted him alive."
13. Sanesi, *La commedia* 267, writes that "I grandi nomi e le grandi gesta della Serenissima, che il gramo poeta rievocò sulla scena, spensero certo sulle labbra degli spettatori il sorriso ma accesero nelle loro anime un'ardente fiamma di entusiasmo e li fecer vibrare di altera e austera commozione" ("the famous names and the great gesta of the Serenissima, which the wretched poet recalled on the scene, certainly wiped the smile off the lips of the spectators, but ignited a burning flame in their hearts and made them shake with proud and stern commotion"). Marina Calore, 309, on the other hand, plays down the emotional impact of the defeat of Cyprus, noting that it was no longer a recent event in the minds of the Venetians ("non troppo d'attualità ormai nel 1579"). Calore does not take into account that in Venice, the battle of Lepanto and the loss of Cyprus

were commemorated every year. John Julius Norwich, 227–8, speaking of Lepanto and all the events that led to it, notes that "from 1572 to the fall of the Republic that day [18 October, St Justina's day and the day Venice learned of the Fall of Lepanto] was annually celebrated with a procession by the Doge and Signoria to the church of that same fortunate patron [St Justina] outside which the captured Turkish standards were displayed to the populace."

14. The length of the performance is not mentioned in *Emilia*. But in *Alteria*, Prologue tells the audience that they will be entertained for three to four hours. In *Thesoro*, Prologue asks chatty women to keep quiet for the length of the performance – that is, three to four hours. Of course, tragedies lasted much longer, mostly because of the stately fanfare that normally accompanied their performance. For details, see Di Maria's *Italian Tragedy* 37–46.
15. In *Thesoro*, Prologue chastises those playwrights who conclude their plays with the usual recognition scenes of long-lost relatives:

    Una gran cosa per certo che i [...] comici
    [non] sappian mettere il fine a una Comedia
    senza far, che fratelli, figli, ò suoceri
    presi nel sacco di Roma, ò Napoli,
    di Messina, o d'Algier si riconoscano.

    [It is certainly an amazing thing that [....] comedy writers / [don't] know how to end a Comedy / without making sure that brothers, sons, or in-laws, / kidnapped during the sack of Rome or Naples / of Messina or Algiers, are finally reunited.]
16. For a full account of the Venetians' conquest of Constantinople, see Roger Crowley's *City of Fortune*, especially chapter 5, "At the Walls," 61–80.
17. The playwright can be very specific about the action's location when he wishes to do so. In *Alteria*, for instance, Prologue reminds the spectators that the city they behold on stage is their Hadria. They should easily recognize its landmarks:

    Vedete l'hosterie, le café, i portici,
    Le loggie, le botteghe, e le torri. Eccovi
    In quel canto il Palagio del Clarissimo
    Podestà [...].

    [You can see the inns, the cafes, the porticos, / the loggias, the shops, and the towers. There it is, / in that corner there, the palace of his Excellency, / the Podestà.]
18. In *Alteria*, Prologue tells the audience that he is a Nigromante and that for the performance he has turned young men into old men and men into women. In this particular case, I believe, there is no intent to subvert

theatre's pretence of realism, but simply a reminder to the audience that what they behold is a fictional world.

19. A similar attempt to undermine the presentation's credibility is found in the prologue of Della Porta's *La furiosa*. Here, Prologue cautions the spectators not to believe what they see or hear on stage. He warns them that the women on stage are actually men pretending to be women and that the old men are young men pretending to be old. He declares, "io non tanto mi vergogno della loro vergogna, quanto della vostra pazzia, che l'ascoltate" ("I am embarrassed not so much by their [the actors'] shameful pretence, but by your [the spectators'] foolish gullibility").
20. Nicola Mancini, 128, notes that two tragedies, Vincenzo Giusti's *Irene* (Venezia 1579) and Valerio Fuligni's *Bragadino* (Pesaro 1589), are based on events from the fall of Cyprus.
21. For a visual image of women's clothing styles in Renaissance Venice, visit *The Realm of Venus: Fashion and Style in Renaissance Italy* at http://realmofvenus.renaissanceitaly.net/.
22. There were essentially two types of courtesans, the learned and refined *cortigiana onesta*, such as Veronica Franco, and a lower class, the *cortigiana di lume*. Clearly, Erifila belongs to the latter group, which was viewed as somewhat better than a common prostitute.
23. It is likely that the spectators recalled Ariosto's salacious play with the word "coda" in his *Lena*, where Prologue reminds the audience that the character Lena is like all the other women who like to feel a tail behind them ("sentirsi dietro la coda") and who despise those who do not want one behind ("ch'averla di rietro non vogliono"). It is also reasonable to assume that most spectators recalled Boccaccio's phallic connotation of the term in *Dec.* 3.1 and, especially, 9.10. In this last story, Brother Gianni sticks his "coda" in the rear end of Compare Pietro's wife. Some spectators might have recalled Aretino's frequent use of the term in his *Ragionamento della Nanna e della Antonia*. In the second day of the *Ragionamento*, Nanna expresses the belief that we are born of the flesh and die with the flesh, for the *coda* makes us and the *coda* undoes us ("noi nasciamo di carne e in su la carne muoiamo; la coda ci fa e la coda ci disfà," 197).

6. *Gli duoi fratelli rivali:* Della Porta Adapts Bandello's Prose Narrative to the Stage

1. The first complete edition of Della Porta's fourteen comedies was published in 1726 by Gennaro Murzio in 4 volumes. In 1910–11, Vincenzo Spampanato published eight of Della Porta's comedies in 2 volumes, which saw ten editions and reprints. Raffaele Sirri's 1978 *Teatro:*

Giambattista della Porta has seen twenty-eight editions. This four-volume opus was last reissued in 2000. In 1965, Louise Clubb translated into English *Gli duoi fratelli rivali*, and in 2000 Donald Beecher and Bruno Ferraro translated, also into English, *La sorella*. For an overview of the critical fortunes of Della Porta's theatre both in Italy and abroad, see Sirri's *L'attività teatrale*, Clubb's *Giambattista Della Porta*, and Beecher's and Ferraro's introduction to their translation of *La sorella*.

2. Unless otherwise noted, citations in English and Italian are from Clubb's bilingual edition.
3. Sanesi, *La commedia* 375, speaking of the influence Italian Renaissance dramatists had on the European continent, observes that Della Porta's comedies had a much greater influence ("eco assai maggiore") than many of his contemporaries. He mentions Della Porta's influence on Tomkins and Ruggle (England), Rotrou (France), and De Castro (Spain). At the turn of the century, Francesco Milano, in his lengthy essay on Della Porta's *Gli duoi fratelli*, compares it with Shakespeare's *Much Ado about Nothing*. He concludes that, though the Italian play is not as good as the Shakespearean comedy, it is "un lavoro mirabile, degno d'esser tratto dall'oblio in cui é caduto" ("a marvellous work, worthy of redemption from the obscurity in which it has fallen," 394). Also, after stating that Della Porta is a better playwright than fellow dramatists such as Borghini and Sforza d'Oddi, Milano adds that *Gli duoi fratelli* can stand next "a quelli degli Spagnuoli e degl'Inglesi [sic]" (399).
4. For Sirri, *La fantesca* is Della Porta's best play ("é ritenuta la prima assoluta," *Teatro* 2.30). Luigi Tonelli, instead, argues that *Gli duoi fratelli* is Della Porta's masterpiece ("il capolavoro portiano"). In his view, the play is "degna di star accanto, non pure alle migliori commedie italiane, sì alle più celebrate del Calderon e del Vega" ("worthy of standing next not only to the best Italian comedies, but also to the best of Calderon's and Lope De Vega's," 150). Louise Clubb notes that the play has "sometimes been called his [Della Porta's] best." Refusing to weigh in on whether the play is actually the best or merely good, she concedes that it is "extraordinarily representative of trends in late *cinquecento* comedy" (*The Two Rival Brothers* 6).
5. For a discussion on when the play's events are supposed to take place, see Clubb's *The Two Rival Brothers* 11–16.
6. In *La fantesca* 4.4, 6, the two braggart soldiers, Dante and Pantalone, speak Spanish through entire scenes (4.4, 6). Also, *Tabernaria*'s Capitan Spagnolo speaks mostly in Spanish.
7. The authors refer to Louise Clubb's comments on Della Porta's favourable view of the Spanish court in Naples. Clubb points to the pro-Iberian feeling expressed by *Trappolaria's* Prologue in order to refute Milano's and

Cecchi's views that the playwright was resentful of the Spanish (Clubb, *Della Porta: Dramatist* 188).

8. Henry Kamen, 240–1, speaking of the general contempt towards the Spaniards, points out that "since the fifteenth century the Spaniards had been the most hated nation in Italy." He also quotes an official in Milan who in 1570 lamented, "I don't know what there is in the nation and empire of Spain that [...] none of the peoples in the world subject to it bears it any affection. And this is much more so in Italy than any other part of the world."
9. The Lionati sided against the Angevins; the Della Portas were involved in the 1485 "Congiura dei baroni" against Ferdinand I. In 1.1 Don Ignazio reminds the servant Simbolo and, inherently, the audience that the Della Portas' property was confiscated following the rebellion in which Eufranone sided with the Prince of Salerno ("avea seguite le parti del Principe de Salerno"). Eufranone brings it up again in 2.6, when he recalls how he lost most of his property because of the rebellion ("l'altre robbe che mi tolse il rigor della rubellione").
10. *Novelle* 1.22.275. I quote from Francesco Flora's edition of *Tutte le opere di Bandello.*
11. Villari, 56, writes, "Il 'gran disordine dell'ottantacinque' aveva rivelato al di là del moto plebeo, una nuova spinta indipendentistica e motivi di opposizione distinti dalla tradizionale difesa delle 'costituzioni' del regno" ("the 'great turmoil of 1585' had revealed, beyond the popular uprising, a new push for independence. It also revealed new reasons for the opposition that were distinct from the traditional defence of the kingdom's 'constitutions'").
12. For Donald Beecher, the "alignment of the serious with the comic is one of the leading markers of the late erudite comedy" (*Renaissance Comedy* I.26).
13. Sirri, speaking of the these characters and the comic situations they create, notes that these are moments in which street life comes to life on stage, "la vita di piazza irrompe nel testo" (2.12)
14. Speaking of the failure to uproot brigandage and crime in the Neapolitan region during the second half of the sixteenth century, Croce, *Storia* 152, writes "e già il viceré Toledo confessava, nel 1550, di aver fatto morire per giustizia diciottomila persone, e che 'non sapeva piú che fare'; e simili statistiche con migliaia di afforcati e decapitati e arrotati misero fuori i seguenti viceré" ("and the Viceroy Pedro de Toledo already in 1550 admitted to having executed eighteen thousand people and that [according to a letter by the Tuscan agent in Naples] he did not know what else to do [...]. The succeeding viceroys produced similar statistics with thousands of people hanged, decapitated, and wheeled [tortured and killed on the wheel]").

7. *Orbecche*: Giraldi's Imitation of His Own Prose Narrative

1. Giraldi, "Lettera" 1.480, writing of the success of *Orbecche*'s performance by the Accademia in Parma, claims that "doppo tanti secoli ho rinovato l'uso dello spettacolo delle tragedie, il quale era poco meno che andato in oblivione" ("after sō many centuries I re-introduced the use of the spectacle of tragedies, which had been almost forgotten"). Luigi Groto, in his 1572 dedicatory letter of his *Dalida* to Alessandra Volta, speaks of *Orbecche* as the model of all subsequent tragedies ("modello dell'altre").
2. Giraldi used *Ecatommiti* as the primary source for most of his tragedies, including *Altile* (II, 3), *Antivalomeni* (II, 9), *Selene* (V, 1), *Euphimia* (VIII, 10), *Arrenopia* (III, 1), *Epitia* (VIII, 5).
3. Horace advised that spectators should be spared the sight of bloody scenes such as Medea's murdering her children or Atreus preparing his banquet on stage:

   Nec pueros coram populo Medea trucidet;
   Aut humana palàm coquat exta nefarius Atreus;
   Aut in avem Progne vertatur, Cadmus in anguem.
   Quodcunque ostendis mihi sic, incredulus odi. (*Ars poetica*, 185–8)
   [Medea must not murder her children before the people; / nor nefarious Atreus prepare his bloody banquet on stage / nor Procne turn into a bird, Cadmus into a snake. / Whatever you show me like this, I hate and refuse to believe.]

   Aristotle, *Poetics* 2.14.26, considered violent scenes inappropriate, noting that "those who, while striving to achieve that which arouses fear, produce only what is monstrous, are total strangers to [the nature and purpose of] tragedy." Renaissance playwrights and theorists such as Giorgio Bartoli argued that violent scenes "molto più movon maraviglia et compassione con immaginarle per via di narazione d'alcuno, che con la vista loro" ("arouse greater marvel and compassion when we imagine them through somebody's narrative than when we see them," quoted in Weinberg, *History* 2.930). Alessandro Piccolomini shared this view and suggested that audiences grant playwrights the poetic licence required by the fiction of the stage and the art of imitation ("l'arte dell'imitare," *Annotationi* 24). Castelvetro was also against the representation of bloody deeds on the grounds that they could not be faithfully executed and could easily appear ridiculous ("producono non effetto di tragedia ma di comedia"). But he appears to contradict himself when conceding that certain horrible acts should be represented on stage, since people are moved more by the sense of sight than by the sense of hearing ("per lo sentimento della veduta che per lo sentimento dell'udita," *Poetica* 3.13.160–1).

4. Greek tragedy seldom featured Prologue as such, and Seneca used it sporadically.
5. Francis W. Kent, 6, reports that Nannina, following an argument with her husband, Bernardo Rucellai, over domestic arrangements, complained to her mother, Lucrezia Tornabuoni, about her unhappiness.
6. Baldacci, 483, and the bibliographical note on p. lii. Later audiences would also be reminded of Beatrice Cenci, the eighteen-year-old who was put to death for her involvement in the murder of her abusive father (1599). The episode, which became the subject of Shelley's tragedy *The Cenci*, bears witness to the ever-abusive patriarchal system and the misogynist practices it engendered.
7. Reflecting a humanist tendency dating back to Petrarch, some men wished that procreation could be attained without marriage so that they did not have to live with women. Pietro Lauro concedes that "se si potesse tener famiglia, haver figliuoli heredi de le facultà e del nome de la casata, senza pigliar moglie, non è dubbio che sarebbe assai meglio il viverne senza [Ma] siamo pur astretti à viver tra tanti incomodi con la moglie" ("if one could have a family, have heirs worthy of the family name, without having to take a wife, there is no doubt that it would be much better to live without one. [But] we are forced to live with the inconvenience of having a wife," quoted by Frigo, 92). The Venetian Giuseppe Passi, in his 1599 *I donneschi difetti* 10, expresses a similar view by paraphrasing the censor Cato the Elder's address to the Roman Senate whereby the old statesman wished that "se la generatione nostra potesse conservarsi senza donne, noi sarebbemo compagni, e simili ai Dei immortali" ("if [we] men could procreate without the help of women, we would be similar to the immortal gods").
8. In *Facezie e motti* 220, p. 122, we read that Messer Marsilio Ficino "usava dire, che le donne si volevano usare chome gl'orinali, che come l'uomo v'à orinato si nascondono" ("used to say that women should be used like bedchamber pots, which are hidden once a man has unrinated in them").
9. For a comprehensive discussion of the position of women in the culture and theatre of the Renaissance, see Di Maria's *The Italian Tragedy*. To see how the issue was represented in Renaissance portraiture, see Dale Kent, *Women in Renaissance Florence*. The article provides a series of portraits and an extensive bibliography.
10. On 23 February 1572, Cosimo ordered the podestà of Barga (Lucca) to leave Giovanni's corpse hanging in public view so that it might serve as an example to others ("afinché sia da tutta la terra visto per esemplo delli altri," *The Medici Archive Project*, www.medici.org).

11. One should keep in mind that audiences for tragic theatre were usually highly educated and therefore informed enough to participate in meaningful cultural debates.

8. Dolce's *Marianna*: From History to the Stage

1. Dolce, in informing Antonio Molino that in 1565 his *Marianna* was presented twice in the palace of the Duke of Ferrara, proudly points out that "quantunque la prima volta per la gran moltitudine fosse turbato il rapppresentarla, la seconda fu confermato il giudizio primiero" ("though the first performance was hindered by the unusually large audience, the second was highly acclaimed," in Cremante, *Teatro del Cinquecento* 745).
2. For the English version of Boccaccio's biography of Mariamne, see Guarino's *Concerning Famous Women* 85, 189–91.
3. On the editorial fortunes of Boccaccio's *De claris* in the Renaissance, see the introduction to Da Casentino, *Volgarizzamento di Mastro Donato Da Casentino Dell'Opera di Messer Boccaccio De claris mulieribus*.
4. Boccaccio's *De claris mulieribus* and its Italian *volgarizzamenti* allude to the old queen's contemptible behaviour, but only in passing and without details. They simply note that the queen turned against her daughter.
5. All quotations are from Cremante's edition.
6. All Josephus quotations are from the Whiston translation, whereby the first number refers to the book, the second to the chapter, and the third to the section.
7. Compare Othello's grief as he stares at Desdemona's lifeless body with Erode's wish to join his now dead Marianna:

   Othello: Man but a rush against Othello's breast,
   And he retires. Where should Othello go?
   Now, how dost thou look now? O ill-starr'd wench!
   Pale as thy smock! when we shall meet at compt,
   This look of thine will hurl my soul from heaven,
   And fiends will snatch at it. Cold, cold, my girl!
   Even like thy chastity. O cursed slave!
   Whip me, ye devils,
   From the possession of this heavenly sight!
   Blow me about in winds! roast me in sulphur!
   Wash me in steep-down gulfs of liquid fire!
   O Desdemona! Desdemona! dead!
   Oh! Oh! Oh! (*Othello* 5.2.313–25)

Erode: A me non saria cosa acerba e grave
Con le mie proprie mani aprirmi il petto.
Ma tu, sì come pura et innocente,
Sciolta da' lacci uman sei gita in cielo,
Et io discenderei da te lontano,
Pieno di sceleraggini a l'Inferno. (5.3248–53)
[For me, it would be neither repugnant nor onerous a deed / to tear open my breast with my own hands. / But you, so pure and innocent, / freed from your human bonds, have gone to heaven. / And I, with all my iniquities, would descend / in Hell, far away from you.]

8. In the play the boys are no more that seven years old, since Mariamme was executed in 29 BCE, eight years after she and Herod were married. In the source, the boys were executed in 6 BCE, when they were well into their twenties.
9. In Cary's *The Tragedie of Mariam, the Faire Queene of Jewry* (1613), the Jewish queen is much more faithful to the historical character, especially in the way she meets her death.

Bibliography

Alonge, Roberto. "Quella diabolica coppia di Messer Nicia e di Madonna Lucrezia." In Alessandro Pontremoli, ed., *La lingua e le lingue di Machiavelli. Atti del Convegno internazionale di studi.* Torino, 2–4 dicembre 1999. Turin: Olschki, 2001.

Ammannati Piccolomini, Jacopo. *Lettere* (1444–79). Ed. Paolo Cherubini. 3 vols. Rome: Ministero per i beni culturali e ambientali, 1997.

Andrews, Richard. *Scripts and Scenarios.* Cambridge: Cambridge University Press, 1993. http://dx.doi.org/10.1017/CBO9780511553073.

Archivio di Stato Fiorentino. Online database: Medici Archive Project: http://www.medici.org.

Arditi, Bastiano. *Diario di Firenze e di altre parti della cristianità (1574–1579).* Ed. Roberto Cantagalli. Florence: Istituto Nazionale di studi sul Rinascimento (Palazzo Strozzi), 1970.

Aretino, Pietro. *Cortegiana. Tutte le opere. Le lettere: Il primo e il secondo libro.* Ed. Francesco Flora. Milan: Mondadori, 1960.

Aretino, Pietro. "*Ragionamento della Nanna e della Antonia.*" *Ragionamento – Dialogo.* Intr. Giorgio Bàrberi Squarotti. Commentary Carla Forno. Milan: Rizzoli, 1988.

Ariani, Marco. *Tra classicismo e manierismo: Il teatro tragico del Cinquecento.* Florence: Olschki, 1974.

Ariani, Marco. "La trasgressione e l'ordine: *Orbecche* di G.B. Giraldi Cinthio." *La Rassegna della Letteratura Italiana* LXXXIII (1979): 117–80.

Ariani, Marco, ed. *Il teatro italiano: La tragedia del Cinquecento.* 2 vols. Turin: Einaudi, 1977.

Ariosto, Ludovico. *Le commedie.* In *Ludovico Ariosto: Opere minori.* Ed. Cesare Segre. Milan: Ricciardi, 1954.

Ariosto, Ludovico. *Le satire.* In *Ludovico Ariosto: Opere minori.* Ed Cesare Segre. Milan, Naples: Ricciardi, 1954.

Aristotle. *The Poetics of Aristotle*. Trans. P.H. Epps. Chapel Hill: University of North Carolina Press, 1970.

Baldacci, Luigi, ed. *Lirici del Cinquecento*. Milan: Longanesi, 1975.

Bandello, Matteo. *Novelle*. In *Tutte le opere di Matteo Bandello*. Ed. Francesco Flora. 2 vols. 2nd ed. Milan: Mondadori, 1942.

Baratto, Mario. *La commedia del Cinquecento*. Vicenza: Neri Pozza Editore, [1975] 1977.

Baron, Hans. *Crisis of the Early Italian Renaissance*. Princeton: Princeton University Press, 1955.

Bartoli, Giorgio. "Poetica." In Bernard Weinberg, *History of Literary Criticsm in the Italian Renaissance*. 2 vols. Chicago: University of Chicago Press, 1961.

Beecher, Donald, trans. and ed. *Renaissance Comedy: The Italian Masters*. 2 vols. Toronto: University of Toronto Press, 2008–9.

Beecher, Donald, and Bruno Ferraro, intr. and trans. [Giambattista Della Porta], *The Sister*. Ottawa: Dovehouse, 2000.

Benvenuti, Giovanni. *Il cieco di Adria. Vita ed opere di Luigi Groto*. Sala Bolognese: Arnaldo Forni, 1984.

Bertelli, Sergio. "When Did Machiavelli Write *Mandragola*?" *Renaissance Quarterly* 24, 3 (1971): 317–26. http://dx.doi.org/10.2307/2859587.

Bibbiena, Bernardo D. *La calandria*. In Nino Borsellino, ed., *Commedie del Cinquecento*, vol. 2. Milan: Feltrinelli, 1967.

Blanché, Chantal. "Entre comédie savante et *commedia dell'arte*: Les *Marioli* de Giambattista Della Porta." In Anna Fontes Baratto, ed., *De qui, de quoi se moque-t-on? Rire et derision à la Renaissance*. Paris: Presses Sorbonne Nouvelle, 2004.

Bluestone, Max. *From Story to Stage*. The Hague: Mouton, 1974.

Boccaccio, Giovanni. *Concerning Famous Women*. Trans. Guido Guarino. New Brunswick, NJ: Rutgers University Press, 1963.

Boccaccio, Giovanni. *Decameron*. Ed. Carlo Salinari. 2 vols. Bari: Laterza, 1966.

Borsellino, Nino. "Per una storia delle commedie di Machiavelli." *Cultura e Scuola*, IX, 33–4 (1970): 229–41.

Borsellino, Nino. *Rozzi e intronati: Esperienze e forme di teatro dal "Decameron" al "Calendaio."* Rome: Bulzoni, 1974.

Borsellino, Nino, ed. *Commedie del Cinquecento*. Milan: Feltrinelli, 1962.

Bosco, Umberto. *Francesco Petrarca*. Bari: Laterza, 1961.

Bracciolini, Poggio. *Facezie di Poggio Fiorentino*. Rome: A. Sommaruga, 1885.

Brown, Nancy M. *The Abacus and the Cross. The Story of the Pope Who Brought the Light of Science to the Dark Ages*. New York: Basic Books, 2010.

Bruni, Leonardo. *Laudatio Florentine Urbis*. Ed. Stefano Baldassarri. Florence: Galluzzo, 2000.

Burckhardt, Jacob. *The Civilization of the Renaissance in Italy*. 2 vols. New York: Harper & Row, 1929; Rpt 1958.

Calore, Marina. "Le commedie di Luigi Groto." In Giorgio Brunello and Antonio Lodo, eds, *Luigi Groto e il suo tempo: Atti del convegno di studi Adria, 27–29 Aprile, 1984*. 2 vols. Rovigo: Associazione Culturale Minelliana, 1987.

Camerini, Eugenio. *Giovan Maria Cecchi, "L'Assiuolo."* Milan: Daelli, 1863.

Camerini, Eugenio. *Nuovi profili letterari*. 3 vols. Milan: Battezzati e B. Saldini, 1876.

Carlson, Marvin. *Theories of the Theater: A Historical and Critical Survey from the Greeks to the Present*. Ithaca, NY: Cornell University Press, 1984.

Caro, Annibale. *Gli straccioni*. In Nino Borsellino, ed., *Commedie del Cinquecento*, vol. 2. Milan: Feltrinelli, 1962.

Carroll, Linda, trans. *Venice, cita' excelentissima: Selections from the Renaissance Diaries of Marin Sanudo*. Ed. Patricia Labalme and Laura Sanguineti White. Baltimore: Johns Hopkins University Press, 2008.

Cary, Elizabeth T. *The Tragedie of Mariam, the Faire Queene of Jewry*. London: Richard Hawkins, 1613. On-line edition: http://digital.library.upenn.edu/women/cary/mariam/mariam.html.

Castelvetro, Lodovico. *Poetica d'Aristotele vulgarizzata, et sposta per Lodovico Castelvetro*. Vienna, 1570. Munich: Wilhelm Fink Verlag, 1968.

Castiglione, Baldesar. *Il libro del cortegiano*. Ed. Giulio Preti. Turin: Einaudi, 1960.

Cavallini, Giorgio. *Interpretazione della "Mandragola."* Milan: Marzorati, 1973.

Cecchi, Giovammaria. *L'Assiuolo*. In Nino Borsellino, ed., *Commedie del Cinquecento*, vol. 1. Milan: Feltrinelli, 1962.

Cecchi, Giovammaria. *Commedie*. 2 vols. Florence: Le Monnier, 1856.

Cecchi, Giovammaria. *Le commedie di Giovammaria Cecchi: Notaio Fiorentino del secolo XVI*. Ed. Gaetano Milanesi. 2 vols. Charlotte, SC: Nabu Press, 2010.

Cecchi, Giovammaria. *The Horned Owl*. Ed. and trans. Konrad Eisenbichler. Waterloo, ON: Wilfrid Laurier University Press, 1981.

Cecchi, Giovammaria. *The Slave Girl*. Ed. and trans. Bruno Ferraro. Ottawa: Dovehouse, 1996.

Cervantes, Miguel de. *El ingenioso hidalgo Don Quijote de la Mancha*. Ed. Luis Andrés Murillo. 2 vols. Madrid: Clásicos Castalia, 1978.

Cherubini, Paolo, ed. *Iacopo Ammannati Piccolomini Lettere (1444–1479)*. 3 vols. Rome: Ministero per i beni culturali e ambientali, 1997.

Cicero, M. Tullius. *M. Tulli Ciceronis: De Re Publica, De legibus, Cato Maior de Senectute, Laelius de amiciti*. Ed. J.G. F. Powell. Oxford: Oxford University Press, 2006.

Clubb, George Louise. *Giambattista Della Porta: Dramatist*. Princeton: Princeton University Press, 1965.

Clubb, George Louise, ed. and trans. [Giambattista Della Porta], *Gli duoi fratelli rivali / The Two Rival Brothers*. Berkeley: University of California Press, 1980.

Cochrane, Eric. *Historians and Historiography in the Italian Renaissance*. Chicago: Chicago University Press, 1981.

Cody, Jane M. "The *senex amator* in Plautus' *Casina*." *Hermes*, 104, 4 (1976): 253–76.

Coletto, Daniela. "Aspetti del linguaggio nelle commedie del Groto." In Giorgio Brunello and Antonio Lodo, eds, *Luigi Groto e il suo tempo: Atti del convegno di studi Adria, 27–29 Aprile, 1984*. 2 vols. Rovigo: Associazione Culturale Minelliana, 1987.

Corrigan, Beatrice M. "Il *Capriccio*: An Unpublished Italian Renaissance Comedy and Its Analogues." *Studies in the Renaissance* 5 (1958): 74–86. http://dx.doi.org/10.2307/2856975.

Croce, Benedetto. *Storia del regno di Napoli*. Bari: Laterza, 1965.

Croce, Benedetto. *I teatri di Napoli*. Bari: Laterza, 1947.

Croce, Benedetto, ed. *Carlo de' Dottori, "Aristodemo": Tragedia*. Florence: Le Monnier, 1948.

Crowley, Roger. *City of Fortune: How Venice Ruled the Seas*. New York: Random House, 2011.

Da Casentino, Donato. *Volgarizzamento di Mastro Donato Da Casentino dell'Opera di Messer Boccaccio De claris mulieribus*. Ed. Luigi Tosti. Milan: Giovanni Silvestri, 1841.

D'Ancona, Alessandro. *Origini del teatro italiano*. 2 vols. Turin: Loescher, 1891.

Dante Alighieri. *Divina commedia*. Ed. Natalino Sapegno. 3 vols. Florence: La Nuova Italia, 1955; Rpt 1985.

Davico Bonino, Guido. *Niccolo' Machiavelli. Teatro: "Andria," "Mandragola," "Clizia."* Turin: Einaudi, 2001.

Da Vinci, Leonardo. *Scritti letterari di Leonardo da Vinci*. Ed. Augusto Marinoni. Milan: Rizzoli, 1974.

De Amicis, Vincenzo. *L'imitazione latina nella commedia italiana del XVI secolo*. 1897. Rome: Studio Bibliografico Adelmo Polla, 1979.

De Grazia, Sebastian. *Machiavelli in Hell*. Princeton: Princeton University Press, 1989.

Della Porta, Giambattista. *Gli duoi fratelli rivali / The Two Rival Brothers*. Ed. and trans. L.G. Clubb. Berkeley: University of California Press, 1980.

Della Porta, Giambattista. *The Sister*. Intr. and trans. Donald Beecher and Bruno Ferraro. Ottawa: Dovehouse, 2000.

Della Porta, Giambattista. *Teatro. Porta, Giambattista della, 1535?–1615*. Ed. Raffaele Sirri. 4 vols. Naples: Istituto universitario orientale, 1978. Repr. Naples: Edizioni Scientifiche Italiane, 2000–3.

De' Medici, Lorenzino. *L'Aridosia*. In Ireneo Sanesi, ed., *Commedie del Cinquecento*, vol. 2. Bari: Laterza, 1912.

De Pisan, Christine. *Cyte of Ladyes*. Trans. B. Anslay. London, 1521. Bk 2, ch. 36. Cited in Julia O'Faolain and Lauro Martines, eds, *Not in God's Image*. New York: Harper & Row, 1973.

Di Maria, Salvatore. "The Ethical Premises for the *Mandragola*'s New Society." *Italian Culture* VII (1986–9): 17–33.

Di Maria, Salvatore. "Fortune and the 'Beffa' in Bandello's *Novelle*." *Italica* 59, 4 (1982): 306–15. http://dx.doi.org/10.2307/478909.

Di Maria, Salvatore. *The Italian Tragedy in the Renaissance*. Lewisburg, PA: Bucknell University Press, 2002.

Di Maria, Salvatore. "Nicomaco and Sofronia: Fortune and Desire in Machiavelli's *Clizia*." *Sixteenth Century Journal* 14, 2 (1983): 201–13. http://dx.doi.org/10.2307/2539946.

Di Maria, Salvatore. "Structure of the Early Form of the 'Beffa' in the Italian Renaissance." *Canadian Journal of Italian Studies* 4 (1980–1): 227–39.

Dolce, Lodovico. "Apologia contra i detrattori dell'Autore." *Orlando furioso di Messer Ludovico Ariosto nobile ferrarese con la giunta, novissimamente stampato e corretto. Con una apologia di M. Lodovico Dolce contra i detrattori dell'autore*. Turin: Martino Cravoto & Francesco Robi de Saviliano, 1536.

Dolce, Lodovico. *Il ragazzo*. In Ireneo Sanesi, ed., *Commedie del Cinquecento*, vol. 2. Bari: Laterza, 1912.

Dolce, Lodovico. *Marianna*. In Renzo Cremante, ed., *Teatro del Cinquecento: La tragedia*, 741–877. Milan, Naples: Ricciardi, 1988.

Donatus, Eugraphius Aelius. *Aeli Donati Commentum Terenti*. 3 vols. Ed. Paulus Wessner. Stuttgart: Teubner, 1902; Rpt 1966.

Doni, Anton Francesco. *I marmi del Doni*. Ed. Ezio Chiòrboli. 2 vols. Bari: Laterza, 1928.

Duckworth, George. *The Nature of Roman Comedy*. 2nd ed. Princeton: Princeton University Press, 1952; Norman: University of Oklahoma Press, 1994.

Eisenbichler, Konrad, ed. and trans. *Giovan Maria Cecchi: The Horned Owl*. Waterloo, ON: Wilfrid Laurier University Press, 1981.

Evans, Oliver, trans. *"Clizia." Niccolo Machiavelli*. Great Neck, NY: Barron's Educational Series, 1962.

Faulkner, Robert. "*Clizia* and the Enlightenment of Private Life." In Vickie B. Sullivan, ed., *The Comedy and Tragedy of Machiavelli*. New Haven: Yale Unversity Press, 2000.

Ferroni, Giulio. *"Mutazione" e "riscontro" nel teatro di Machiavelli*. Rome: Bulzoni, 1972.

Ficino, Marsilio. *Facezie e motti. In Scelta di curiosità letterarie inedited o rare. Facezie e motti dei secoli XV e XVI*. Vol. 138. Bologna: Commissione per i testi di lingua, 1968.

Fiske, George Converse. *Lucilius and Horace: A Study in the Classical Theory of Imitation*. Vol. 1. Madison: Wisconsin University Press, 1920.

Frazier, Alison K. *Possible Lives: Authors and Saints in Renaissance Italy*. New York: Columbia University Press, 2004.

Frigo, Daniela. "Dal caos all'ordine: Sulla questione di 'prender moglie' nella trattatistica del sedicesimo secolo." In Marina Zancan, ed., *Nel cerchio della luna: Figure di donna in alcuni testi del XVI secolo*. Venice: Marsilio, 1983.

Gaeta, Franco, ed. *Niccolo' Machiavelli: Lettere*. Milan: Feltrinelli, 1961.

Gannon, J. "Literary Imitation in Renaissance Poetic." *United College Journal* 4 (1965): 1–11.

Garin, Eugenio. *La cultura del Rinascimento*. 1964; Milan: Il Saggiatore, 1995.

Giannetti, Laura, and Guido Ruggiero, ed. and trans. *Five Comedies from the Italian Renaissance*. Baltimore: Johns Hopkins University Press, 2003.

Giannotti, Donato. *Dialogi di Donato Giannotti, de' giorni che Dante consumò nel cercare l'inferno e 'l purgatorio*. Ed. Deoclecio Redig de Campos. Florence: Sansoni, 1939.

Gilbert, Felix. *Machiavelli and Guicciardini*. Princeton: Princeton University Press, 1965.

Giraldi, Giambattista Cinthio. *Altile*. Ed. Peggy Osborn. Lewiston, NY: The Edwin Mellen Press, 1992.

Giraldi, Giambattista Cinthio. *Arrenopia*. In Gaetano Poggiali, ed., *Teatro italiano antico*, 5: 51–191. Milan: Società Tipografica de' Classici Italiani, 1808–12.

Giraldi, Giambattista Cinthio. *Cleopatra Tragedia*. Ed. Mary Morrison and Peggy Osborn. Exeter: Short Run Press, 1985.

Giraldi, Giambattista Cinthio. "Discorso intorno al comporre delle commedie e delle tragedie." In Camillo Guerrieri Crocetti, ed., *Scritti critici*. Milan: Marzorati, 1973.

Giraldi, Giambattista Cinthio. *Gli "Ecatommiti" ovvero Cento novelle di Gio. Battista Girali Cintio*. In *Biblioteca portatile del Viaggiatore*, vol. 5. *Raccolta di novellieri italiani*, parte II. Florence: Borghi e Compagni, 1833.

Giraldi, Giambattista Cinthio. "Lettera sulla tragedia (1543)." In Bernard Weinberg, ed., *Trattati di poetica e retorica del Cinquecento*, vol. 1: 471–86. Bari: Laterza, 1970.

Giraldi, Giambattista Cinthio. *Orbecche*. In Renzo Cremante, ed., *Teatro del Cinquecento: La tragedia*, 281–448. Milan, Naples: Ricciardi, 1988.

Giraldi, Giambattista Cinthio. *Selene*. Ed. Philip Horne. Lewiston, NY: The Edwin Mellen Press, 1996.

Gordan, Phyllis Walter Goodhart, ed. *Two Renaissance Book Hunters*. New York: Columbia University Press, 1991.

Grazzini, Anton Francesco. *"Le cene" di Anton Francesco Grazzini detto il Lasca*. 3 vols. Milan: Giovanni Silvestri, 1815.

Grazzini, Anton Francesco. *Commedie di Anton Francesco Grazzini detto il Lasca*. Florence: Le Monnier, 1859.

Grazzini, Anton Francesco. *Opere di Anton Franscesco Grazzini*. Ed. Guido Davico Bonino. Turin: UTET, 1974.

Grazzini, Anton Francesco. *Le rime burlesche di Anton Francesco Grazzini*. Ed. Carlo Verzone. Florence: Sansoni, 1882.

Greenblatt, Stephen. *The Swerve: How the World Became Modern*. New York: W.W. Norton & Company, 2011.

Greene, Thomas. *The Light in Troy: Imitation and Discovery in Renaissance Poetry*. New Haven: Yale University Press, 1982.

Groto, Giuseppe. *La vita di Luigi Groto, cieco d'Adria*. Rovigo: Gio. Jacopo Miazzi, 1777.

Groto, Luigi. *La Alteria. Comedia di Luigi Groto, cieco d'Hadria. Novamente ricorretta e ristampata*. Venice: Antonio Turino, 1612.

Groto, Luigi. *La Dalila, tragedia nova di Luigi Groto cieco di Hadria con privilegio*. Venice, 1572.

Groto, Luigi. *La Emilia. Commedia nova di Luigi Groto*. Venice: Francesco Ziletti, 1597.

Groto, Luigi. *Il Thesoro. Comedia nova di Luigi Groto cieco d'Hadria. Novamente stampata*. Venice: Agostin Zopini & Nepoti, 1599.

Gurevic, Aron Ja. "Il mercante." In Jacques Le Goff, ed., *L'uomo medievale*. Bari: Laterza, 1987.

Hale, J.R. *Machiavelli and Renaissance Italy*. New York: The Macmillan Co., 1960.

Hankins, James. "Petrarch and the Canon of Neo-Latin Literature." Proceedings of the conference *Petrarca, l'Umanesimo e la civiltà europea*. Florence, Italy, December 2004, sponsored by the Comitato Nazionale per il VII Centenario della Nascita di Francesco Petrarca. To be published in *Quaderni petrarcheschi*. Downloaded from Harvard University's DASH Repository.

Herlihy, David, and Christiane Klapisch-Zuber. *Tuscans and Their Families: A Study of the Florentine Catasto of 1427*. New Haven: Yale University Press, 1985.

Herrick, Marvin. *Comic Theory in the Sixteenth Century*. Urbana: University of Illinois Press, 1964.

Herrick, Marvin. *Italian Comedy in the Renaissance*. Urbana: University of Illinois Press, 1960.

Herrick, Marvin. *Italian Tragedy in the Renaissance*. Urbana: University of Illinois Press, 1965.

Hopkins, T.C.F. *Confrontation at Lepanto: Christendom vs. Islam*. New York: Tom Doherty Associates, 2006.

Horace. *The Satires and Epistles of Horace*. Ed. J.B. Greenough. Boston: Ginn & Company, 1888.

Horace. *Satires, Epistles and Ars Poetica*. 1929. Trans. H. Rushton Fairclough. London: William Heinemann Ltd, 1942.

Ianziti, Gary. "Bruni on Writing History." *Renaissance Quarterly* 51, 2 (1998): 367–91. http://dx.doi.org/10.2307/2901571.

Ingegneri, Angelo. "Della poesia rappresentativa e del modo di rappresentare le favole sceniche. Discorso di Angelo Ingegneri." In Ferruccio Marotti, ed., *Storia documentaria del teatro italiano: Lo spettacolo dall'umanesimo al manierismo*, 271–308. Milan: Feltrinelli, 1974.

Josephus, Flavius. *The Works*. Trans. William Whiston. 1737. http://www.sacred-texts.com/jud/josephus/index.htm.

Kamen, Henry. *Philip of Spain*. New Haven, London: Yale University Press, 1997.

Kent, Dale. "Women in Renaissance Florence." In David Alan Brown, ed., *Virtue and Beauty: Leonardo's Ginevra de' Benci and Renaissance Portratis of Women*. Princeton: Princeton University Press, 2001.

Kent, Francis, W. "Sainted Mother, Magnificent Son: Lucrezia Tornabuoni and Lorenzo de' Medici." *Italian History & Culture* 3, 3 (1997): 3–35.

Khan, Victoria. " 'Virtu' and the Example of Agathocles in Machiavelli's Prince." In Albert Russell Ascoli and Victoria Kahn, eds, *Machiavelli and the Discourse of Literature*, 195–217. Ithaca, NY: Cornell University Press, 1993.

King, Margaret L. *Women of the Renaissance*. Chicago: University of Chicago Press, 1991.

Labalme, Patricia, and Laura Sanguineti White, eds. *Venice, cita' excelentissima: Selections from the Renaissance Diaries of Marin Sanudo*. Trans. Linda L. Carroll. Baltimore: Johns Hopkins University Press, 2008.

Larivaille, Paul. "*L'Orazia* de l'Arétin, tragédie des ambitions déçues." In A. Rochon, ed., *Les écrivains et le pouvoir en Italie à l'époque de la Renaissance*, 2: 279–360. Paris: Université de la Sorbonne Nouvelle, 1973.

Lettieri, Michael, and Julius A. Molinari, eds. *Il "Capriccio": Commedia anonima del Cinquecento*. Welland, ON: Soleil, 1999.

Lotz, Wolfgang. *Architecture in Italy: 1500–1600*. Trans. Mary Hottinger. New Haven: Yale University Press, 1995.

Luther, Martin. "Preface to the German Theology." *Works*. Ed. J. Pelikan. Philadelphia: Fortress Press, 1954.

Macek, Josef. *Il Rinascimento italiano*. Trans. Hana Kubistova Casadei. Rome: Editori Riuniti, 1992.

Machiavelli, Niccolò. *"Clizia." Niccolò Machiavelli and the United States of America*. Trans. Anthony J. Pansini. Vol. IV. New York: Greenvale Press, 1969.

Machiavelli, Niccolò. *Clizia*. Trans. Oliver Evans. Great Neck, NY: Barron's Educational Series, 1962.

Machiavelli, Niccolò. *The Comedies of Machiavelli: "The Woman from Andros," "The Mandrake," "Clizia."* Ed. and trans. David Sices and James B. Atkinson. Bilingual edition. Hanover, NH: University Press of New England, 1985.

Machiavelli, Niccolò. *Niccolo' Machiavelli: Lettere*. Ed. Franco Gaeta. Milan: Feltrinelli, 1961.

Machiavelli, Niccolò. *Opere di Niccolò Machiavelli*. Ed. Ezio Raimondi. Milan: Mursia, 1967.

Machiavelli, Niccolò. *"The Prince" by Nicolo Machiavelli*. Trans. William K. Marriott. St Petersburg, FL: Red and Black Publishers, 2008.

McLaughlin, L. Martin. *Literary Imitation in the Italian Renaissance*. Oxford: Clarendon Press, 1995.

Malara, Francesca. "Appunti sulla *Clizia*." In Alessandro Pontremoli, ed., *La lingua e le lingue di Machiavelli. Atti del Convegno internazionale di studi. Torino, 2–4 dicembre 1999*. Turin: Olschki, 2001.

Mamone, Sara. "La *Mandragola* e la scena di città." In Alessandro Pontremoli, ed., *La lingua e le lingue di Machiavelli. Atti del Convegno internazionale di studi. Torino, 2–4 dicembre 1999*. Turin: Olschki, 2001.

Mancini, Nicola. "Il teatro veneto al tempo della Controriforma." In Giorgio Brunello and Antonio Lodo, eds, *Luigi Groto e il suo tempo. Atti del Convengo di studi Adria, 27–9 Aprile, 1984*. 2 vols. Rovigo: Minelliana, 1987.

Manes, Yael. *Motherhood and Patriarchal Masculinities in Sixteenth-century Italian Comedy*. Burlington, VT: Ashgate Publishing Co, 2011.

Mansfield, Harvey C. "The Cuckold in Machiavelli's *Mandragola*." In Vickie B. Sullivan, ed., *The Comedy and Tragedy of Machiavelli*. New Haven: Yale University Press, 2000.

Marcus Aurelius. *Meditations*. Intr. and trans. Gregory Hays. New York: Modern Library, 2002.

Martin, Thomas. "Michelangelo's Brutus and the Classicizing Portrait Bust in Sixteenth-century Italy." *Artibus et Historiae* 14, 27 (1993): 67–83.

Martinez, Ronald L. "Benefit of Absence: Machiavellian Valediction in *Clizia*." In Albert Russell Ascoli and Victoria Kahn, eds, *Machiavelli and the Discourse of Literature*. Ithaca, NY: Cornell University Press, 1993.

Milano, Francesco. "Le commedie di Giovanbattista della Porta." *Studi di letteratura italiana*, 2: 311–411. Naples: Giannini & Figli, 1900.

Moore, Timothy J. *The Theater of Plautus: Playing to the Audience*. Austin: University of Texas Press, 1998.

Murphy, Caroline P. *Murder of a Medici Princess*. Oxford: Oxford University Press, 2008.

Napier, Henry Edward. *Florentine History*. London: Edward Moxon, 1846.

Neri, Ferdinando. *La tragedia italiana nel Cinquecento*. Florence: Galletti e Cocci, 1904.

Newell, James, trans. *Rosario Villari, "The Revolt of Naples."* Cambridge: Polity Press, 1993.

Norwich, John Julius. *Venice: The Greatness and the Fall*. London: Penguin Books, 1981.

Oddi, Sforza degli. *Comedie del s. Sforza degl'Oddi, cioe "Il duello d'Amore, & d'Amicitia." "Li morti viui," & "La prigione d'Amore."* Venice: Gio. Battista & Gio. Bernardo Sessa, 1597.

O'Faolain, Julia, and Lauro Martines, eds. *Not in God's Image*. New York: Harper & Row, 1973.

Pacelli, Paolo. "Dialogo del Pacelli, fatto alla partenza del Sig. Don Pietro Girone Duca di Ossuna il Primo nel 1586." In Giuseppe De Montemayor, ed., *Diurnali di Scipione Guerra*, 43–4. Naples: Francesco Giannini & Figli, 1891.

Paleotto, Galeazzo, intr. *Comedie del S. Sforza degl'Oddi, cioé "Il duello d'Amore & d'Amicizia," "Li morti vivi," & "La prigione d'Amore."* Venice: Gio. Battista & Gio. Bernardo Sessa, 1597.

Palmieri, Matteo. *Della vita civile*. Bologna: Zanichelli, 1944.

Parronchi, Alessandro. "La prima rappresentazione della *Mandragola*." *La Bibliofilia* LXIV (1962): 37–86.

Pansini, Anthony J. *Niccolò Machiavelli and the United States of America*. Vol. IV. New York: Greenvale Press, 1969.

Passi, Giuseppe. *I donneschi difetti nuovamente formati e posti in luce da Giuseppe Passi*. Venice: Iacobo Antonio Somascho, 1599.

Pesca, Carmela. *La città maschera: Geometria e dinamica della città rinascimentale*. Ravenna: Longo, 2002.

Petrarca, Francesco. *Epystole familiares*. In *Francesco Petrarca, Opera omnia*. Ed. Pasquale Stoppelli. Rome: Lexis progetti editoriali, 1997. Available at: http:// www.bibliotecaitaliana.it/xtf/view?docId=bibit000921/bibit000921.xml.

Petrarca, Francesco. *Epystole seniles*. In *Francesco Petrarca, Opera omnia*. Ed. Pasquale Stoppelli. Rome: Lexis progetti editoriali, 1997. Available at: http:// www.bibliotecaitaliana.it/xtf/view?docId=bibit000921/bibit000921.xml.

Petrarca, Francesco. *Francis Petrarch: Letters of Old Age: Rerum senilium libri.* Trans. Aldo Bernardo, Sail Levin, and Reta A. Bernardo. Baltimore: The Johns Hopkins University Press, 1992.

Petrarca, Francesco. *Rerum Familiarum Libri.* In *Prose.* Ed. Guido Martellotti, Pier Giorgio Ricci, Enrico Carrara, and Enrico Bianchi. *La letteratura italiana. Storia e testi.* Milan, Naples: Ricciardi, 1955.

Petrarca, Francesco. *"Rerum Senilium Libri." Opere di Francesco Petrarca.* Ed. Emilio Bigi. Milan: Mursia, 1963; Rpt 1968.

Phillimore, M. Catherine. "The Italian Drama." *Macmillan's Magazine* 36 (May–October 1877): 218–27.

Piccolomini, Alessandro. *Annotationi nel Libro della Poetica d'Aristotile, con la traduttione del medesimo libro in lingua volgare.* Venice: Giovanni Guarisco e Compagni, 1572.

Plautus, Titus Maccius. *"Casina." Six Plays of Plautus.* Ed. and trans. Lionel Casson. Garden City, NY: Doubleday & Co, 1963.

Plautus, Titus Maccius. *Epidicus.* In *Plauti Comoediae.* Ed. F. Leo. Berlin: Weidmann, 1895–6. The Latin Library: http://www.thelatinlibrary.com/.

Plautus, Titus Maccius. *"Epidicus."* Trans. Constance Carrier. In *Plautus: The Comedies.* Ed. David R. Slavitt and Plamer Bovie. Vol. 3. Baltimore: The Johns Hopkins University, 1995.

Plautus, Titus Maccius. *Plautus: The Darker Comedies.* Intr., notes, and trans. James Tatum. Baltimore: Johns Hopkins University Press, 1983.

Plautus, Titus Maccius. *T. Maccius Plautus. Plauti Comoediae.* Ed. F. Leo. Berlin: Weidmann, 1895.

Poliziano, Angelo. *"Stanze per la giostra." Le stanze, "l'Orfeo" e le rime di messer Angelo Ambrogini Poliziano.* Ed. Giosuè Carducci. Florence: Barbera, 1863.

Pullini, Giorgio. "Stile di transizione nel teatro di Giambattista Della Porta." *Lettere Italiane* 8 (1956): 299–310.

Quintilian, Marcus Fabius. *Institutio oratoria.* Vol. 3. Loeb Classical Library. Cambridge, MA: Harvard University Press, 1920.

Quintilian, Marcus Fabius. *Institutio oratoria.* Trans. H.E. Butler. Cambridge, MA: Harvard University Press, 1963.

Radcliff-Umstead, Douglas. *The Birth of Modern Comedy in Renaissance Italy.* Chicago: University of Chicago Press, 1969.

Radcliff-Umstead, Douglas. *Carnival Comedy and Sacred Play. The Renaissance Dramas of Giovan Maria Cecchi.* Columbia: University of Missouri Press, 1986.

Raimondi, Ezio. *Politica e commedia.* Bologna: Il Mulino, 1972.

Ricchi, Agostino. *I tre tiranni.* In Ireneo Sanesi, ed., *Commedie del Cinquecento,* vol. 2. Bari: Laterza, 1912.

Riposio, Donatella. *Nova comedia v'appresento. Il prologo nella commedia del Cinquecento.* Turin: Tirrenia-Stampatori, 1989.

Rizzi, Fortunato. *Le commedie osservate di Giovan Maria Cecchi e la commedia classica del sec. XVI.* Rocca S. Casciano: Licinio Cappelli, 1904.

Roscoe, William. *The Life of Lorenzo de' Medici, called the Magnificent.* 5th ed. 3 vols. London: J. M'Creery, 1806.

Rucellai, Giovanni. *"Le api." Le opere di Giovanni Rucellai,* 1–40. Ed. Guido Mazzoni. Bologna: Zanichelli, 1887.

Russo, Luigi. "La tragedia nel Cinque e Seicento." *Belfagor* 1 (1959): 14–22.

Russo, Luigi, ed. *Commedie e Belfagor di Niccolo' Machiavelli.* Florence: Sansoni, 1943.

Sanesi, Ireneo. *Storia dei generi letterari italiani: La commedia.* Vol. I. Milan: Vallardi, 1911.

Sanesi, Ireneo, ed. *Commedie del Cinquecento.* 2 vols. Bari: Laterza, 1912.

Sanudo, Marino. *I diarii di Marino Sanuto (MCCCCXCVI-MDXXXIII) dall'autografo Marciano ital. cl. VII codd. CDXIX-CDLXXVII.* Ed. Rinaldo Fulin, Federico Stefani, Niccolò Barozzi, Guglielmo Berchet, and Marco Allegri. Auspice la R. Deputazione veneta di storia patria. Venice: F. Visentini, 1879–1903.

Scaglione. Aldo. "Petrarch 1974: A Sketch for a Portrait." In Aldo Scaglione, ed., *Francis Petrarch, Six Centuries Later: A Symposium.* Chapel Hill: University of North Carolina, 1975.

Scoti-Bertinelli, Ugo. *Sullo stile delle commedie in prosa di Giovan Maria Cecchi.* Citta' di Castello: S. Lapi, 1906.

Seigel, Jerrod E. " 'Civic Humanism' or Ciceronian Rhetoric? The Culture of Petrarch and Bruni." *Past & Present* 34, 1 (July 1966): 3–48. http://dx.doi.org/10.1093/past/34.1.3.

Seneca. *Ad Lucillum epistulae morales.* 3 vols. Trans. Richard Gummere. Loeb Classical Library, vol. 2. Cambridge, MA: Harvard University Press, 1920; Rpt 1963.

Seneca. *Seneca's Tragedies.* Trans. Frank Justus Miller. Vol. 2. 1917. Cambridge: Harvard University Press, 1953.

Serlio, Sebastiano. "Il secondo libro di prospettiva." In Ferruccio Marotti, ed., *Storia documentaria del teatro italiano: Lo spettacolo dall'umanesimo al manierismo,* 190–205. Milan: Feltrinelli, 1974.

Shelley, Percy B. *The Cenci, A Tragedy in Five Acts.* London: C & J Ollier, 1819.

Sices, David, and James B. Atkinson, ed. and trans. *Machiavelli, Niccolò. The Comedies of Machiavelli: "The Woman from Andros," "The Mandrake," "Clizia."* Bilingual edition. Hanover, NH: University Press of New England, 1985.

Sirri, Raffaele. *L'attività teatrale di G. B. Della Porta*. Naples: Libreria De Simone, 1968.

Sirri, Raffaele, ed. *Giambattista della Porta. Teatro*. Vol. 2. Naples: Istituto Universitario Orientale, 1980.

Sirri, Raffaele, ed. *Giambattista della Porta. Teatro*. Vol. 3. Naples: Istituto Universitario Orientale, 1985.

Sobel, Dava. *Galileo's Daughter*. New York: Penguin Books, 2000.

Sorella, Antonio. *Magia lingua e commedia nel Machiavelli*. Florence: Olschki, 1992.

Stefani, Luigina, ed. *Il formicone*. Ferrara: Bovolenta, 1980.

Storey, John. *Cultural Studies and the Study of Popular Culture*. Athens: University of Georgia Press, 1996.

Strathern, Paul. *The Artist, the Philosopher, and the Warrior*. New York: Bantam Books, 2010.

Sumberg, Theodore. "*La Mandragola*: An Interpretation." *Journal of Politics* 23, 2 (1961): 320–40. http://dx.doi.org/10.2307/2126708.

Tacitus. *The Histories*. Books I–III. Trans. Clifford H. Moore. Loeb Classical Library, vol. 1. Cambridge, MA: Harvard University Press, 1925; Rpt 1956.

Tatum, James, ed. and trans. *Plautus: The Darker Comedies. "Bacchides," "Casina," and "Truculentus"*. Baltimore: Johns Hopkins University Press, 1983.

Tenenti, Alberto. "La religione di Machiavelli." *Studi storici* X (1969): 709–48.

Terence [Publius Terentius Afer]. *Eunuchus*. In *Opera Omnia*. Bibliotheca Latina. IntraText Digital Library. Copyright Eulogos, 2007.

Terpening, Ronnie H. *Lodovico Dolce: Renaissance Man of Letters*. Toronto: University of Toronto Press, 1997.

Toffanin, Giuseppe. *Il Cinquecento*. Milan: Vallardi, 1929.

Tonelli, Luigi. *Il teatro italiano: Dalle origini ai giorni nostri*. Milan: Modernissima, 1924.

Torelli, Pomponio. *Merope*. In Marco Ariani, ed., *Il teatro italiano: La tragedia del Cinquecento*, 2:561–637. Turin: Einaudi, 1977.

Trexler, Richard. *The Women of Renaissance Florence*. 2 vols. Binghamton, NY: Medieval & Renaissance Texts & Studies, 1993.

Trissino, Giovan Giorgio. *Sofonisba*. In Renzo Cremante, ed., *Teatro del Cinquecento: La tragedia*. Milan, Napoli: Ricciardi, 1988.

Ubersfeld, Anne. *L'école du spectateur: Lire le theatre* 2. Paris: Éditions.

Ulivi, Ferruccio. *L'imitazione nella poetica del Rinascimento*. Milan: Marzorati, 1959.

Vanossi, Luigi. "Machiavelli." In Gianfranco Folena, ed., *Lingua e struttura del teatro italiano del Rinascimento*. Padua: Liviana Editrice, 1970.

Varchi, Benedetto. *"L'Ercolano." Opere di Benedetto Varchi.* Ed. A. Racheli and G. Battista Busini. Trieste: Lloyd Austriaco, 1859.

Vasari, Giorgio. *Le vite de' più eccellenti pittori scultori ed architettori scritte da Giorgio Vasari pittore aretino.* Ed. Gaetano Milanesi. Vol. 6. Florence: Sansoni, 1906.

Villani, Giovanni. *Nuova cronica*. Ed. Giuseppe Porta. 3 vols. Parma: Ugo Guanda, 1990–1.

Villari, Rosario. *La rivolta antispagnola*. Bari: Laterza, 1973.

Villari, Rosario. *The Revolt of Naples*. Trans. James Newell. Cambridge: Polity Press, 1993.

Viroli, Maurizio. *Niccolò's Smile. A Biography of Machiavelli.* Trans. Anthony Shugaar. New York: Hill and Wang, 2000.

Weinberg, Bernard. *History of Literary Criticsm in the Italian Renaissance.* 2 vols. Chicago: University of Chicago Press, 1961.

Index